$ 35.

BORODINO-THE MOSKOVA

The Battle for the Redoubts

F.-G. HOURTOULLE

Uniforms plates by André Jouineau
Maps by Morgan Gillard
Translated from the French by Alan Mc Kay

HISTOIRE & COLLECTIONS - PARIS

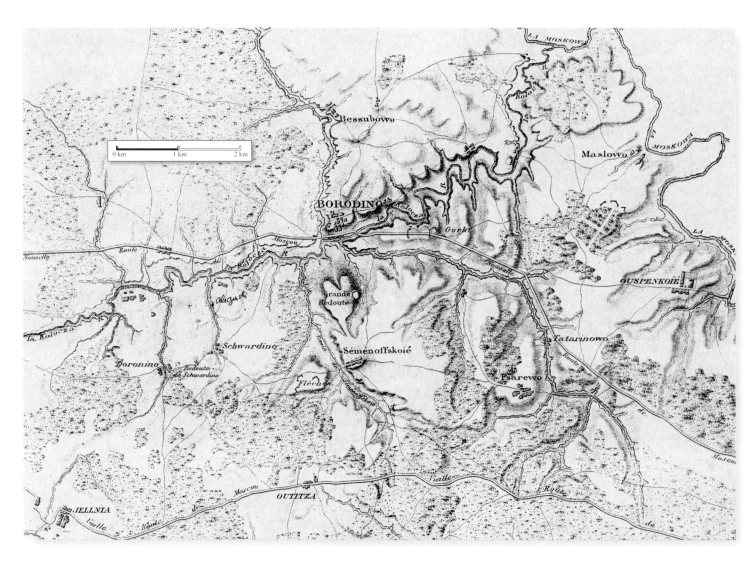

Map from the "Atlas de Thiers".

CONTENTS

Introduction   3

THE FORCES PRESENT
   The Russians   6
   The "Grande Armée"   37

THE BATTLE
   5 September 1812   39
   6 September 1812   41
   7 September: The Big fight   44

THE FRENCH PARTICIPANTS

                                                 54

CASUALTIES   118

Conclusions   122

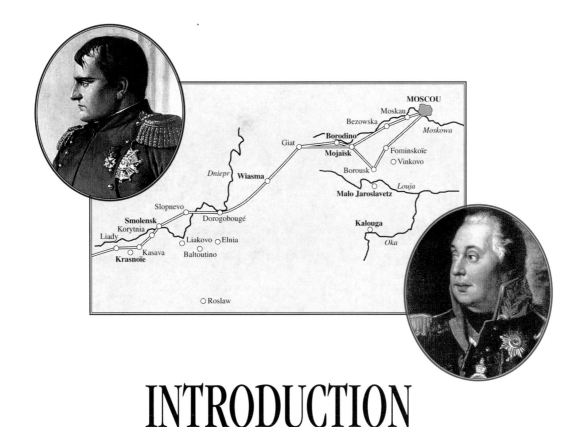

INTRODUCTION

The Battle of the Moskova has given rise to a multitude of partisans and controversial theories about the validity of the victory, the mistakes the Emperor made, his behaviour, the number of soldiers in the two opposing armies, the relative scale of the losses and what followed the battle.

I have tried to get close to the truth by consulting the extensive statistics in the archives, the witnesses and by especially not including the spectre of the subsequent retreat which always tends to cloud objectivity.

This is why it is necessary to accompany these soldiers on the long road to Moscow, towards this much sought-after battlefield, to discover it with them, but without taking into account this retreat. It is necessary to take part in the battle, and live through the different episodes in the midst of all the confusing details of the real participants, who only saw the place where they charged, fired, attacked, or gave ground before the enemy's attacks.

The accounts of the staff officers are often only a gathering of misformed and misinterpreted indirect reports.

First the forces involved with all their uniforms and different details so that you can place them more easily. The Russian Army, homogenous, fanatical, defending its territory with passion, was much simpler than Napoleon's army which consisted of a variety of troops, French and foreign, regrouped or integrated into the different French corps. In order to have enough of an army, Napoleon had to call on the rest of Europe, then under his domination, because his old soldiers had been left behind in Spain, far from their leader. It was a far cry from the proud *Grande Armée* of the beginning of the Empire, proud of the quality of its men, proud of its enthusiasm and not just its uniforms.

The army which had entered Russia included doubtful and disenchanted allies, and reluctant conscripts. The hard core of the army was made up of men from Germany forged by Davout from old regiments, and of the Garde. It was with this assorted army that the Emperor thought he could win, compensating all its deficiencies by his genius for organising and handling battles. Would he be right?

With her gold, England was pulling the strings and watching very closely those who were fighting for her unawares.

THE PRELUDE TO THE BATTLE

NAPOLEON AND THE MOOD IN 1812

During the first years of the Empire, the rules of war had been defined quite well. The attacker sought to create the most favourable conditions in which to fight a big battle, to win this big battle and get hold of the adversary's capital.

The winner and the loser would then meet to sign a peace treaty, but in an atmosphere of social courtesy, like at Tilsitt.

BY 1812 QUITE A FEW THINGS HAD CHANGED

Guerrila warfare had broken out in Spain. The guerillas, avoiding confrontation, laid ambushes, harassed communication lines and showed how cruel they could be.

In the diplomatic field, England was showing its usual skill, multiplying its initiatives. She obtained that Turkey make peace with Russia, which freed Tchichagov's army, enabling it to march up onto the French right flank.

Bernadotte, who had been promised Norway, took sides with Russia which was thus able to bring back its army from Finland to reinforce Wittgenstein. Under duress, the Prussians were obliged to send 10 000 men to Riga with MacDonald's 10th Corps. They were ready to turn at the first opportunity and did not actually show any great enthusiasm.

Although he was Napoleon's father-in-law, the Austrian Emperor secretly renewed his friendship with the Russians. He did send Schwarzenberg's Corps to help Reynier's Saxon Corps against Tomasov on the right flank towards Lithuania, but this was without conviction. In Spain, English action was even stronger because it was upholding the rebellion and Wellington's army was gathering strength in its Portuguese base. Wellington had wisely waited until Napoleon was too deeply engaged in Russia, at the other end of Europe to come out of his base. He had just beaten Marmont at Los Arapiles and Napoleon had not yet received the news. Marmont, who had yet again underestimated this redoutable adversary, had not wanted to wait for the support of his colleagues before fighting this battle. The English knew only too well that there was no real single command in Spain capable of coordinating operations. Neither King Joseph nor his adviser Jourdan could do this and the disagreements between the marshals was facilitated Wellington's progress. And thus a second front was created, wearing down and tying down the excellent troops that was the Armée d'Espagne. History has shown that a war on two fronts is always strategically fatal.In Italy, Napoleon's attitude towards the Pope, had shocked the country which became hostile. Moreover, in Naples, Murat was thinking more about his crown than about imperial conquests. He had come nevertheless to command the cavalry and to get carried away with these fights that he adored. When things started to go badly, he dropped Napoleon and try to save his throne by all available means.

PRINCE EUGENE WAS ALSO THINKING OF HIS ITALIAN FUTURE

The most serious point was that the Emperor had changed too. Thanks to his immenses intellectual abilities, Bonaparte had succeeded in becoming Emperor, carried along by the enthusisam of his republican volunteers, by the support of men attracted by the philosophy of the «Enlightenment» who saw their ideas spreading in the wake of the conqueror, dismantling kingdoms with out-of-date priviledges.

France admired this "Man of Providence", straight from the Revolution. He won battles, organised everything, knew everything; the country had made an Emperor of him.

In this new world, men could hope for everything, the most competent and the most meritorious were rewarded no matter what their origins were. What counted was the «quality of men» and no longer "men of quality". The French people were living with enthusiasm.

But Napoleon's absolute power was like a virus. The disease of power had begun to undermine him. This power virus which finishes by carrying off the patient, has been seen in other clinical cases and in those who have this power disease, all lesser men than Napoleon.

With Napoleon this disease had developped into the Conqueror's disease. The symptoms had already been noticed during the Egyptian Campaign where he dreamt of following through to India to chase out the damned English and take their riches away from them. He talked of Alexander, the genial golden young man and of Caesar; he wanted to equal them and if possible outdo them by becoming the most illustirous conqueror in the world. At St John of Acre which he attacked without having the means to do so, he saw his dream of the moment collapse. He was not strong enough in these Egyptian deserts with his small band of elite troops. He had had to come back , think and create an immense force worthy of his dreams. The severe attack had been calmed, but the virus was still there.

Napoleon had won in these good old lands of Europe. He had beaten his adversaries though England on its island, with its elite Navy, remained untouchable. This was a thorn in the Emperor's side, but he was carried away by his conquests on the continent; he was the best and he could make no mistakes. The worse thing for somebody who has the power disease is to be surrounded by courtisans who fortify this idea of infallibility with their subtle permanent flattery. Old compagnons who occasionally dared to contradict him, irritated him more and more often. Courtisans were so much more pleasant! He had become a prisoner of his own dream. He had his star and for him nothing was impossible.

He himself had changed, for his army and for the French people. The soldiers of 1812 were no longer the volunteers of 1792. Men were needed, so there was more and more conscription and, in the departements, the police tracked down the draft dodgers, and re-grouped them in battalions. Of course there were conscripts who were happy to take part in the adventure, there were the passive conscripts whom the officers shaped in their own way and like the old campaigners, cried *"Vive l'Empereur»*, joining the conqueror's army to share in the glory. The world of war was a world of risk, adventure, a mirage for the young of 18 to 20. And then there were promotions, decorations, the discovery of other countries, other women...

Napoleon had changed his way and his ideas. He was no longer the republican general, he had abandoned that position. He had been impressed by the apparel and the pomp of the royal or imperial courts, by the atmosphere of the palaces, of the castles and by eveything that surrounded the large princely families gathered together in their innate world of superiority, their nomenclatura. Napoleon created his own nobility, with new knights of merit come up from the people. He had his barons, his counts, his dukes and his princes. He made members of his family whom he moved around at will into kings. All this since 1808. By deciding to found a dynasty, he got even more out of hand.

Josephine was repudiated and the Austrian Emperor gave him the hand of his daughter Marie-Louise. They had a son and thus started a dynasty which was bound to be grandiose. A page had been turned and Napoleon thought that he had joined the great lineage. He had already started by making it easy for the old families of France to come back, and by integrating in his Court young people from the French high nobility who were indeed very European considering all the branches of the family trees. In the Emperor's Household that followed him to Russia, the young noblemen found themselves *en famille*. Certain had relatives who had remained with the Tsar. Some even claimed to have found their Russian cousins during the campaign.

Napoleone was marching towards Ghjat and Borodino from Viasma. The Emperor had been trapped by the English, who had manipulated the Tsar into making this conflict inevitable.

Napoleon had let himself be attracted by this challenge worthy of his position because the conqueror's virus had reappared a second time with the scale of the problems

he had to solve. This disease was in the critical phase, he was speaking once more of Alexander and Caesar and was dreaming again of India. The Emperor's hope was that, once beaten - for he always needed a great battle in his scenarios - Alexander would agree to join forces and boot the English out of India.

In Davout's wagons, captured on 18th November at Krasnol, the Russians found maps of Russia and also maps marked with the passage to India. Was this dream realisable?

The Emperor had made several mistakes, the most important of which was the war in Spain. He thought that the capture of Madrid and his brief stay there had settled everything. The failures in his moves towards Portugal and the general hostility of the people towards this occupation should have made him think.

But have being called back to Austria, he considered Spain as a side-show and left his marshals (some of whom only saw an opportunity for pillage and loot), to sort it out. There were thus 300 000 good troops stuck in this arid country full of hatred, led by generals who could not get their act together.

The second mistake was the return to a type of super-royalty, well coming the old nobility who found a taste for their old priviledges again.

Napoleon thus cut himself off from his popular and revolutionary base. The republicans did not understand this about-turn and the men of the enlightenment who had helped him so much, became hostile then finally opposed him. Before, the advance of the French armies was made in the name of liberty and the Russian nobility was very frightened that the people would rise up, that the Polish and the Lithuanians would rise *en masse* against the power of their cast.

In the French army, this created a problem and I will quote General Berthezène, commanding a brigade of the New Guard. He wrote: *"A swarm of young people from the old and the new families, often without capability and definitely without modesty and without experience, having got into the army, brought with them a completely different spirit. Hungry for rank and distinctions, they sought to obtain these rather than merit them, and all too often they were seen to move up instead of those with good service and talent who had neither recommendation nor protection."* The marshals and in particular the Major-Generals, were surrounded only by this type of man and their headquarters became a machine for producing generals and colonels. The light cavalry regiments were endowed with these briliant officers who chose them because of the richness and the elegance of their uniforms and maybe because of a ridiculous feeling of superiority; thus these corps degenerated rapidly. Whereas the infantry with its simple uniform and the difficult nature of the tasks it had to carry out, preserved itself from such a disease ...

In Russia, Napoleon also made the mistake of not controlling the supply system

The French 4th Corps on its way to Borodino.

adequately. He was used to letting the army feed itself off the conquered countries but there, in Russia, ressources were non-existent. The army lost many men through illness or desertion, who organised themselves into bands at the rear and one general from Minsk complained about these marauding bands who were almost 100 000 strong. The impressive number of foreign troops whose motivation was not always sincere during this war was the cause of progressive defections, thereby increasing the numbers of laggards. In the French regiments it must not be forgotten that there were a number of conscripts from departments called "conquered", now within the new frontiers of the Empire, their number often reaching 30% of a regiment and even the regiments of the Guard, new and old had a certain percentage of these new Frenchmen. In the regiment of the Fusilier-Grenadiers of the *Moyenne Garde*, Roguet's Division, I have noted from the registers that 21% of the fusiliers lost or captured were originally from conquered departments. This proportion fell to 16% for those who came back directly. The old units in Spain would have been useful on this main front.

There was also a serious problem concerning horses, whose number diminished all along the progression of the army. The size of the Imperial Household with all its carriages and its horses, was a scourge devouring a large part of the available ressources.

Finally Napoleon was confronted with an unforeseen scenario which developped progressively as a result of the Russian command's hesitations and weaknesses. The Tsar had quietly been put out to graze on the sidelines and had given up the military command, knowing full well that it was not his cup of tea. The military advisers who had prepared the plans were in fact pseudo-scientists who had read a lot of books, and frequented the General Staffs a lot, playing their war on their maps, in a sort of Kriegspiel. This was the case of Pfuhl and their learned theories impressed the generals, for a while at least.

Their latest wild idea, separating the army into two with the camp at Drissa, was totally stupid. Bagration's Army of the South, the second army, just avoided annihilation. Fortunately for Bagration, Jerome's stupidities, dawdling with his Westphalians, enabled him to join up, just, with the first army near Smolensk with a minimum of losses. Without a real battle, the Russians had given away a lot of territory. Barclay with his back to Smolensk was in risk of being turned. Sacrificing rearguard troops each time, he left for Moscow. And it is on this road that Napoleon's thinned out army was to be found chasing after the big, indispensible and decisive final battle.

A lot has been written about the decision to march on Moscow. Reinventing histo-

ry, some have said that the Emperor would have been wiser to stay in conquered territories, preparing his winter quarters, reorganising his army, mobilising the Poles, etc. The reaction of Napoleon's entourage has been analysed; Berthier who was tired and had had enough, Murat's advice changing several times a day. As if the Emperor was a man capable of listening seriously to their advice! Berthier ran things with his elite secretariat, Murat charged with his cavalry, every man true to character.

All these hypotheses and analyses have been made with the advantage of hindsight and one can feel the ever-present spectre of the dramatic Retreat from Russia looming. One has the impression that the historians have only one idea: how could he have avoided this final disaster? It is much better to consider the problem the other way around with an obvious question: on the road from Smolensk to Moscow at the end of that month of August 1812, should the march forwards be continued?

Napoleon and only Napoleon could take the decision. Was he not the best of them all, was he not infallible? He did not know that he had the conqueror's disease and that this disease was at its critical phase. At any rate his vanity opposed any decision to withdraw without a battle. Such a conqueror giving up without defeating the enemy was unthinkable. The shades of Alexander and Caesar who were fellow travellers had to be considered, Napoleon could only march towards a new victory, and a parade in the Russian capital with all the honours.

This is what he said to Duroc, on 23 August: *"I need a huge victory, a battle before Moscow; my taking Moscow must astound the world."* Such an exceptional conqueror was responsible for astounding the world and he was a prisoner of the person and the dream he had created.

He must have weighed up all the elements which had been entrusted to his exceptional organising genius but like all conquerors he had his gambler's side, relying on his star and his luck. Alone he decided: «Forwards!»

NAPOLEON CHASING AFTER HIS BATTLE

He left Smolensk on the 24th August after ensuring the organisation of the rear. He left the Young Guard in Smolensk; it would catch up later. Murat led with his cavalry, followed by Davout, Ney, Junot and the Guard. On the roads more to the right, Poniatowski advanced with Latour-Maubourg's cavalry.

On the other side, was Prince Eugène supported by Grouchy's 3rd Cavalry Corps. The principal road had been devastated; however on the side roads, there were some welcome ressources.

Murat who adored cavalry charges, wasted his vanguard and the horses. Coming upon a group which was a bit too strong for him, he shouted for the support of Davout's infantry. The Maréchal, always so sparing of his soldiers' blood, was furious. The argument worsened and Murat told Napoleon that he had been insulted. The Emperor who had to humour Murat, decided in his favour and detached Compans' division under the direct orders of the King of Naples. Davout was appalled, but he knew only too well that he irritated Napoleon especially when he was right. A conqueror right in the middle of the critical phase of his dream, always preferred slightly mad attackers like Murat and Ney to reasonable strategists. This episode was settled at Viasma. The army left this town and reached Ghjat on 1 September. It rained heavily but briefly. In certain books this rain is presented as an omen that made Napoléon hesitate. Did he envisage returning to Smolensk? Were these dusty roads so suddenly turned into mud an obstacle to the troops' progress? It was more likely the opposite since the officers told of the overwhelming heat and the excessive dust thrown up on the road and of being relieved by this short outburst of rain.

They had to wait in this town a little and regroup. The main thing for the Emperor was it not that this ghost of a Russian army at last end up fighting a battle to protect Moscow?

ON THE RUSSIAN SIDE

In their camp there had been problems since Smolensk and a clan had formed against Barclay and his eternal retreats. Bagration was furious against this traitor and he was backed by a number of others.

The decision to nominate a commander in chief was taken finally and for this delicate position only one man was possible: General Kutuzov, aged 67, a subtle and crafty old warrior. He knew that he had to fight this battle and he accepted the place found by Toll as a favourable battlefield.

The scene was set, terrassing began in order to make the redoubts and ditches; the troops spread out over this large battlefield before the curtain rose for the big carnage.

THE FORCES THAT WERE PRESENT

THE RUSSIAN ARMY

Wilson, the English advisor, whose role during this campaign was considerable.

General Benningsen, a close friend of the Tsar, commander of the army at Eylau.

General Yermolov.

General Miloradovitch.

KUTUZOV'S GENERAL STAFF

The Chief of Staff was **Bennigsen.**

Miloradovitch had rejoined Kutuzov with some reinforcements (1 000 cavalry and militiamen from Moscow). Wilson, the English adviser was there to watch.Wilson seems to have suggested falling back to Rostopchin with a scorched earth policy and burning Moscow after the Moscova.

The numbers for each corps according to Boutourlin, the Russian historian, will be given. His book on 1812 was published in 1824.

Colonel Toll.

General Koutaissov, commanding the artillery.

General Barclay de Tolly.

THE FIRST ARMY OF THE WEST

This was the army of **Barclay de Tolly** with, from the general staff, the Chief of Staff **Yermolov** and as Quartermaster, Colonel **Toll**. General **Kutaissov** commanded the artillery.

BAGGOVUT'S 2nd CORPS (11 500 men)
● THE PRINCE OF WURTEMBERG'S 4th DIVISION.
Infantry
Infantry regiments from Krenechug (or Kremenstug), Minsk, Tobolsk, Volhynia, and the 4th and 34th Chasseur regiments.
Artillery
The 6th Heavy Company and the 7th and 8th light Companies.
● OLSUFIEV'S 17th DIVISION
Infantry
Infantry Regiments from Riazan, Belozersk (or Belo-ozero), Wilmanstrand, Brest and the 3rd and 48th Jäger Regiments.
Artillery
The 17th Heavy Company, the 32nd and 33rd Light and the Mounted 4th.
Cavalry
The 8 squadrons of Elisabethgrad Hussars.

TUTCHOV'S 3rd CORPS (7 000men)
● STROGONOV'S 1st DIVISION
Infantry
The Grenadier Regiments of Count Aracczeyev, Pavlov, and the grenadiers from Ekaterinoslav, Saint Petersburg and Tauride.
Artillery
The 1st Heavy Company, the 1st and 2nd Light, and the Mounted Company.
● KONOVNITZIN'S 3rd DIVISION
Infantry
Murom (or Murmansk), Revel, Tchernigov and Korporie infantry regiments, and the 20th and 21st Jäger regiments.
Artillery
The 3rd Heavy Company, the 5 and 6th Light Companies.
Cavalry
The Cossacks of the Guard with 4 squadrons, with a squadron of Black Sea Cossacks and a regiment of Teptiarsk Cossacks.

OSTERMAN-TOLSTOY'S 4th CORPS (10 000 men)
● GENERAL TCHOGLOKOV'S 11th DIVISION
Infantry
Kexholm, Pernau, Polotsk, Jelets infantry regiments and the 1st and 35th Jäger regiments.
Artillery. The 2nd Heavy, and the 3rd and 4th Light Companies.
● BAKHMETIEV'S 23rd DIVISION
Infantry
Kylsk, Ekaterinburg, Selinguisk infantry regiments and the 18th Jägers .
Artillery
The 23rd Heavy and the 43rd and 44th Light Companies.
Cavalry
8 squadrons of Isum hussars.

The 5th CORPS, the GUARD (17 000 men)
(theoretically the Corps of the Grand-Duke Constantin, who was absent)

● THE GUARDS DIVISION
Infantry
Preobrajenski, Izmailovski, Semenovski, Lithuanian infantry regiments, the Jägers of the Guard, the Battalion of Sailors of the Guard.

General Baggovut,
Commander in Chief
of the 2nd Corps, Army of the West.

General Tutchkov,
Commander in Chief
of the 3rd Corps, Army of the West.

General Osterman-Tolstoy.

General Dokhtorov.

General Ouvarov.

General Korf.

7

General Pahlen.

General Platov.

The Prince of Wurtemberg.

General Strogonoff.

General Konovnitzin.

General Bakhmetiev.

General Olsufiev.

Artillery of the Guard

2 heavy companies, 2 light and one mounted.

● THE COMBINED GRENADIERS DIVISION
Infantry
Combined grenadier regiments from the 1st, the 4th and the 27th divisions (each unit having two battalions), the grenadiers of the 23rd division (with one battalion only). Two companies of pioneers.
Cavalry
The 1st division of Deperadovitch's cuirassiers. The regiments (with 4 squadrons) of the Chevalier-Garde, the Horseguards, the Emperor's Cuirassiers, the Empress's Cuirassiers and the Astrakhan Cuirassiers.

DOKHTOROV'S 6th CORPS (8 500 men)
● KAPTSEVITCH'S 7th DIVISION
Infantry
The Moscow, Pskov, Libau, Sofia infantry regiments and the 11th and 36th Jägers .
Artillery
the 7th Heavy and the 12th and 13th Light companies.
● LIKHATCHEV'S 24th DIVISION
Infantry
The Oufa, Chirwan, Tomsk, Butirki infantry regiments and the 19th and 40th Jägers .
Artillery
The 24th Heavy and the 45th and 46th Light companies and the 7th Horse battery.
Cavalry
The 8 squadrons of Soum Hussars.

OUVAROV'S 1st CAVALRY CORPS (2 500 cavalrymen)
Cavalry of the Guard
The Hussars, Dragoons and Uhlans of the Guard (regiments with 4 squadrons).
Cavalry of the Line
The Kourland, Kasan, and Negin dragoons (regiments with 4 squadrons)
Artillery
One company of light artillery.

KORF'S 2nd CAVALRY RESERVE CORPS (3 500 men)
The Moscow, Pskov, Ingria (Finland) and Kargopol dragoons (regiments with 4 squadrons). The Polish Uhlans (regiments with 8 squadrons.
Artillery
The 6th Light Company and the 28th, 29th and 30th heavy Companies.

PAHLEN'S 3rd CAVALRY RESERVE CORPS (2 500 men)
(as Fain has noted, Boutourlin forgot to mention this corps in his account of the numbers)
The Siberian, Irkutsk and Orienburg Dragoons (regiments with 4 squadrons). The Mariupol Hussars (regiments with 8 squadrons)
Artillery
The 9th Light Company.

PLATOV'S COSSACKS (7 000 Cossacks)
(7 000 Cossacks minimum, divided into 72 squadrons for 8 regiments)

The Ataman, Denisov, Illovaskoi, Karitinov, Vlassov, Bug, Gardeyev, and Simpheropol Cossacks, Tatars from Perecop, Kalmuks and Bashkirs.
Artillery
One Light Company from the Don.

General Likhatchev.

RUSSIAN FLAGS

This is a most complicated area and the principal references have been consulted, beginning with Zwegintzov who based himself on Viskovatov and also Brauer, Fortoffer, Gayda and Wise's synthesis. Accuracy is unattainable for the following reasons:
— successive reforms.
— the creation of new regiments.
— the tradition that kept the original flags for the "old" regiments. In 1815 more than 60 regiments still had them. The most probable emblems that were borne at the Moskova have been presented. First, however, are the original types of flags with their doubtful points.

From Andolenko

Colour Variation

The first 1797 model

This was a 1.42 metres square, with an orange centre and the symetrical two-headed eagle; a vertical cross of one colour and angles of another colour. In order to distinguish the 82 regiments, 5 types were created varying the disposition of the colours and dividing the basic zones. We have reproduced them in the drawing opposite.

The number of the flags varied. There was a colonel's flag per regiment with a white flag at the beginning, then all-white in 1812.

There were also colour flags for the battalions. In 1812, the first battalion had the colonel's flag in one colour and the others had flags with two colours.

The 1800 model flag

From Paul 1st. The eagle in the middle was dissymetric and there was embroidery at each angle with the monogram.

The 1803 Alexander Flag

The colours in the medallion were changed and monogram became "A".

A unification by inspection was carried out (as for the uniform distinctives on the collar and the farings). For these inspection flags, the angles were white and the cross was the colour of the inspection, the embroidery was «gold». The distinctives for the inspections were:

Brest : straw; **Caucasus :** blue; **Crimea :** natural colour; **Dniestr :** lilac; **Finland :** yellow; **Kiev :** strawberry; **Lithuania :** light green; **Livonia :** turquoise; **Moscow :** orange; **Orenburg:** buff; **Siberia :** grey; **Smolensk :** white.

These colours were given to new regiments and regiments who were waiting for their emblem.

Other modifications concerned certain regiments and in 1807, Alexander created the St George flags, awarded to the regiments for a special exploit. The first was given to the Kiev regiment in 1807. It was distiguishable by its pike containg the St George Cross, an orange and black cordon and an inscription in gilt letters parallel with the edges of the flag, stating the feat of arms.

For the Moskova we shall try to state the case of each regiment by giving if possible, the variants according to the sources.

The Cavalry Standards.

These appear to be simpler since in 1812, there was a standard type, green with gold, sometimes silver embroidery for the squadrons and the white colonel flag.

Only the cuirassiers and the dragoons had their own standards.

This did not take into account the traditions to be respected and the Cuirassiers, no doubt, kept their initial emblem with their distinctive colour, like some of the older dragoon regiments. The colonel flags and standards have not been reproduced on the plates since in 1812 they were all white in principle, except for the Guard which is shown apart.

For the old regiments of this guard (according to Terence Wise), the colonel flag and the battalion flags were the same between 1803 and 1813, date of the big change. So after the Moskova, only the colour of the staves changed from one regiment to another.

The Lithuanians and the Finns of the Guard are illustrated. The Jägers of the Guard did not have a flag in 1812. Below are the colour plates with the different Russian corps.

On each plate, details proper to each regiment have been noted when necessary, with details about the flag.

Inspection type

Colonel Standard

Squadron Standard

Squadron standard, Old model, Pskov Dragoons.

FIRST ARMY
2nd ARMY CORPS, 4th DIVISION

In 1812, most of the old regiments had kept their colour flags of the 1797-type. The colonel flag was in principle white for all regiments. All the white 1797-type flags have been given. the green of the uniforms has been deliberately lightened so that no details are lost. Normally, the green worn by the Tsar's army was very dark gren, almost black.

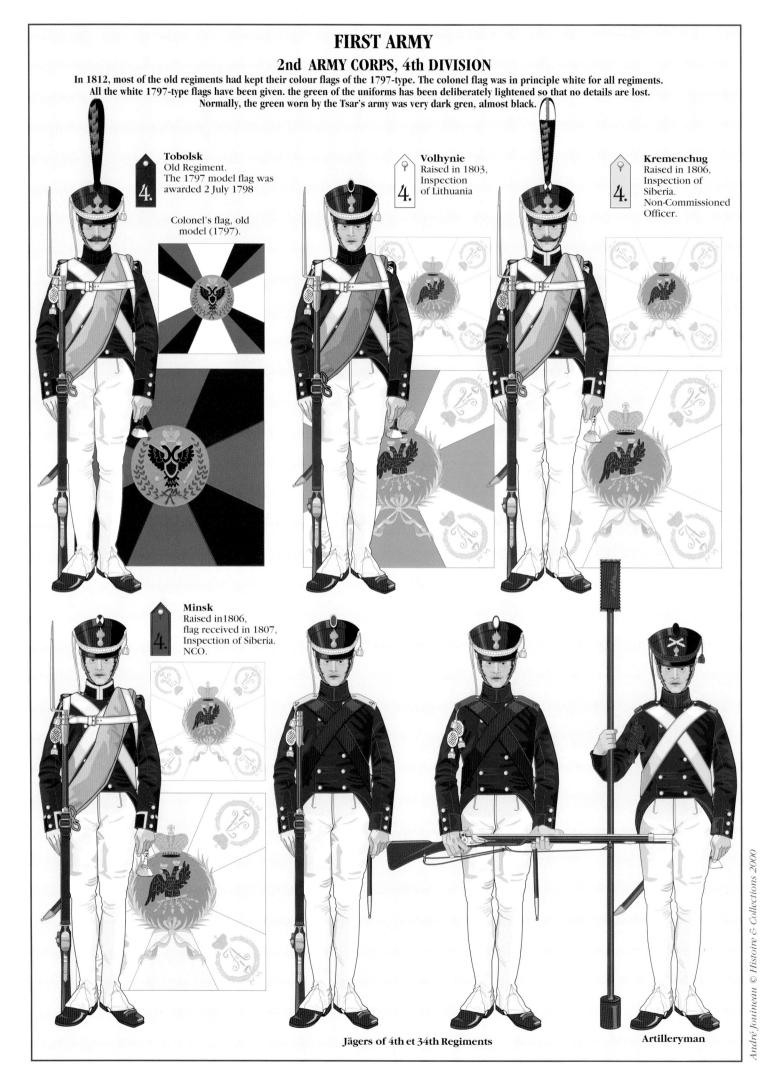

Tobolsk
Old Regiment.
The 1797 model flag was
awarded 2 July 1798

Colonel's flag, old
model (1797).

Volhynie
Raised in 1803,
Inspection
of Lithuania

Kremenchug
Raised in 1806,
Inspection of
Siberia.
Non-Commissioned
Officer.

Minsk
Raised in1806,
flag received in 1807,
Inspection of Siberia.
NCO.

Jägers of 4th et 34th Regiments

Artilleryman

André Jouineau © Histoire & Collections 2000

FIRST ARMY
2nd ARMY CORPS, 17th DIVISION

17. Colonel's flag, old model (1797).

17. Colonel's flag, old model (1797).

17.

Riazan
Old regiment.
1797 model flag
received
21 August 1798

Bielozerkov
Old regiment.
1797 model flag
received 8 February
1798

Brest
Raised in 1806,
Inspection of Siberia

Wilmanstrand
Raised in 1806,
Inspection of Siberia.
NCO.

17.

**Elizabethgrad
Hussars,
cavalryman**

**Horse Artillery,
4th company**

André Joutineau © Histoire & Collections 2000

FIRST ARMY
3rd ARMY CORPS, 1st DIVISION

Colonel's flag, old model (1797).

Leib Grenadier. This regiment only entered the Guard in 1813 with a new flag with a yellow cross with blue and black angles, of the St George type.

On the collar and the flap fairings, there were white button holes, very rare distinctives close to those of the Guard which were golden.

Colonel's flag, old model (1797).

Pavlovski Grenadier. This regiment only entered the Guard in 1813 with a new flag with a yellow cross with blue and white angles, of the St George type.

Colonel's flag, old model (1797).

Iekaterinoslav Grenadier. Formed in 1642, the regiment received a flag, model 1797 on 30th July 1797.

Riazan

Colonel's flag, old model (1797).

Colonel's flag, old model (1797).

Colonel's flag, old model (1797).

Arakcheyev Grenadier. Coming from the Rostov Regiment created in 1700, received a flag, model 1797 on 5th September 1798.

St Petersburg Grenadier. Formed in 1726, the regiment received a flag, 1797 model on 22nd September 1798.

Tauride Grenadier. Formed in 1756, the regiment received a flag, 1797 model with a coffee and yellow cross, then in 1800, the new model, above, black and red.

André Jouineau © Histoire & Collections 2000

FIRST ARMY
3rd ARMY CORPS, 3rd DIVISION

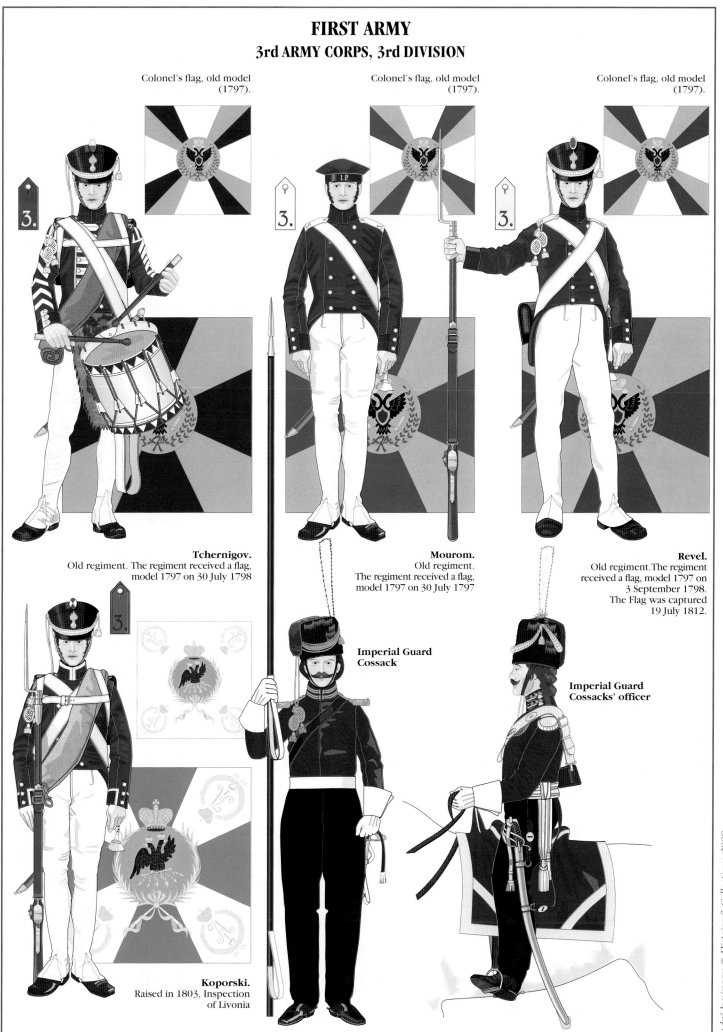

Colonel's flag, old model (1797).

Colonel's flag, old model (1797).

Colonel's flag, old model (1797).

Tchernigov.
Old regiment. The regiment received a flag, model 1797 on 30 July 1798

Mourom.
Old regiment.
The regiment received a flag, model 1797 on 30 July 1797

Revel.
Old regiment. The regiment received a flag, model 1797 on 3 September 1798. The Flag was captured 19 July 1812.

Imperial Guard Cossack

Imperial Guard Cossacks' officer

Koporski.
Raised in 1803, Inspection of Livonia

André Jouineau © Histoire & Collections 2000

FIRST ARMY
4th ARMY CORPS, 11th DIVISION

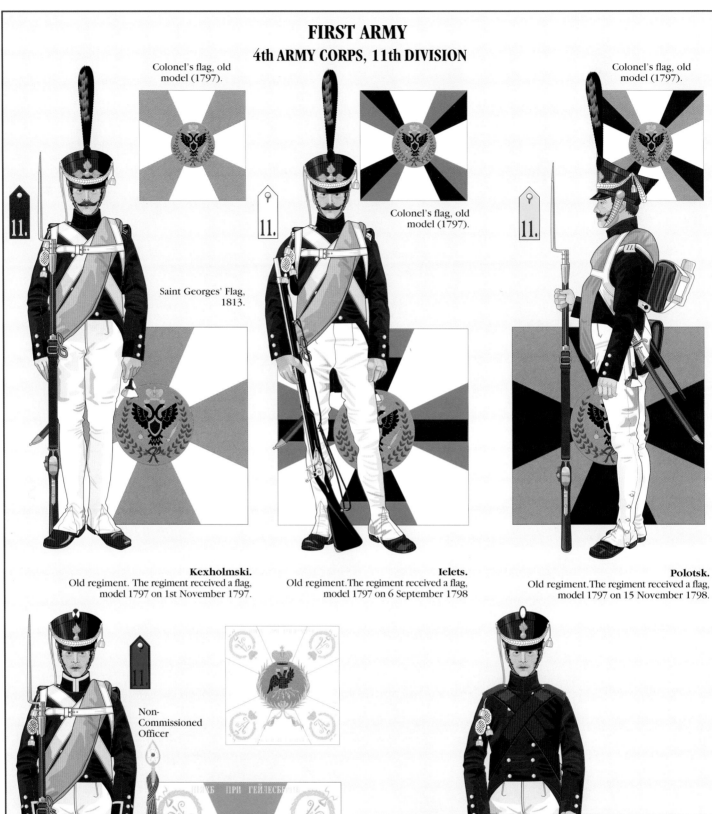

Colonel's flag, old model (1797).

Colonel's flag, old model (1797).

Colonel's flag, old model (1797).

Saint Georges' Flag, 1813.

Kexholmski.
Old regiment. The regiment received a flag, model 1797 on 1st November 1797.

Ielets.
Old regiment. The regiment received a flag, model 1797 on 6 September 1798

Polotsk.
Old regiment. The regiment received a flag, model 1797 on 15 November 1798.

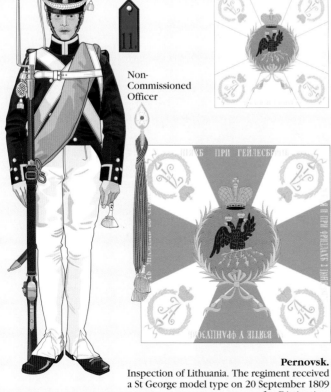

Non-Commissioned Officer

Pernovsk.
Inspection of Lithuania. The regiment received a St George model type on 20 September 1809 for *Distinction*.

Jäger

André Jouineau © Histoire & Collections 2000

FIRST ARMY
4 ARMY CORPS, 23rd DIVISION

Colonel's flag, old model (1797).

Colonel's flag, old model (1797).

Colonel's flag, old model (1797).

Rylsk
Old regiment. The regiment received a flag, model 1797 on 20 November 1798

Iekaterinbourg
Old regiment. The regiment received a flag, model 1797 on 9 January 1798

Selenguinsk.
Old Regiment. The regiment received a flag, model 1797 on received 21 January 1799.
Officer

Cavalryman, Izioumski Hussars

Jäger 18th regiment, Officer

André Jouineau © Histoire & Collections 2000

FIRST ARMY
5th ARMY CORPS, DIVISION OF THE GUARD

Colonel flag
and Battalion flag
of the Guard.
The shafts were straw
yellow for the
Preobrajenski,
black for the Semenovski
and white
for the Ismailovski.

Colour Flag (Battalion)
1813 model

Preobrajenski

Semenovski

**NCO-Drummer
Ismaïlovski Regiment**

**Flags of the
Lithuania Regiment**
The Regiment was
raised with the
Preobrajenski
4th Battalion.
In 1813, the Guards'
flags are the Saint
George model.

Colonel's flag, 1812

Colours flag in1812.

Lithuania

Finnish Jägers

NCO, Sailors of the Guard

André Jouineau © Histoire & Collections 2000

FIRST ARMY
5th ARMY CORPS, DIVISION OF THE GUARD

Artillery man and NCO of the Guard
Foot Artillery Regiment

Drummer and Officer of the Guard
Foot Artillery Regiment

Officer and Trumpeter,
the Guard Horse Artillery
Regiment

Combined
Grenadiers
Division

André Jouineau © Histoire & Collections 2000

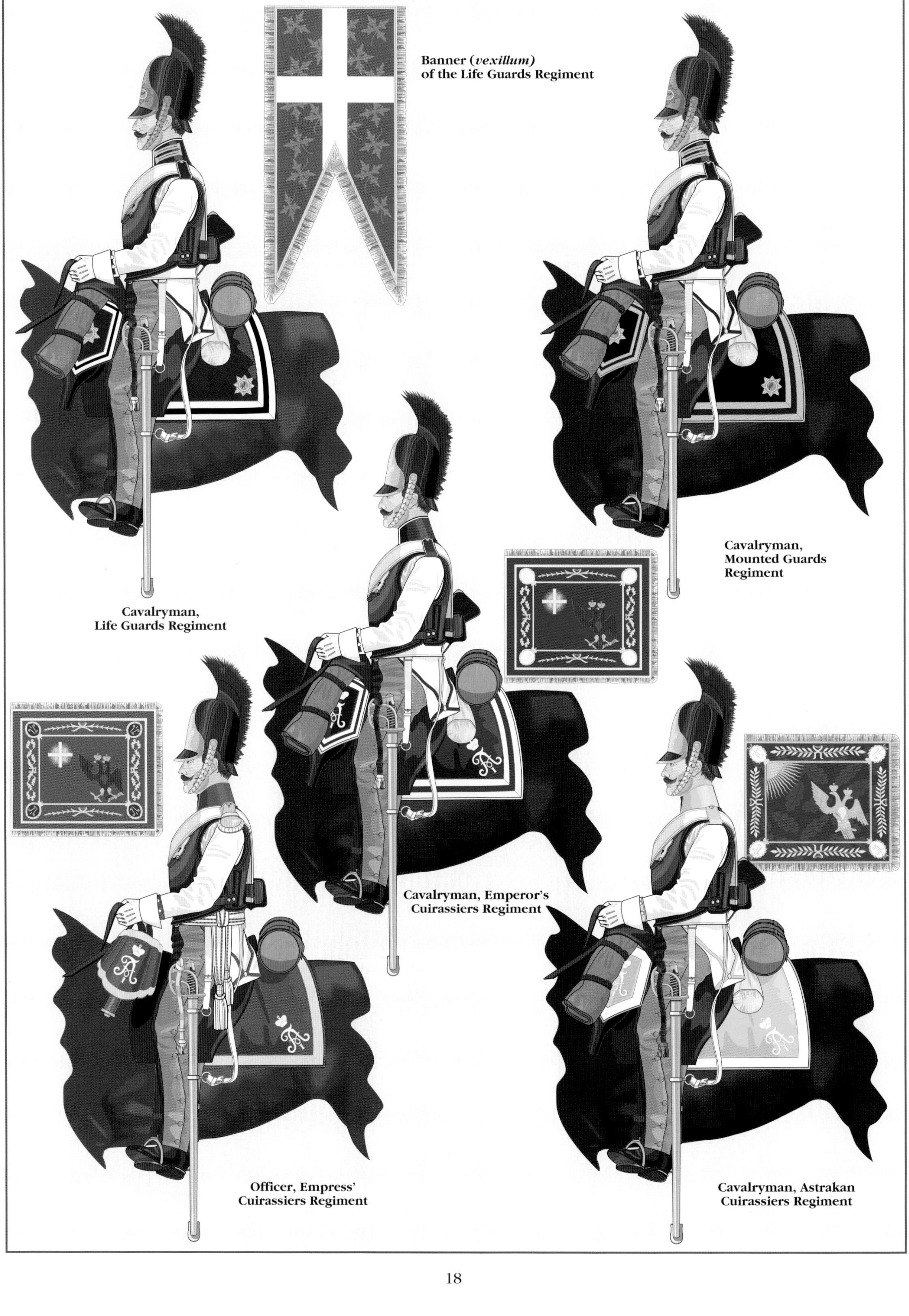

Banner (*vexillum*)
of the Life Guards Regiment

Cavalryman,
Mounted Guards
Regiment

Cavalryman,
Life Guards Regiment

Cavalryman, Emperor's
Cuirassiers Regiment

Officer, Empress'
Cuirassiers Regiment

Cavalryman, Astrakan
Cuirassiers Regiment

André Jouineau © Histoire & Collections 2000

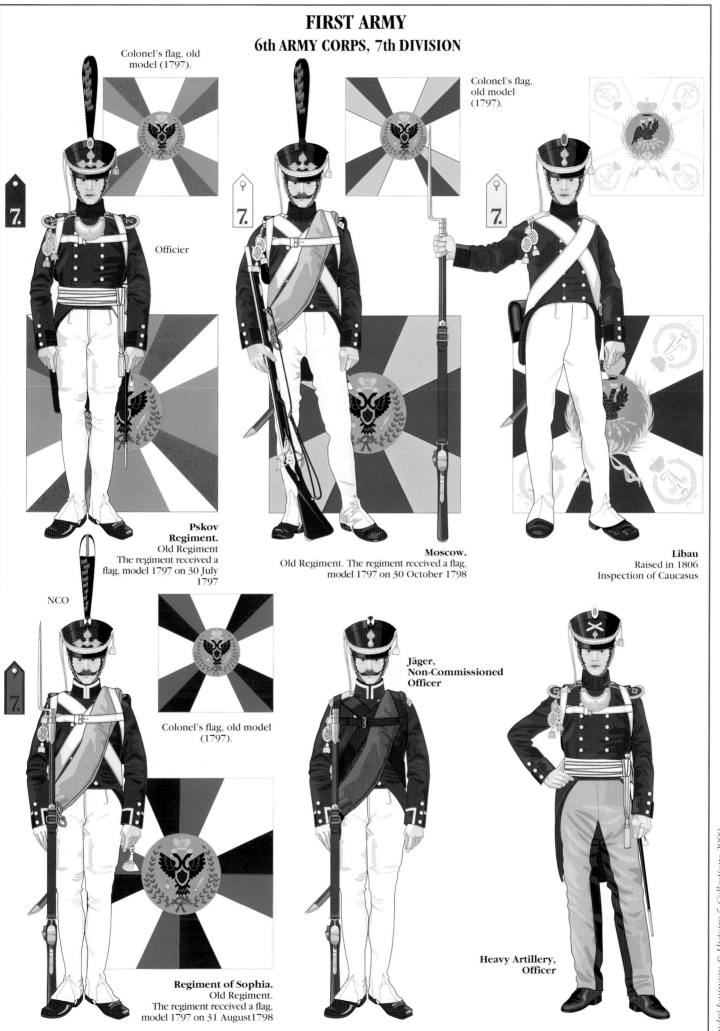

FIRST ARMY
6th ARMY CORPS, 7th DIVISION

Colonel's flag, old model (1797).

Officier

Colonel's flag, old model (1797).

Colonel's flag, old model (1797).

Pskov Regiment.
Old Regiment
The regiment received a flag, model 1797 on 30 July 1797

Moscow.
Old Regiment. The regiment received a flag, model 1797 on 30 October 1798

Libau
Raised in 1806
Inspection of Caucasus

NCO

Colonel's flag, old model (1797).

Regiment of Sophia.
Old Regiment.
The regiment received a flag, model 1797 on 31 August 1798

Jäger,
Non-Commissioned Officer

Heavy Artillery, Officer

André Jouineau © Histoire & Collections 2000

FIRST ARMY
6th ARMY CORPS, 24th DIVISION

Colonel's flag, old model (1797).

Officer

Colonel's flag, old model (1797).

Colonel's flag, old model (1797).

Drummer, Oufa Regiment.
Old Regiment. The regiment received a flag, model 1797 on 9 January 1798.

Chirwan.
Old Regiment
The regiment received a flag, model 1797 on 1st January 1799

Bourtiski.
Old Regiment.
The regiment received a flag, model 1797 on 5 July 1798.
Officer

Colonel's flag, old model (1797).

NCO

Tomsk Regiment.
Old Regiment. The regiment received a flag, model 1797 on 1797 21 January 1799

Cavalryman, Soum Hussars

Heavy Artillery, 24th Company Light Artillery, 45th and 46th Companies Horse Artillery, 7th Battery

André Jouineau © Histoire & Collections 2000

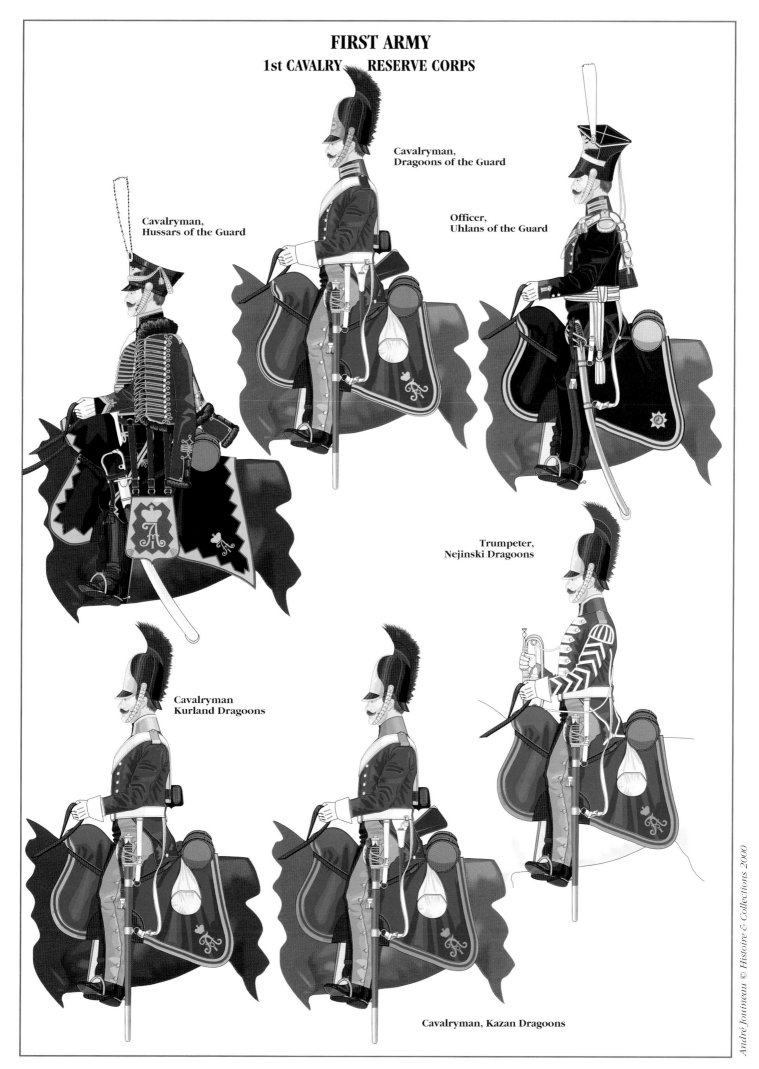

FIRST ARMY
1st CAVALRY RESERVE CORPS

Cavalryman,
Dragoons of the Guard

Cavalryman,
Hussars of the Guard

Officer,
Uhlans of the Guard

Trumpeter,
Nejinski Dragoons

Cavalryman
Kurland Dragoons

Cavalryman, Kazan Dragoons

André Jouineau © Histoire & Collections 2000

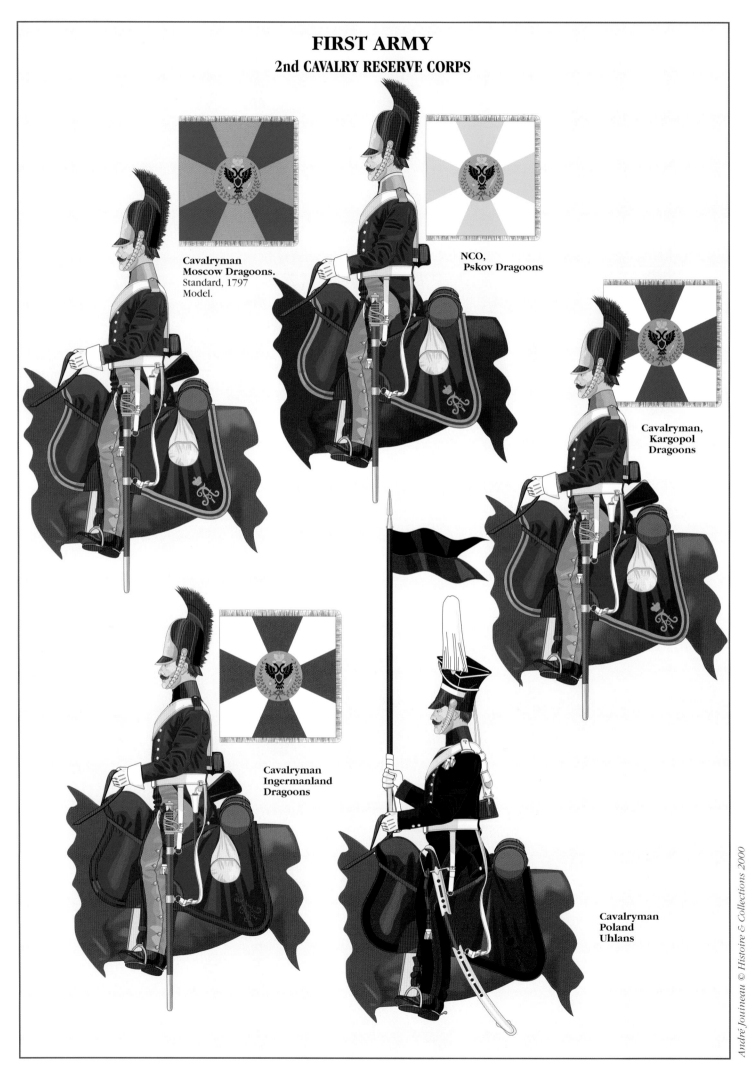

FIRST ARMY
2nd CAVALRY RESERVE CORPS

Cavalryman Moscow Dragoons.
Standard, 1797 Model.

NCO, Pskov Dragoons

Cavalryman, Kargopol Dragoons

Cavalryman Ingermanland Dragoons

Cavalryman Poland Uhlans

André Jouineau © Histoire & Collections 2000

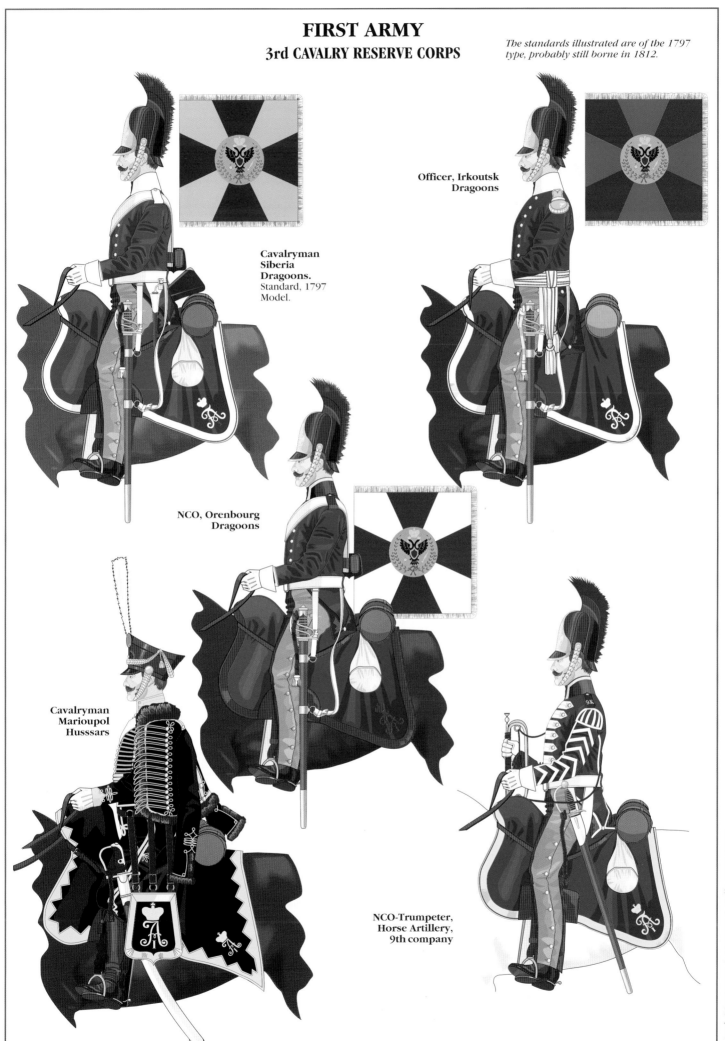

FIRST ARMY
3rd CAVALRY RESERVE CORPS

The standards illustrated are of the 1797 type, probably still borne in 1812.

Officer, Irkoutsk Dragoons

Cavalryman Siberia Dragoons.
Standard, 1797 Model.

NCO, Orenbourg Dragoons

Cavalryman Marioupol Husssars

NCO-Trumpeter, Horse Artillery, 9th company

André Jouineau © Histoire & Collections 2000

General Bagration commanding
the Second Army of the West.

BAGRATION'S 2nd ARMY OF THE WEST

Chief of Staff was **Count Saint Priest**.

RAYEVSKI'S 7th CORPS (14 000 men)

● PASKIEVITCH'S 26th DIVISION.

Infantry

The Ladoga, Poltava, Nigegorod, Orel Regiments, and the 5th and 42nd Jägers.

Artillery

The 26th Heavy and the 47th and 48th Light Companies.

● KOLUBAKIN'S 12th DIVISION

Infantry

The Narva, Smolensk, New Ingria, Alexopol regiments and the 6th and 41st Jägers.

Artillery

The 12th Heavy and the 22nd and 23rd Light Companies; the 8th Company of Light Artillery (attached to the Hussars).

Cavalry

The 8 squadrons of Akhtyrsk Hussars.

BOROSDIN'S 8th CORPS (20 000 men)

● VORONZOV'S COMBINED GRENADIER DIVISION

Combined grenadier regiments from the 2nd, 7th, 12th, 20th 24th and 26th division, two battalions in a division.

● THE PRINCE OF MECKLEMBURG'S COMBINED GRENADIER DIVISION

Combined grenadier regiments from Kiev, Moscow, Astrakhan, Fanagoria, Siberia, and Little Russia, two battalions in a regiment).

Artillery

The 11th Heavy and the 20th and 21st Light Companies.

● DOUKA'S 2nd CUIRASSIER DIVISION

The Cuirassiers from the Ekaterinoslav, the Military Order Regiments. Douka's Cuirassiers with the Gluchov, New Russia and Novgorod Regiments, all these regiments having 4 squadrons.

Artillery

The 31st and 32nd Heavy Companies.

The following particularly have to be mentioned.

● NEVEROWSKI'S 27th DIVISION

As far as Boutourlin was concerned, this division had to be included in the total for Borosdin's Corps.

This was not an Army Corps, but a division which had been heavily committed in order to delay the advance of the French towards Smolensk. It had resisted well against the rather disorganised charges that Murat threw against it but which nevertheless caused severe losses. Because of these losses, the division included 4 regiments with two battalions each:

The Vilna, Simbirsk, Odessa and Tarnopol infantry and the 49th and 50th Jäger regiments. It had lost its artillery.

SIEVER'S 4th CAVALRY CORPS (3 000 men)

The Kharkov, Tchernigov, Kiev and New Russia Dragoons, with 4 squadrons in a regiment. The 8 squadrons of Lithuanian Lancers (Uhlans).

Artillery-Engineers

The 10th Light Artillery Company and the 4th Company of pontoneers and a company of pioneers.

THE ILOVAISKI COSSACKS

These cannot be counted in Platov's 7 000 cavalrymen with their 30 squadrons. Counting 100 Cossacks per squadron, which is few, this repre-

General Raïevski

General Borosdine.

General Duka.

General Sievers.

SECOND ARMY
7th ARMY CORPS, 12th DIVISION

Colonel's flag,
old model (1797).

Colonel's flag,
old model (1797).

Colonel's flag,
old model (1797).

Smolensk.
Old Regiment.
The regiment received
a flag, model 1797 on
15 September 1798

Narva.
Old Regiment raised in 1797.

Alexopol.
Old Regiment. The regiment
received a flag, model 1797 on
30 October 1798

Colonel's flag,
old model (1797).

**Cavalryman,
Achtyrka Hussars**

New Ingermanland Regiment
Old Regiment. The regiment received a flag,
model 1797 on 15 November 1798

André Jouineau © Histoire & Collections 2000

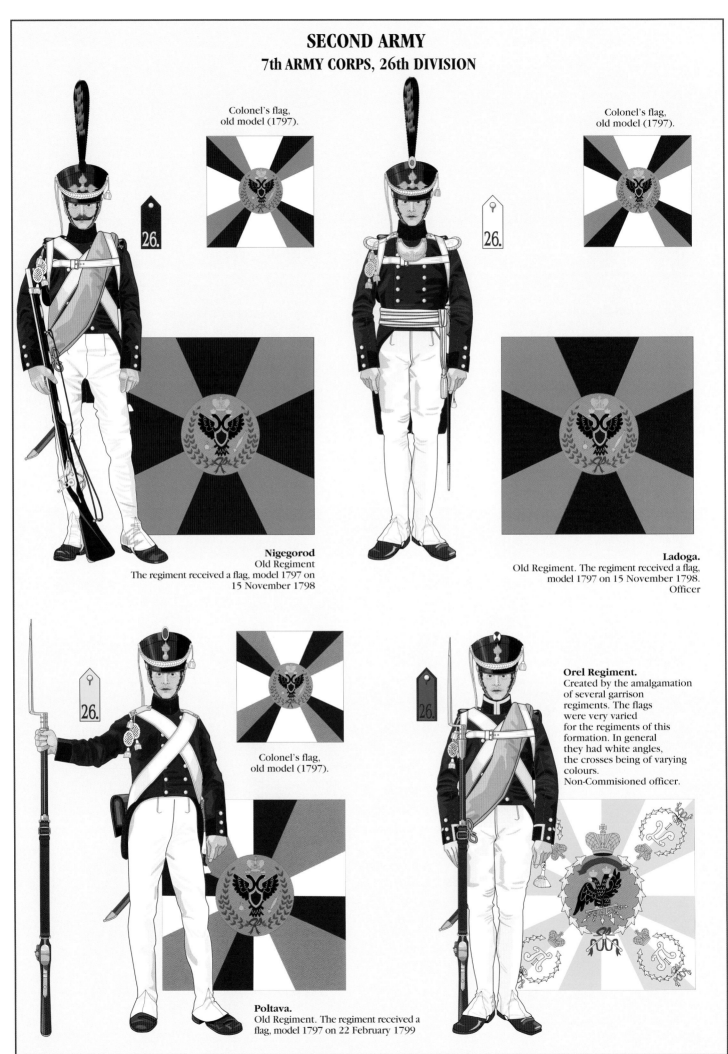

SECOND ARMY
7th ARMY CORPS, 26th DIVISION

Colonel's flag,
old model (1797).

Colonel's flag,
old model (1797).

Nigegorod
Old Regiment
The regiment received a flag, model 1797 on
15 November 1798

Ladoga.
Old Regiment. The regiment received a flag,
model 1797 on 15 November 1798.
Officer

Colonel's flag,
old model (1797).

Poltava.
Old Regiment. The regiment received a
flag, model 1797 on 22 February 1799

Orel Regiment.
Created by the amalgamation
of several garrison
regiments. The flags
were very varied
for the regiments of this
formation. In general
they had white angles,
the crosses being of varying
colours.
Non-Commisioned officer.

André Jouineau © Histoire & Collections 2000

SECOND ARMY
8th ARMY CORPS, VORONZOV AND PRINCE OF MECKLENBURG'S GRENADIERS' DIVISONS

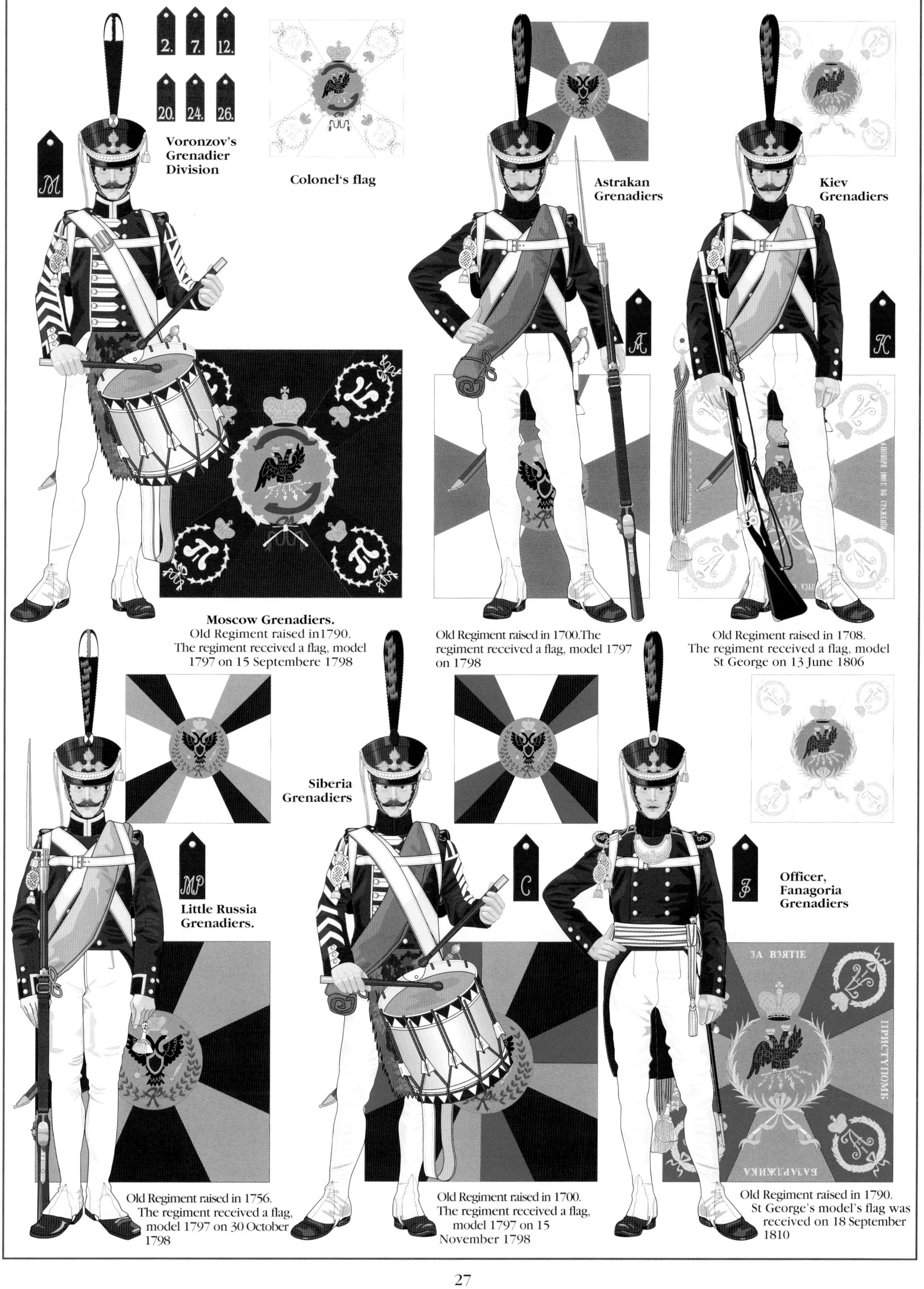

Voronzov's Grenadier Division

Colonel's flag

Astrakan Grenadiers

Kiev Grenadiers

Moscow Grenadiers.
Old Regiment raised in1790. The regiment received a flag, model 1797 on 15 Septembere 1798

Old Regiment raised in 1700.The regiment received a flag, model 1797 on 1798

Old Regiment raised in 1708. The regiment received a flag, model St George on 13 June 1806

Siberia Grenadiers

Little Russia Grenadiers.

Officer, Fanagoria Grenadiers

Old Regiment raised in 1756. The regiment received a flag, model 1797 on 30 October 1798

Old Regiment raised in 1700. The regiment received a flag, model 1797 on 15 November 1798

Old Regiment raised in 1790. St George's model's flag was received on 18 September 1810

André Jouineau © Histoire & Collections 2000

SECOND ARMY
8th ARMY CORPS, 27th DIVISION

Odessa
Regiment raised in 1805
This flag was used since 1811

Vilna
Regiment raised in 1805

Tarnopol.
Regiment raised in 1811

NCO, Simbirsk Regiment.
Regiment raised in 1811

André Jouineau © Histoire & Collections 2000

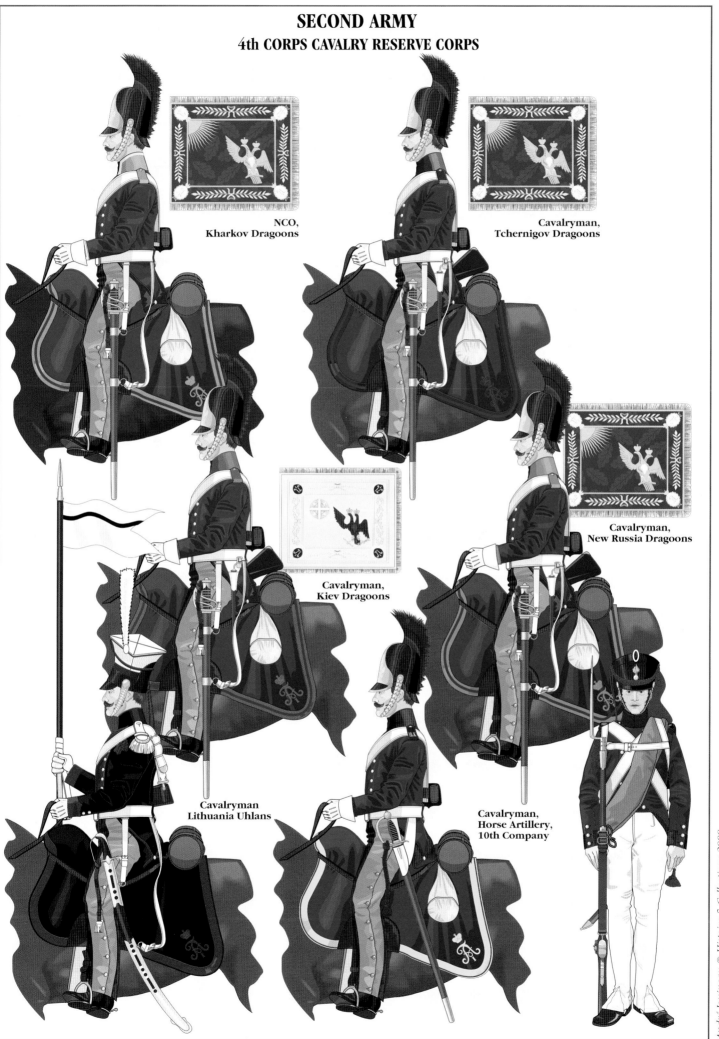

NCO,
Kharkov Dragoons

Cavalryman,
Tchernigov Dragoons

Cavalryman,
New Russia Dragoons

Cavalryman,
Kiev Dragoons

Cavalryman
Lithuania Uhlans

Cavalryman,
Horse Artillery,
10th Company

André Joutineau © Histoire & Collections 2000

sents 3 000 Cossacks forgotten by Boutourlin. These Cossacks were assimilated to a force of 30 squadrons.

Cossack regiments of Ilowaïski (4), of Bug, Oussarev, Syssoiev, Karpov and Andreinov.

Artillery

A company of Don Light Artillery

MILORADOVITCH'S REINFORCEMENTS

These are to be named apart. He only brought back about a thousand Cavalrymen and the Moscow Militia.There were already 3 000 - 5 000 militiamen brought back from Smolensk, the Mocow contingent formed 11 regiments numbering 27 772 men. For the Russians, there were only 20 000 organised into regular troops, the remainder being used for work and for evacuatiing the wounded from the battlefield. They can be thus estimated at 20 000 utilisable fighters. A lot of militiamen served to make up regiments which had been hard hit.

A letter sent on 5th September from Mojaisk, to Rostopchin by Markov, the commander of the Moscow Militia says that eight of his regiments had joined the first army and six the second. He was left with 3 000 men to look after the safety of the villages, of which several had been pillaged and burnt by the camp followers in the baggage train and by Cossacks. He kept a reserve of 4 000 men on the left wing.

RUSSIAN NUMBERS AT BORODINO

BARCLAY DE TOLLY'S ARMY

In his book published in 1824 and dedicated to the Tsar, Boutourlin gave a total of 150 battalions, 134 squadrons of the Line, 72 irregular squadrons and 43 artillery companies (including 2 companies of Pioneers). A battalion corresponded to 650 combattants theoretically, a squadron to 170 cavalrymen, and an artillery company to 230 men; we are a long way from reality.

BAGRATION'S ARMY

There were 58 battalions, 52 squadrons and 17 artillery companies. Taking the theoretical figures, a figure of 50 000 mcn could be reached, but in their report of 27 August, the Russians gave the number of 34 125 soldiers with 73 cannon. Boutoulin gave however 54 200 men for this figure.

THE TOTAL

Boutourlin gave a total figure of 131 200 men present at Borodino for the whole Russian Army; but he forgot Pahlen's cavalry, a certain number of Cossacks and 5 000 militiamen, a total of about 10 000 men. So a grand total of 140 000 men.

THE PROBLEM OF THE MILITIAMEN

The Russian figures estimate more than 30 000 men in the field, but they were used to complete some regiments and were also used for work by the campaigning army. They were only 15 000 combattants regrouped and regimented, who were not actually used, being left in the second line as a reserve on the extreme left.

SOME GENERALITIES ABOUT THE 1812 RUSSIAN ARMY

Like all armies, it had gone through a lot of changes, especially in the spread of the regiments; the basic structure however was fixed.

General Paskievitch.   **General Voronzov.**

General Neverovski.   **Saint-Priest, Chief of Staff.**

The Prussian influence could be felt at every level of the organisation.

I. THE INFANTRY

The regiment. Regiments were made up of three battalions and had: 1 Colonel, 1 Lieutenant-Colonel, 4 Majors, 5 Captains, 14 Lieutenants of which 1 Quartermaster and 1 Pay Officer, 15 Second-Lieutenants, 13 Cadets and 420 Non-Commissioned Officers, 660 Grenadiers and 1 315 musketeers in time of war.

The musicians had 41 Drummers, 8 fifes for the Grenadiers. The Medical Service numbered 19 people. To which be added 6 scribes, 19 armourers, 18 smiths or carpenters, 43 wagonners, 1 Veterinary Surgeon, 1 Judge and 3 provosts. Combattants were: 53 officers, 420 NCOs and about 2 000 soldiers. But grenadier regiments were formed apart from the others and a part of the regiment was left at the depot. At the Moskova, only two battalions of musketeers were present in each regiment, except for the Guard which had three.

Indeed, like in Prussia, the Grenadiers were regrouped in battalions with companies coming from the other regiments of the division and made up grenadier regiments, often elite divisions, like the Voronzov Division, for example. Normal divisions had 4 regiments of musketeers, 2 regiments of jägers and a company of heavy and two companies of light artillery. A regiment of hussars was attached to a division or replaced by regular Cossacks.

THE DIFFERENT TYPES OF INFANTRY AND THEIR UNIFORMS

1. THE INFANTRY OF THE LINE

The soldiers wore a dark green coat with the collar, the facing and the edges red. They had white trousers in summer, fixed on the calves by buttons on the outside. In winter, the trousers were covered with black tanned leather on the legs. The shako was a new model called Kiwer, and had a white cordon with *raquettes* slipping under the right *épaulette*. On the

SECOND ARMY
8th ARMY CORPS, 2nd CUIRASSIERS' DIVISION

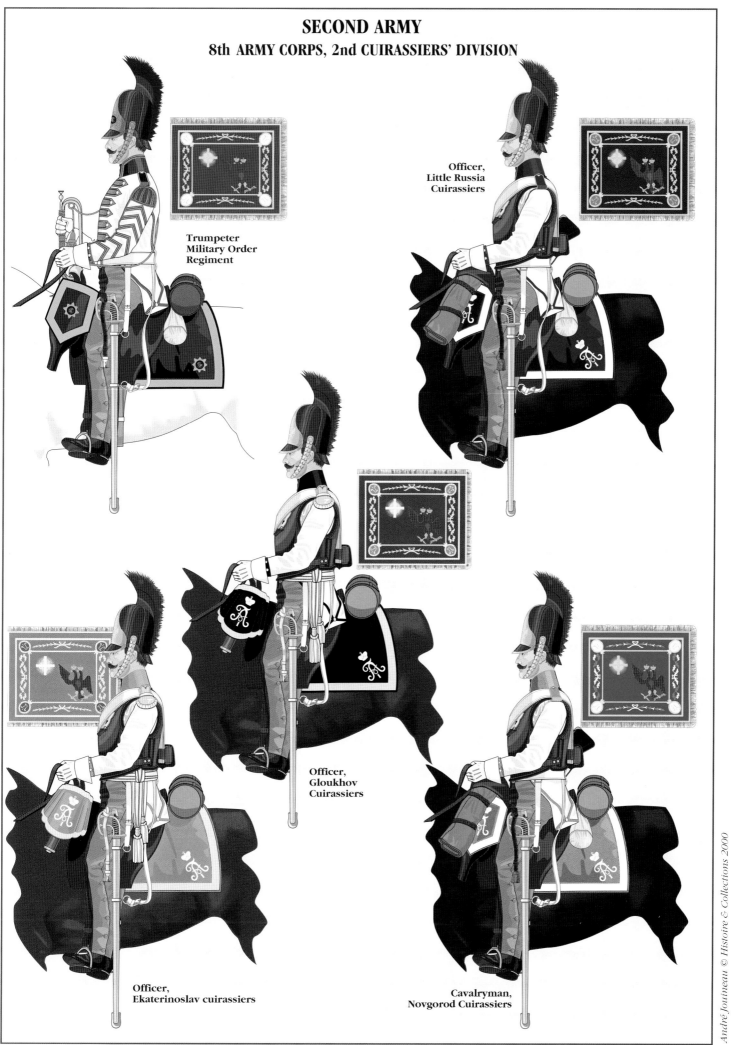

Trumpeter
Military Order
Regiment

Officer,
Little Russia
Cuirassiers

Officer,
Gloukhov
Cuirassiers

Officer,
Ekaterinoslav cuirassiers

Cavalryman,
Novgorod Cuirassiers

André Jouineau © Histoire & Collections 2000

Officers, NCO and drummer of the Infantry of the Guard.

front of the shako a single brass grenade and above a pompom which enabled the battalion and the company to be distinguished by the colour of the centre and the surrounds. The surround for the 1st Battalion was white, green for the 2nd, blue for the 3rd. For the companies, the centre was white for the 1st, 4th and 7th companies, light blue for 2nd, 5th and 8th, and orange for the 3rd, 6th and 9th. The brass grenade was also on the cartridge pouch.

For the grenadiers, they wore a long black plume and the pompom was

A Colonel's flag and two coloured flags (Russian artwork).

entirely red for the 1st Battalion, but for the 2nd battalion, the lower third of the plume was dark green, for the 3rd, light blue and for the skirmishers yellow. On the front of the shako they also had a grenade with three flames which was repeated on the cartridge pouch.

The sword-knots of the sabres were different according to the colours of the three rolls which preceded the white fringes and were as follows for the musketeers: 1st battalion, white; 2nd, dark green; and 3rd light blue; the three rings were red for the grenadiers, yellow for the skirmishers for the 1st battalion and the lowest ring was the battalion colour for the 2nd and the 3rd. (*see illustrations*).

The shoulder flaps enabled one to see the rank of the regiment in its division whose number was as follows: for the 1st regiment of the division, the shoulder flap was red with the number in yellow; for the 2nd white flap and red number; for the 3rd, yellow flap with red number; for the 4th, dark green flap and red number; in the case of a 5th regiment, light blue flap and red number.

They wore their cape rolled over their left shoulder and slipped under the leather harness on that side. NCOs had a quartered shako pompom with the upper and lower parts black mixed with orange, and the side quadrants white. They had a golden stripe round the collar and on the top of the facings. They carried a stick.

The officers had a pompom edged with gilt for the Line, and silver for the Jägers, their epaulettes of rank and a belt scarf mixed with red and gilt, or silver. The musicians had button-holes with white stripes on the front of the coat and on the facings, 6 chevrons on the sleeves topped with litzens.They wore a red plume.

2. THE JÄGERS

They corresponded to the French light infantry. At the Moskova, they covered the front line, forming a mobile curtain in front of the infantry of the line. They were regrouped in regiments wearing a number which was on the shoulder flap and the cartridge pouch. The number of regiments had been raised to 50. In summer they wore a dark green coat with green collar, facings and curls with red edges, with white trousers. In winter the trousers were dark green with leather leggings.

3. THE GUARD

Its particular distinguishing elements were the shako plate with the two-headed eagle, the two yellow stripes on each side of the collar and the facing buttonholes with three stripes. On the cartridge pouch a golden star, with the two-headed eagle in the centre.

— *the old division* included the Preobragenski , Semenovski, Ismaïlovski regiments, the Jägers of the Guard, the Lithuanian Regiment, the Finnish Jägers and the Sailors of the Guard.

The famous Pavlovsk or Pavlovski Regiment which had kept the old mitre as a reward for its conduct at Eylau and the regiment of the Grenadiers of the Guard in 1812 wore the ordinary uniform of the grenadiers of the Line and had not yet been incorporated into the Old Guard. This happened in 1813.

4. THE FLAGS OF THE RUSSIAN INFANTRY

This is a complicated problem which began in 1797 influenced by the Prussian models. Paul 1st began a first modification in 1800 and Alexander continued, reducing the number of flags per regiment still with the white colonel's flag and coloured flags for the battalions, in principal 5 colour flags per regiment, i.e. 2 per battalion or a single colour one as this painting seems to show.

The embroidery was gold for all the regiments, but this applied to the newly-formed regiments; the older ones kept their old flags, in principle. In 1806, the Saint George model appeared with its new lance. The colour of the shaft is that of the 4 regiments of the division: Yellow shaft for the 1st regiment, black for the 2nd, white for the 3rd, yellow for the 4th and black for an eventual 5th.

So in 1812 at the Moskova, several types of flags were used together, with the old and new regiments. They have been illustrated in the most rational way possible. It seems that the colours attributed to each regiment were transfered to Alexander's models in service in 1812. The grenadiers had their own flags, the Jägers had none.

II. THE CAVALRY

The basic element was the squadron. There were 174 cavalrymen per squadron counting all the accompanying services. In the Guard, the number was a little higher, 179 cavalrymen and in wartime, it seems better to count 200 officers and men for a squadron.

1. The CAVALRY of the GUARD

At that time there were only two regiments properly considered as being in the Guard: the Life Guards and the Horse Guards. The Prussian influence was found everywhere in the organisation of this army.

— **The Life Guards**. With their white uniform, they wore scarlet collars and facings and wore the insignia of the Guard which were the two buttonholes on the collar and three on the facings. There were also the Stars of Saint Andrew, one of which was on the helmet and the other on the cartridge pouch; they were also on the saddle blanket and on the hoods which were scarlet bordered with a black stripe between two yellow stripes. On officers the ornaments were silver. Only 19 flankers had a carbine that was rifled. In this regiment, as with the Prussians, the Standard was a vexillum which was left in a safe place during the battle.

— **The Horse Guards.** They have the same insignia as the Guards. The dust cover and the hood were dark blue edged with a red stripe between two yellow stripes. For both regiments the trumpets were made of silver.

— **The Dragoons and the Uhlans.** They were formed in 1809 by the separation of the 10 Uhlan squadrons of Grand Duke Constantine. They wore a green coat but with red lapels. Collars and facings were red and they wore the insignia of the Guard, but the stars were only on the helmet and the cartridge pouch.

The horse's equipment had a green background with a red stripe between two yellow ones and the red imperial monogram. Buttons were yellow and ornaments gold for officers who did not have a cartidge pouch.

For the Hulans or Uhlans (the word was of Turkish origin?), the colours were the same and the details are illustrated. They were in Ouvarov's Corps, like the Hussars.

— **The Hussars of the Guard.** They had a red dolman with dark blue collar and facings, two yellow stripes on the collar and three on the facings. The trousers were dark blue with a yellow stripe. The belt was blue with yellow knots. The pelisse was red with yellow braid edged with fur.

The shako was black with the Imperial eagle, with yellow cord and a white plume. The horse equipment was dark blue, edged with a jagged yellow stripe bordered with red, bearing the imperial monogram. The sabretache was red with yellow ornaments. Only sixteen flankers had a rifled rifle. For the officers, the ornaments were silver and the fur of the pelisse was black

— **The Cossacks of the Guard.**, attached to Touchkov's corps, they are illustrated below.

2. THE CUIRASSIERS

At the Moskova, only the following regiments were present: the Emperor's, the Empress' and the Astrakhan. These three regiments were the first division with the two regiments of the Guard.

The Cuirassiers of the Military Order, the **Ekaterinoslav Cuirassiers,** the **Gloukhov Cuirassiers,** the **Little Russia Cuirassiers,** the **Novgorod Cuirassiers.**

3. THE DRAGOONS.

They wore a green coat with red facings and a *casque à brosse* (helmet with a brush - like top piece). The regiments had 4 war squadrons present and were distinguishable by the colour of the button and that of their distinctive which was on the collar, on the facings and on the horse's equipment, on the saddle stripe. Below are the regiments present at the battle and the colour of their buttons and their distinctives.

— **Courland Dragoons,** turquoise distinctive, yellow buttons.
— **Kasan Dragoons,** light strawberry distinctive, yellow buttons.
— **Negin Dragoons,** turquoise distinctive, yellow buttons, founded in 1806 this regiment was marked by the colours of Courland.
— **Pskof Dragoons,** capucine distinctive, yellow buttons.
— **Moscow Dragoons,** pink distinctive, white buttons.
— **Kargopol Dragoons,** capucine distinctive, white buttons.
— **Finnish Dragoons,** white bordered with red distinctive, yellow buttons.
— **Orenburg Dragoons,** black distinctive, yellow buttons.
— **Siberian Dragoons,** white distinctive, white buttons.
— **Irkhutsk Dragoons,** white distinctive, yellow buttons.
— **Kharkov Dragoons,** orange distinctive, yellow buttons.
— **Tchernigov Dragoons,** ultramarine distinctive, white buttons.
— **Kiev Dragoons,** light strawberry distinctive, white buttons.
— **New Russian Dragoons,** turquoise distinctive, white buttons.

We have presented the trumpeters with red plumes and their stripes. The coat holder was green and often a brass mess tin was attached on the left end. They had their rifles until November 1812.

4. THE UHLANS

This word is of Tartar origin. From 1813 they became more numerous, replacing dragoon regiments. At the Moskova there were apart from the Uhlans of the Guard.

— **the Polish Uhlans.** They had a dark blue uniform, leathered trousers with a double band. On their schapska there was a plume of cock's feathers. There were eight squadrons in the line.

— **the Lithuanian Uhlans.** They were with Bagration, also with eight squadrons.

5. THE HUSSARS

At the Moskova, there were five regiments each with 8 squadrons.

— **The Soum Regiment** wearing a pelisse and a grey dolman with red collars and facings. The trousers were red, the buttons and the fur of the pelisse were white. The belt was red with white loops; the saddlecloth was grey edged with red teeth and the sabretache was red edged and decorated with white.

— **the Isum Regiment** had a dark-blue pelisse, a red dolman with dark-blue collar and facings and trousers of the same colour; white fur. Dark-blue saddle blanket with red teeth, sabretache with a red background

Cuirassiers of the Line

and white decoration. White braid and buttons, blue belt with white loops.

— **the Elizabethgrad Regiment** had entirely grey pelisses and dolmans and dark-green trousers. Braids and buttons were yellow. Shabrack was dark-green with yellow teeth and monogramme. Sabretache was dark-green with yellow ornaments. Red and green belt.

— **the Mariupol Regiment** wore blue pelisses, dolmans and trousers. These were lighter than the Isum Regiment. The collar and the facings of the dolman were yellow.The shabrack was blue with yellow teeth and the sabretache blue with yellow ornaments. Grey belt.

— **the Akhtyrsk Regiment** had a brown pelisse and dolman. The dolman's collar and facings were yellow as well as the braids and the buttons. The trousers were dark blue. The saddle blanket was brown with yellow teeth and the sabretache brown with yellow ornaments.

In all these regiments the NCOs usually had a stripe on the collar and the fur of their pelisse was black. The so-called hussar rifles were abandoned and only 16 flankers per squadron were equipped with them.

6. THE COSSACKS

These irregular troops were allowed all sorts of variations. The Don Cossacks were the most organised with their blue coats striped with red. Several types of Cossacks from different origins have been illustrated; their standards were very fanciful.

III. THE ARTILLERY

1. THE HEAVY ARTILLERY

What distinguished them were the black collars and the facings edged with a red border. The kiwer had a red pompom and red cords. The number of the company was marked on the shoulder straps. The drummers had white striping. The Artillery of the Guard had two collar buttons and the three on the facings were yellow and the eagle on the kiwer was copper. Officers had a star on their horse equipment.

2. THE LIGHT ARTILLERY

Wearing a green-collared coat with black red-edged facings, they had the cavalry helmet and green saddle blanket with a orange-yellow striping. The number of the company was on the red épaulettes. The Light Artillery of the Guard wore the shako with red pompom and cords with the eagle. The plume was red and white for the trumpeters; the striping of their coats was yellow; their trousers were green with a double red stripe. The saddle blanket was green with a double yellow stripe.

There were three types of company with 12 pieces each.

— the Heavy Companies

These had 8 12-pounders of which 4 were medium and 4 short; and 4 heavy 24 - or 16-pounder *unicorns* . All these pieces were pulled by 6 horses.

— the Light Companies

These had 8 6-pounders and 4 12-pounder *unicorns* pulled by 4 horses. Two 3-pounder *unicorns* pulled by only two horses were entrusted, it seems, to the Jägers.

—The Mounted Companies

These had 6 6-pounders and 6 12-pounder *unicorns*, all pulled by 4 horses. The unicorns were particular to the Russian artillery. They could fire cannonballs with a longer range than ordinary pieces; they could also send off grenades.

The little 3-pounder unicorns could shoot off bombs. The official representation of these pieces is given here thanks to our friend Pierre Brétégnier who has the official period plans in his private collection. In the redoubts and the trenches of the Moskova, there were also classic 12-pounders.

A unicorn, particular to the Russian Artillery.

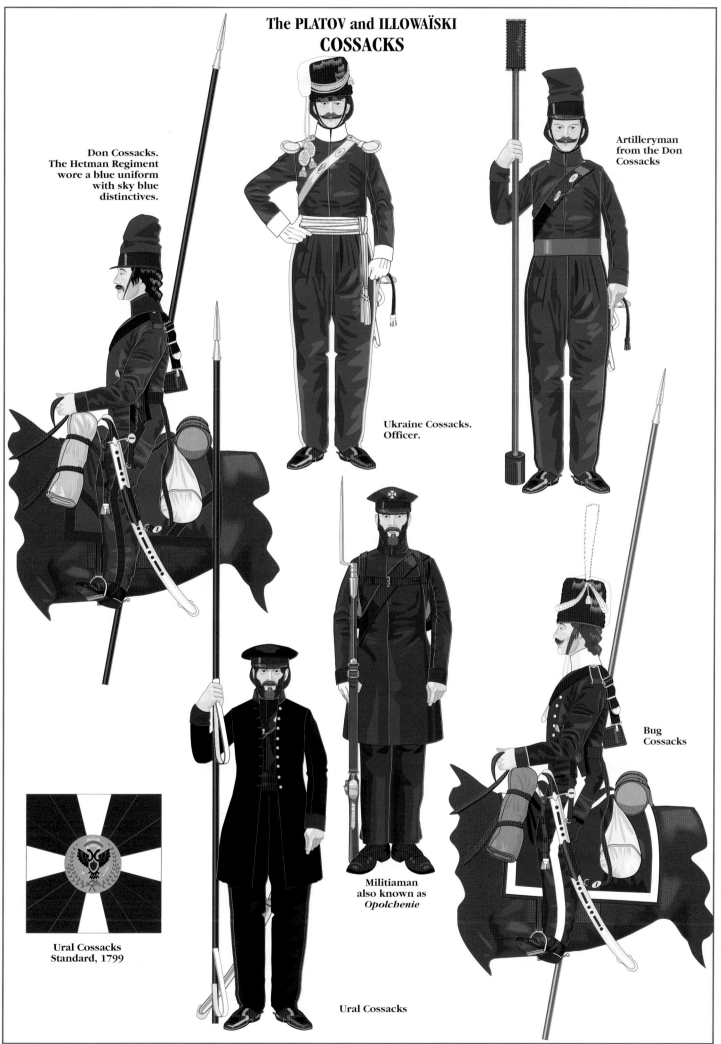

The PLATOV and ILLOWAÏSKI
COSSACKS

Don Cossacks.
The Hetman Regiment
wore a blue uniform
with sky blue
distinctives.

Artilleryman
from the Don
Cossacks

Ukraine Cossacks.
Officer.

Bug
Cossacks

Militiaman
also known as
Opolchenie

Ural Cossacks
Standard, 1799

Ural Cossacks

André Jouineau © Histoire & Collections 2000

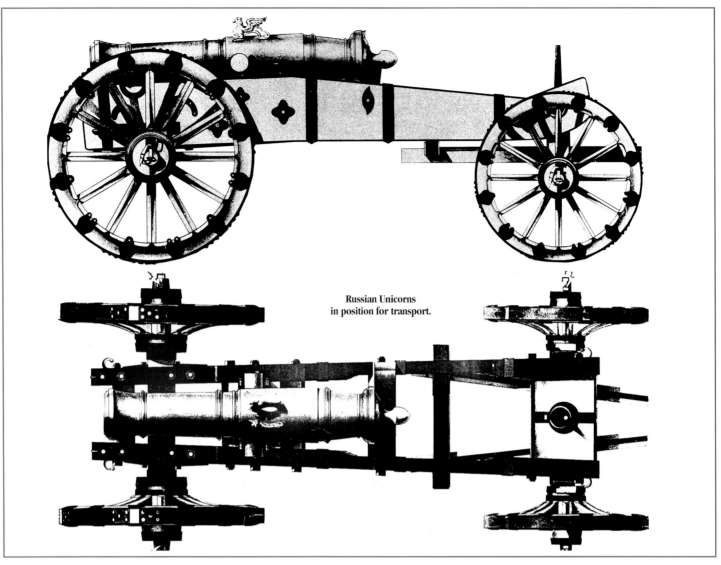

Russian Unicorns
in position for transport.

IV. THE MILITIAMEN OF THE *OPELCHENIE*

At the Moskova, there were the Smolensk and the Moscow militiamen. In their peasants dress, they had a copper cross with the imperial number on their hat or bonnet. Their equipment was just as varied and not all of them had rifles.

The militias had varied banners. The drawings of the banners of the Moscow Militia reproduced in Svegintzov's work and in the Russian work on Borodino are shown below.

At Moscow, two cavalry regiments were better equipped, they were the Black Hussars of Count Saltikov and the Cossacks of Count Mamounov.

The Banner of the Moscow Militia.

THE *GRANDE ARMÉE*

All details concerning this army will be taken up in the chapter concerning the combattants of the Moskova. Here only the general plan is given.

The EMPEROR'S HOUSEHOLD

Duroc was Grand Maréchal du Palais. The cabinet was under the orders of Bacler d'Albe. Napoleon's aide de camps and their suite. The ordnance officers. The Headquarters Staff and General Berthier's staff. The general administration with Matthieu-Dumas.

The IMPERIAL GUARD

Only the Artillery participated at the Moskova.

— **The INFANTRY.** Maréchal Mortier.

The Old Guard: Maréchal Lefebvre. 1st, 2nd, 3rd (ex-Dutch) Grenadier Regiments, 1st, 2nd, 3rd Infantry Regiments.

The Middle Guard. General Roguet. The Fusilier-Grenadiers, the Fusiliers, the 1st Skirmishers, the 1st Light Infantry. The Flankers were left at Smolensk.

The Young Guard. General Delaborde. **Berthezène's Brigade:** the 4th and 5th Light Infantry Regiments and the 4th Skirmishers. **Lanusse's Brigade,** with the 6th Light Infantry and the 5th and 6th Skirmishers. On the 5th September these troops were on the road from Smolensk, where they had been left.

— **The CAVALRY.** Maréchal Bessières.

General Guyot: Cavalry and Mameluks.

General Saint-Sulpice: the Dragoons.

General Krasinski: the 1st Light Horse.

General Colbert: the 2nd Light Horse.

General Durosnel: the Gendarmes d'élite.

— **The ARTILLERY.** General Sorbier.

The only one to participate in the battle, it included:

General Drouot's Heavy Artillery, General Desvaux de Saint-Maurice's Light Artillery, the Pool commanded by General Pellegrin.

— **The SERVICE CORPS**

There was an affectation to each division of the Guard and units of the line reinforced the numbers of this troop. At the beginning there were: 24 12-pounders, 80 6-pounders, 32 4-pounders and 40 howitzers of which 8 were heavy. This made a total of 176 guns taken into the Guard. With 2 000 artillerymen. The line troops came from the 8th Heavy Artillery and the 1st Light Artillery Regiments.

— **The ENGINEERS OF THE GUARD.** General Kirgener.

At Moscow on 1st October, these numbered 5 officers, 150 men and 37 horses. With the Sappers of the Guard there were Berg's Sappers under Captain Blaux.

DAVOUT's FIRST CORPS

By far the largest and the best controlled, it consisted of:

— **The MORAND DIVISION:** the 30th and the 17th of the Line, the 13th Light. 2nd Baden Regiment had a battalion at headquarters and one at Smolensk.

— **The FRIANT DIVISION:** the 15th light, the 33rd and the 48th of the Line. The Joseph Napoleon Regiment. Only two battalions were present with Friant (2nd and 3rd).

— **The GERARD DIVISION** (ex-Gudin): the 7th Light, the 12th and 21st of the Line. The recent 127th Regiment was not at the Moskova.

— **The DESSAIX DIVISION:** the 33rd Light was left in the rear and did not take part in the battle, like the Hessian Battalion. The 85th and the 105th of the line were the only ones present.

— **The COMPANS DIVISION:** with the winners of Schwardino: the 25th, 57th, 61st and 111th of the Line.

— **The 1st CORPS' CAVALRY:** Commanded by Pajol up to 9th August 1812; he was put at the head of the 2nd Division of Montbrun's Cavalry Corps. So at the Moskova, the two Brigadier-Generals assumed the command. They were Bordessoulle with the 2nd Chasseurs and the 9th Polish Lancers, and Girardin with the 1st and 3rd Chasseurs. He was the appointed replacement.

— **The 1st CORPS' ARTILLERY:** commanded by General de Pernety aided by Generals Baltus and Jouffroy.

Total Equipment: 12 12-pounders with 50 6-pounders and 64 regimental 3-pounders. 12 howitzers of which 4 heavy. In all 138 guns, theoretically.

— **The ENGINEER's CORPS:** commanded by Haxo, it had 6 companies of sappers at its disposal and one Service Corps company.

NEY 'S 3rd CORPS.

— **The LEDRU DIVISION** (10th Division): the 24th Light, the 46th and 72nd of the Line. The 1st Portuguese with two weakened battalions.

— **The RAZOUT DIVISION:** (11th Division): the 4th, 18th and 93rd of the Line. The two battalions of the 2nd Portuguese, also weakened. The Illyrian Regiment was at the rear and did not participate in the battle.

— **The WURTEMBURGERS** (25th Division): they were commanded, from the 9th August by General Marchand. They consisted of 2 battalions of Chasseurs, 2 regiments of Light Infantry. 4 Line Regiments of two battalions and 4 artillery companies, of which 2 were Light Artillery.

Many men were left in the rear and there were only about 2 000 at the Moskova.

— **The CAVALRY:** Mourier's Brigade, with the 11th Hussars, the 28th French Chasseurs and the 4th Wurtemburgers attached afterwards.

Beurmann's Brigade with the 4th and 28th Chasseurs and the 1st and 2nd Wurtemburger Light Horse.

— **The ARTILLERY:** commanded by Foucher du Carteil with 7 companies of Heavy Artillery. From Wurtemburg two companies of Heavy and two of Light Artillery. Total Equipment: 18 12-pounders, 34 6-pounders, 20 howitzers of which 4 heavy.

— **The ENGINEER's CORPS:** three companies of sappers.

PRINCE EUGENE's 4th CORPS.

The Italian division of General Pino did not participate in the Battle of the Moskova. This considerably reduced the numbers of this corps for the battle. There remained for Prince Eugene:

— **The DELZONS DIVISION** (13th Division): the 8th Light, the 84th, 92nd and 96th of the Line. The Provisional 1st Croatian took part at the Moskova with its two battalions.

— **The BROUSSIER DIVISION** (14th Division): the 18th Light and the 9th, 35th and 53rd of the Line. Two battalions of the Joseph Napoleon (the 1st and 4th). The other two battalions were with Friant in the 1st Corps.

— **The ITALIAN GUARD:** the Guard of Honour, two battalions of Velites,

FRENCH FORCES AT BORODINO

It is possible to spend hours discussing this subject and the results will always be approximate. Baron Fain in his 1812 manuscript published in 1827, gave a total of 120 000 men present at the battle on the French side. Relying on the archives, on certain witnesses and on the precise position of the regiments at the beginning of September 1812, a reasonably close estimate can be reached.

For the French, the Russians gave very high figures which had already been reduced by 15% because they knew that Napoleon always exaggerated his figures to impress his opponents. The basis for the Russian figures was furnished by the documents that Czernitchev obtained in Paris. He had bribed a certain Michel, a clerc in the War Department. This Michel was discovered and shot. Boutourlin gave 152 000 Frenchmen present at the battle. This is very much exaggerated and impossible. Here is a rough analysis taking into account the toll, the figures given by the generals or colonels concerning their own regiments and the regiments left in the rear. It is known that thousands of laggards pillaged the country around Minsk and that the foreign regiments in particular just melted away.

It is also necessary to take into account the numerous fights along the way which caused heavy losses for certain units. The hospitals were filled with the wounded of which a certain number were evacuated towards Germany. A lot of sick conscripts were also in these hospitals because they had not had the streng-

th to follow and the lack of ressources in the country worsened their condition.

Finally the conquered towns had to be occupied and lines of communication protected. Battalions of draft dodgers coming from Walcheren and prisoners from Spain were used; they were not very enthusiastic, ready to desert at any moment. Thus laggards, deserters and the sick disappeared along the way in addition to the casualties from the various fights.

Berthezène, who commanded a brigade of the Young Guard said that at the beginning of the campaign an infantry regiment had to be counted as 2 500 men on average, a regiment of light cavalry at 800 horsemen and a regiment of heavy cavalry at 400 men. Starting from this base, it is possible to evaluate the numbers in a regiment taking into account its origin and its activities before reaching the battlefield of the Moskova.

General van Dedem commanding the 35th of the Line and 2 battalions of the Joseph Napoleon Regiment belonging to the most solid and the best commanded of the corps - the first - said simply that the figures given on the 1st September had been increased by 35 000 men, who were absent on the field. For him, on the battlefield of the September 1812 only 115 000 men on the French side. Some works give 130 000 Frenchmen present. It must not be forgotten that at Moscow, there were more than 90 000 men left with of course the arrival of the marching battalions coming up in reinforcement and the return of certain regiments or even divisions like Pino's. The most realistic figure, in my opinion is that already given, namely 115 000 present at the battle.

Each corps and each regiment has been scrutinised together with its problems and with this backtracking, a figure of this order will be reached. It must be known that as well for the cavalry, there were men present though only mounted men were sent forward into the line. The increasing dearth of horses led to this weakness in that cavalrymen who had become infantrymen were present but not used in the battle.

It can be admitted that the Russians had a slight numerical advantage as they had between 130 000 and 140 000 men. However, in this number the irregular troops, the Moscow and Smolensk militiamen and the Cossacks who were much less efficent in a set battle, have also been included. It must be remembered that Napoleon did not commit his Guard. Only the artillery was used and certain regiments did not actually fight during this day.

THE UNIFORMS OF THE *GRANDE ARMEE* IN 1812

These are presented with the details of the regiments. The French uniforms are well known, bearing in mind that the famous ordnance of 1812 which was to regulate dress was only applied after this campaign. As far as the flags are concerned, there was a new model, with three vertical bands, but certain flags of the old model were no doubt present, like that of the 1st Grenadiers of the Guard, by tradition or for some regiments coming from afar.

The uniforms of the foreign troops are more interesting. Only the corps having taken part in the battle of the Moskova. are detailed below with the study of the regiments.

---

two battalions of infantry and two battalions of conscripts. Dragoons of the Guard and the Queen's Dragoons, two squadrons.

— **PREYSSING's BAVARIAN CAVALRY** should have followed the 6th Corps, but was attached to the 4th Corps with Ornano. 3rd, 4th,5th and 6th Light Horse and Bidermann's light battery.

— **The ARTILLERY:** partly with Pino's Division. From the 2nd Heavy Artillery Regiment, 7 companies. From the 4th Light Artillery Regiment, the 2nd and 3rd Companies.

From the Italian Guard: two heavy artillery and one light companies. plus 2 heavy artillery companies in reserve.

The equipment: 24 12-pounders, 46 6-pounders, 24 3-pounders and 22 howitzers.

— **The ENGINEER's CORPS:** three companies of sappers.

PONIATOWSKI's 5th CORPS

Dombrowski's 17th Regiment was left in the rear and ended up at Borisov.

— **ZAYONCHEK's 16th INFANTRY DIVISION:** including the 3rd, 13th, 15th and 16th Polish Regiments.

— **KAMENIEKI's 18th DIVISION:** including the 2nd, 8th and 12th Polish Regiments.

— **The CAVALRY:** including the 7th, 8th and 11th Polish Lancers with in principle the 13th Hussars and the 5th Chasseurs. In fact the Polish cavalry regiments were numbered from 1 to 17 no matter what their speciality. Thus the Cuirassiers were the 14th regiment although there was only one regiment of this type in the army of the Grand Duchy of Warsaw.

— **The ARTILLERY:** 2 companies each of Heavy and Light Artillery equipped with 6 12-pounders, 30 6-pounders and 12 howitzers.

JUNOT's 8th CORPS

These were the Westphalians who had been deserted by their King, infuriated by his unfortunate beginnings and refusing to take orders from Davout. It was Junot who was given the command, but he was on the verge of madness and was incapable of commanding efficiently.

They had already left behind them a lot of stragglers and looters since Vilna.

— **OCHS' 25th INFANTRY DIVISION.** The 2nd and 3rd light battalions. The 2nd, 3rd, 6th and 7th regiments of the Line with two battalions.

— **THARREAU's 24th DIVISION.**The battalion of Carabiniers, the

battalion of Chasseurs of the Guard, the battalion of Grenadiers Guards and the 1st Light battalion.

Three regiments were left in the rear and were not present at the Moskova (1st, 5th and 8th of the Line).

— **The CAVALRY:** the 1st and 2nd Hussars of 4 squadrons.The Light Horseguards of 4 squadrons.

— **The ARTILLERY** included 26 6-pounders and 8 24-pound howitzers.

MURAT's CAVALRY RESERVE

It included 4 corps.

NANSOUTY's 1st CORPS

— **The De BRUYERES LIGHT DIVISION:** including the 7th and 8th Hussars, the 9th Light Horse, the 16th Chasseurs, the 6th and the 8th Polish Lancers together with the 2nd Prussian Hussars.

— **The SAINT-GERMAIN DIVISION:** including the 2nd, 3rd and the 9th Cuirassiers and the 1st Light Lancers.

— **The VALENCE DIVISION:** including the 6th, 11th and 12th Cuirassiers and the 5th Light Horse.

— **The PAJOL LIGHT DIVISION:** the 5th and 9th Hussars, the 11th and 12th Chasseurs plus the 1st Prussian Lancers, the 3rd Wurtemburger Chasseurs and the 10th Polish Regiment (Hussars).

— **The WATIER DE SAINT ALPHONSE DIVISION:** the 5th, 8th and 10th Cuirassiers plus the 2nd Light Horse.

— **The DIVISION DE FRANCE:** the 1st and 2nd Carabiniers, the 1st Cuirassiers and the 4th Light Horse.

GROUCHY's 3rd CORPS.

— **The CHASTEL LIGHT DIVISION** with the 6th Hussars, the 6th, 8th and 25th Chasseurs.

— **The La HOUSSAYE DIVISION** with the 7th, 23rd, 28th and 30th Dragoons.

LATOUR-MAUBOURG's 4th CORPS.

— **The ROZNIECKI LIGHT DIVISION** with the 3rd, 15th and 16th Polish Lancers.

— **The LORGE DIVISION** with the Saxon Lifeguards, Zastrov's Saxon Cuirassiers, the Polish Cuirassiers (14th Regiment) and the 1st and 2nd Westphalian Cuirassiers.

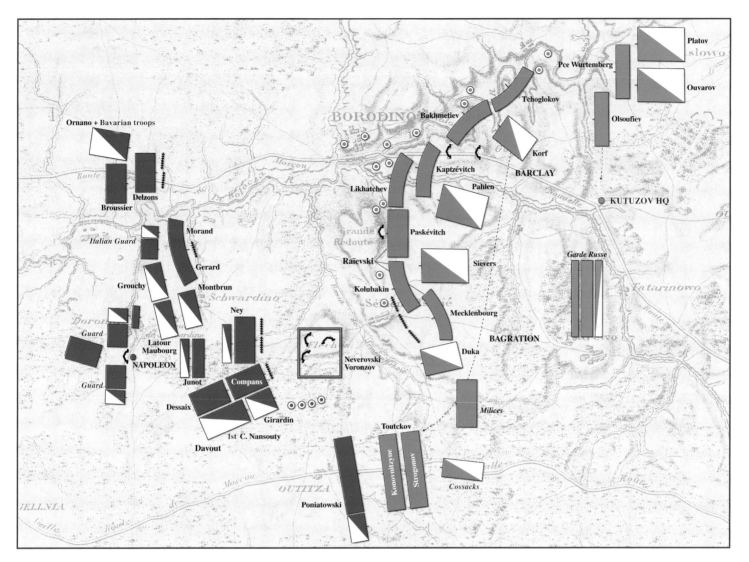

THE BATTLE

5th SEPTEMBER 1812

THE CAPTURE OF THE REDOUBT AT SCHWARDINO

On the 5th September, in the morning at 6 o'clock, the French were on the march. Konovnitzin who was commanding the Russian rearguard was on a level with the Abbey of Koloshoi, but was constantly being pushed back and eventually rejoined the Russian lines towards Borodino.

Murat's vanguard had been supported by Compans' Division from the 1st Corps ever since Viasma. Poniatowski's Corps came up on the right following the old Smolensk-Moscow road, towards the village of Jelnia and the 4th Corps of the Viceroy Eugène which marched on Borodino on the left of this big road. Napoleon arrived at the front to examine the enemy dispositions.

Discovering on the right of the Kolocha, the very numerous Russian Jägers, spread out in skirmishing formation, and seeing behind them the forward redoubt of Schwardino, he ordered this "curtain" which protected the Russian left to be "torn". General Compans was ordered to undertake this mission, with the support of Poniatowski who advanced with great difficulty throught the wood situated to the south of the redoubt, and with the support of Murat's cavalry. It was late in the afternoon, towards 5 o'clock, when the attack began.

On the Russian side, Colonel Toll, who was in the redoubt at the beginning, warned that large forces were approaching. The defence was given to General Gortchakov, the nephew of old Souvarov. Neverovski's 27th Division was in the front line. When necessary, Bagration had them supported by Gluckov's curassiers and by those of Little Russia taken from the

Russian artillerymen

2nd Cuirassier Division, and also by dragoons from Siewers' 4th Corps and the 2nd division of Vorontsov's grenadiers. The Akhtyrsk Hussars were also present, as well as two batteries of 12 cannon, including one mounted.

COMPANS' DIVISION ATTACKS

Compans formed a combined corps of light infantrymen made up of the 57th with the 61st and the 25th. The latter marched ahead of the 57th with its five battalions, followed by the 61st.

It was Major Duchesne, of the 25th who commanded these light infantrymen forming two little battalions made up as follows: The 1st Battalion included the 1st Light Infantry Company of the 25th and the 1st and 2nd of the 57th. The 2nd had the 3rd and 4th Companies of the 57th and the 1st of the 61st. Going through Famkino, the forward elements, the light infantrymen, the 57th and the 61st marched on Doronino. The 1st Battalion attacked this village, but needed the support of 6 companies of the regiment to overwhelm the defenders. Duchesne's 1st Light Infantry Battalion cleaned up the woods around Doronino. Meanwhile the 25th advanced towards the village of Schwardino, supported by the 111th, which was a little further to the north, towards Alzinski.

The Russian Cuirassiers had come to grips with the Cavalry of Montbrun's 2nd Corps and reached the infantry which had to fight them off; the 2nd, 3rd and 4th Battalions of the 61st and the Grenadiers of the 57th took charge of this. The French Cavalry reinforcements cleaned up the area and the redoubt set up on the top of the little hill was now isolated.

To the west of the redoubt, Compans used a hill to install the 1st Light Infantry Battalion with some artillery whose 12-pounders had a good position within range and could fire on the redoubt.

A first attack was launched with a column of the 61st (2nd and 3rd Battalions) to the left and one column with the 2nd Battalion of the combined Light Infantry followed by the 1st Battalion of the 61st. The other two battalions were kept in reserve in support of the artillery; the 57th was on the right. When the French arrived on the brink of the redoubt, the defenders sent down a wall of fire which drove back the attackers whose impetus was thus broken. Compans then brought up 4 artillery pieces loaded with grapeshot, hidden behind the 2nd Battalion of the 57th. On the edge of the redoubt, the infantry opened up and the pieces went into action decimating the defenders and opening a breach into which poured the 57th , supported by the 2nd Light Infantry and the 1st Battalion of the 61st. The redoubt was taken together with its 12-pounders. For Charriere, the Colonel of the 57th, there were 12 pieces; another witness counted only 8. The occupants of the redoubt were killed or thrown out. Morand's division of the 1st Corps came up in support. The 17th Regiment of the line had 2 officers killed.

It was eight o'clock in the evening; Bagration tried to counter-attack; he claimed even to have recaptured the redoubt, but it was the Russian dragoons in particular that bore the brunt of the action. The Karkov and the Tchernigov Dragoons fell on the 111th and captured two regimental pieces. The Akhtyrsk Hussars who were protecting a battery of 6-pounders charged as well. The Kiev Dragoons and the Karpov Cossacks fought against the Poles, and the Russian infantry recaptured the outposts which protected the Russian left to the rear. This night fighting was very disorganised and almost impossible to trace exactly.

It was ten o'clock at night when calm fell again on this terrible field; the prelude was over.

THE FRENCH LOSSES

It is possible to be more precise here for we possess the reports and the rolls for the French. Moreover, on 10 October, in Moscow, the Emperor

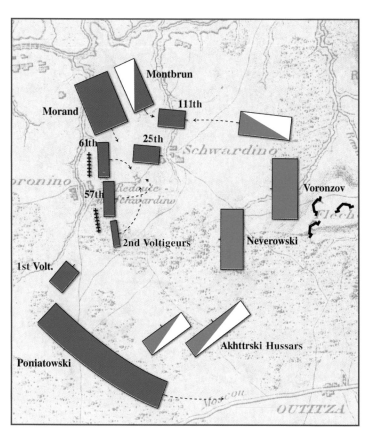

The Redoubt at Schwardino

reviewed only the Compans Division, thus recognising its merits; he granted a lot of rewards to these men. The 57th lost three officers killed, including the Battalion Commander Gelée de Laboulaye and three other officers who died of their wounds in Kolochoi Abbey which had become the main hospital for the battle and afterwards. Thirty-three soldiers were killed.

THE REDOUBT AT SCHWARDINO

Eight officers and 336 men were wounded, but many continued to serve. For the light infantry, 2 officers and 71 men were wounded.

For 11 other companies no figures are available. Many received a citation for bravery. The 61st lost one officer and 29 men killed and 12 officers and 226 men wounded, among them a light infantry officer.

Captain Duhoux was mentioned as the first to enter the redoubt at the head of the Grenadiers of the 1st Battalion. Wounded in Egypt, he was battalion commander at Moscow and was killed at Waterloo. Many received citations on 7th September. Also at Moscow, 18 officers and 8 NCOs were awarded the *Légion d'Honneur*. 20 second-lieutenants were appointed. The 111th had the following losses on the 5th September: 4 officers and 82 men killed and 15 officers and 540 men wounded. 171 men were captured or got lost.

The 25th lost three officers and 25 men killed and two officers and 216 men wounded on the 5th September. For the 5th September, the total losses for the Compans Division were 14 officers and 169 men killed, 37 officers and 1 118 men wounded and 171 missing from the 111th during the night attacks by Russian dragoons. So for Schwardino the total was 1 472 men out of action; this figure is theoretical because a good number of the wounded took part in the battle on the 7th; this is clear from the reports.

THE RUSSIAN LOSSES

3 000 men are said to have been lost. The Russians say that Neverowski had received 4 000 recruits to fill the ranks, that he had 6 000 men at Schwardino and left with 3 000. They estimated that 6 000 men were lost on both sides, which was false as far as the French were concerned but gives an idea of the Russian losses on the 5th September.

PREPARATIONS FOR THE BATTLE

THE 6th OF SEPTEMBER 1812

THE FRENCH LAYOUT

Napoleon had the enemy installations reconnoitered and set out his army accordingly.

ON THE LEFT, UNDER THE COMMAND OF PRINCE EUGENE

Since the 4th Corps was rather weakened and Pino's Division was missing, he removed two divisions from Davout - Morand's and Gérard's (ex-Gudin). These two divisions by chance were placed on the most exposed spot, facing the big redoubt. Grouchy's 3rd Cavalry Corps was affected to this wing in support.

ON THE CENTRE NEY'S CORPS, AND FURTHER BEHIND, JUNOT'S

They were reinforced by a powerful 60-strong battery of Guards Artillery. They faced the two Russian outposts furthest on the left, below the village of Semenovskoï. Foucher, commanding Ney's artillery set up a second strong battery facing these outposts. Friant's division from the 1st corps was placed in reserve on their right flank. Montbrun's cavalry corps and on his right, Latour-Maubourg's, were to operate in the centre, they were to the left of Ney's Corps, and slightly behind it.

ON THE RIGHT DAVOUT ONLY HAD

Compans' and Dessaix's divisions, the light cavalry division of the 1st Corps, Nansouty's 1st Cavalry Corps and the artillery.

ON THE FAR RIGHT, PONIATOWSKI'S POLES

They were facing the village of Utitsa on the old Smolensk to Moscow road.Napoleon's command post was on the heights. It was set up in front of the Schwardino redoubt and afforded a good view of the whole layout, except for two distant zones. It was a little more than half a mile from the

The troops set up camp and the Emperor had his tents placed on a height behind the village of Valuïeva.

Russian front line, facing Semenovskoï and Bagration's outposts. With his telescope he could see the redoubt which was about a mile away. In such a frontal battle, it was not understood why Napoleon himself should have moved up so close to the lines of fire; this has often been criticised even though it was the Emperor's habit to be close so that all information would converge on him. Towards 4 o'clock he moved even further forward to evaluate the effect of his offensive; the front line had moved away and he had to decide which attacks and tactics to adopt.

THE SETTING UP OF THE RUSSIAN LINES

They were out of place in relation with the French lines. Kutusov placed his command post behind Gorki, situated near the Moscow road. The Russian Commander-in-Chief did not budge from his seat, a little bench, seeing nothing of the battle. Colonel Löwenstein was with Barclay de Tolly and he followed him on visits made to Kutuzov at rare moments in the battle. The colonel relates that:

"The Prince, with a brilliant headquarters staff, did not move from the main road, in front of Mojaïsk. He had taken up, so to speak, an unassailable position, sitting, in the middle of the fields on a folding chair which an orderly carried around with him everywhere. Nothing could be seen from this point, but then nobody could see them either. Thus, on the evening after the battle, the two or three hundred people who had been with him were perfectly safe."

The battlefield was very spread out since 3 miles separated Gorki from Utitsa and the reserves situated to the left of Gorki were nearly four miles

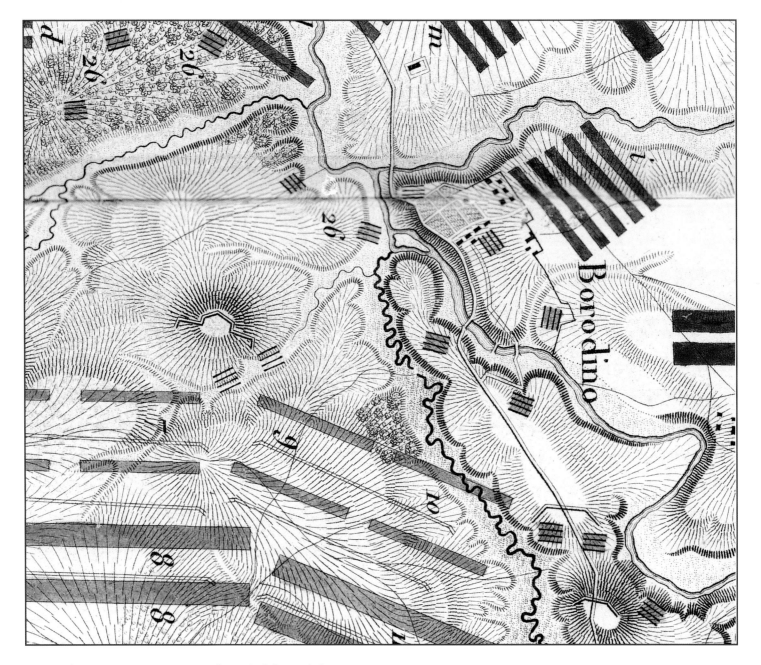

The Great Redoubt (Boutourlin's Map, 1823)

away. As these reserves were sent to reinforce the left, it took them some time to move across, particularly in the middle of the battle.

Looking at the map of the battle carefully we get the impression that it took place to the side of the terrain and not at all in the direction that the genial thinkers on the Russian General staff had chosen.

They had prepared everything as if the French army was actually going to follow the road to Moscow and attack along its axis. The principal redoubts were the two positioned in front of Gorki and the great redoubt which alone was to become famous. It was a mile further to the left, turned towards the Moscow road. So naturally Napoleon attacked the weakest point, the Russian left, whose first section, Schwardino, had fallen on 5th July.

To defend this vast two mile wide sector, there was only Bagration's army to start with, strung out between the great redoubt occupied by Paskevitch from Rayevski's Corps, and the woods at Outitsa. The main army, Barclay's, was centered on Kutuzov's headquarters set up behing Gorki.Barclay, who had lost his post as commander in chief, remained passive, trying only to expose himself rather than really fighting.

This curious glaring discrepancy between the adversaries' positions did not over-alarm the Russian strategists who had all the day of the 6th to think about it. The only measure taken was to send Tutchov's Corps to the far left in front of Ouititsa. The remainder of the set up was kept in place as if

Napoleon was in front of Borodino and not along the axis of the burnt out village of Semenovskoi, where he in fact had chosen to be. At this point the access to the plateau is easier, the defences being only outlined in the form of earthen outposts. The little ravine of the stream nevertheless protected Semenskoi and in front of the burnt out village some artilery pieces were lined up. Looking at the map, this all appears evident when the disposition of these two totally offset armies on this terrain is considered.

DISPOSITION OF THE RUSSIAN TROOPS

GORKI, THE CENTRE OF THE RUSSIAN ARMY

It was on the heights overlooking the hollow in which Borodino was situated and was separated from it by the two terrassed redoubts, cutting the Moscow road. Kutuzov's headquarters were behind them.

TO THE RIGHT OF GORKI

Under the command of Miloradovitch, in the line there were Schuvalov's 4th Corps: Bakhmetyev's and Tchogolov's divisions. Behind them, Korf's 2nd cavalry corps.

Further right, Baggovut's 2nd corps, the Olsufiev and Prince Eugen of Wurtemberg's Divisions. Even more to the right, Ouvarov's cavalry with Platov's Cossacks spread out further north.

TO THE LEFT OF GORKI

Between the village and the great Rayevski redoubt there were Dokhtourov's 6th corps: the Kapsevitch and Likhatchev divisions. Behind them, Pahlen's 3rd Cavalry Corps.

BETWEEN THE GREAT REDOUBT AND THE VILLAGE OF SEMENOVSKOI

There were the soldiers of Bagration's second army whose positions started from there, covering the village of Semenovskoï and the three outposts. Paskievitch occupied the redoubt. The first in line was Rayevski's 7th Corps. Behind him, Sievers' cavalry. On the heights of Semenovskoï, the village had been burnt and a series of artillery pieces set up. Borosdin's 8th Corps covered this sector. In the outposts, were the remaining elements of Neverovski's 27th division and Voronzov's grenadiers. Behind them were Douka's cuirassiers.

ON THE RUSSIAN FAR RIGHT

Tutchov's 3rd Corps had been sent towards Utitsa. Behind it were the Moscow Militia. For cavalry, there were only Karpov's Cossacks.

THE RUSSIAN JÄGERS

They were in the front line or used as flankers all along the front. It was they who occupied Borodino and the little ravine of the Semenovskoï stream. They also formed the front line on the wings.

THE DEFENCE WORKS

The Russians were still working on them on 6th September. The redoubts at Gorki were only used as artillery bases; however the great redoubt, cal-led the Rayevski redoubt, was one of the key points of the battle. Here is a detailed description, given by a Pioneer lieutenant, Bogdanov, who had just joined General Rayevski who was directing construction work. The map in Boutourlin's atlas gives a perfect picture.

The front of the redoubt was almost straight, with an pointed angle of 160 degrees, towards the junction of the two little streams, the Semenovskoi and the Kolocha. It was 180 metres wide with a central point hiding 19 or 21 12-pounder cannon.

The trench in front of it was 10 yards wide with deep pits, wolf holes, over a depth of 120 yards in front of it and slightly more concentrated on the Moscow road side to halt frontal cavalry attacks. On either side, earthen shoulders had been begun and the gorge which was not a gorge was very open behind, no doubt so that the infantry could intervene more easily inside this battery which was cluttered with artillery equipment.

Indeed, the artilery pieces totally occupied the forward space and the infantry in support was placed in a fold of the ground situated just behind the redoubt, in an area protected from enemy fire. As the redoubt was slightly offset and turned towards the Moscow road, the best place to attack was on its left flank, more open and further from the Gorki battery.

Bagration's three outposts.

They were simple shoulders of earthworks whose front made a very wide angle.

The southernmost outpost was turned towards the west, the others to the north west, covering the little ravine of the Semenovskoi stream. in each position there were at least 8 12-pounders. Other works were in progress on the road to Mojaisk.

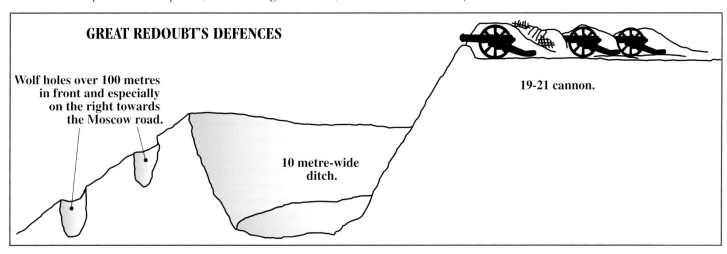

GREAT REDOUBT'S DEFENCES

Wolf holes over 100 metres in front and especially on the right towards the Moscow road.

10 metre-wide ditch.

19-21 cannon.

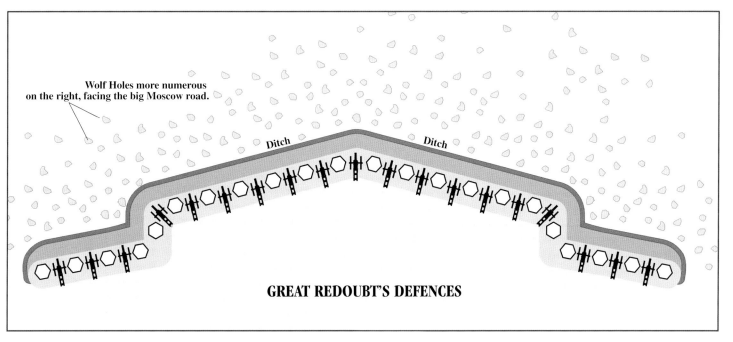

Wolf Holes more numerous on the right, facing the big Moscow road.

Ditch   Ditch

GREAT REDOUBT'S DEFENCES

EVENTS IN THE TWO CAMPS.

In the Russian camp, Kutusov organised a procession with the Holy Virgin of Smolensk. Kneeling Russian soldiers were ready to die for God, the Tsar and Holy Russia. With the French, the Prefet Bausset arrived from Paris bringing a portrait of the King of Rome. Very happy, Napoleon had it exposed in front of his tent.

There was also Colonel Fabvier who coming from Spain, brought bad news: Marmont, who had not wanted to wait for the support of his colleagues, had been defeated at Los Arapiles, by Wellington's army. Napoleon had let himself be trapped: he now had a war to wage on two fronts, separated by the whole width of Europe.

One thing was certain: the Russian campaign must be ended as soon as possible.

Napoleon displays a portrait of the King of Rome.

THE BIG BATTLE

THE 7th OF SEPTEMBER 1812

THE BIG DAY OF THE MOSKOVA

The Emperor came out of his tent at 5 in the morning. At sunrise, he said *"it's the same sun as at Austerlitz"*. At the signal given by the drums, the troops took up arms. The colonels had the drum beaten and the captains read out the following proclamation to their companies:

"Soldiers,

Here is the battle that you have been waiting for. From now on, victory depends on you. We need it, it will give us abundance, good quarters and a prompt return to our homeland. Behave like you did at Austerlitz, at Friedland, at Witepsk, at Smolensk and may posterity cite your names with pride on this day; let them say of you :'He was there at that big battle on the plains before Moscow!"

The French wore full dress. The brilliant Guard surrounded its Commander in front of Schwardino. The Vistula Legion was next to them.

The first cannon shot was fired by Sorbier's battery at 7 o'clock.

ON THE LEFT, THE FIRST ACTIONS OF PRINCE EUGENE

General d'Anthouard had set up a powerful battery on the heights in front of the great redoubt; it had to be moved up, however, into range. Meanwhile General Poitevin had installed four bridges across the Kolocha enabling it to be crossed easily. Behind the heights where the artillery had been installed, there was a little ravine sheltered from the enemy front where the reserves were regrouped. This beginning of an attack by the left seemed to have had the objective of fixing the Russians in this zone so that they did not move away.

THE ATTACK AT BORODINO

It was General Plauzonne who led this first offensive with the 106th Regiment. It was 7 o'clock. He hit the Jägers of the Russian Guard. The village was taken but the General, who was at the head of his troops, fell mortally wounded. The regiment, carried away by its enthusiasm, engaged the bridges which the Russians had set across the Kolocha behind the village. The Russian Jägers re-inforced by the two regiments threatened to destroy the audacious 106th and the 92nd had to be engaged to get these all-too-

adventurous troops out. The Adjutant-Commandant Boisserolle, who had replaced Plauzonne, brought them back into Borodino, improving this position which had to be kept and not over-run, for the moment. The losses of the 106th were great. Borodino remained occupied by the 106th for the rest of the day without any problems.

THE FIRST ATTACK OF THE GREAT REDOUBT

Towards 9 o'clock, this attack seemed more intended to fix the enemy's centre rather than take the redoubt since only the 30th of the line was engaged from Morand's Division, without real support. General Morand was wounded in the jaw and General Bonnamy at the head of this *élite* unit succeeded in getting inside this redoutable bastion. But this success was short-lived for General Yermolov and Count Koutaïssov, commanding the artillery had regrouped forces from General Likhatchev's 24th Division to throw them into an attack on this lost redoubt. Oufa's Regiment, the Jägers of the 19th, 40th and also 11th, attacked followed by the forces Paskevitch still had at his disposal. The 30th of the line, overwhelmed by bigger and bigger forces had to abandon its conquest. General Bonnamy, crib-

The 106th against the Russian Chasseurs

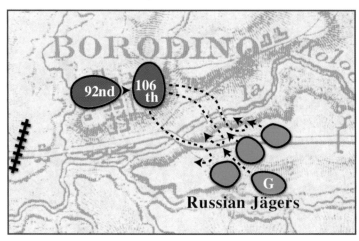

Russian Jägers

bled with bayonet blows, was taken. General Koutaïssov was killed and Yermolov suffered concussion.

General Bonnamy survived and came back from Russia in 1814. The 30th, exhausted by this effort, fell back, but with severe losses.

ON THE RIGHT THE ATTACK ON BAGRATION'S OUTPOSTS

This was the most important part of the day's beginning. Attacks and counter-attacks followed each other. Preceded and accompanied by a "flying" battery organised by Pernety, Compans' and Dessaix's divisions marched against the outpost on the right and Compans chose to move into the little wood which extended on his south flank, to reappear at the outpost furthest to the right. It was at this moment that Compans was wounded and replaced by Duppelin, so they had to fall back on the wood.

Leading the 57th himself, Davout repulsed Neverovski's soldiers and Voronsov's grenadiers and captured the outpost. General Teste was wounded and evacuated, and his aide-de-camp killed.

Bagration immediately sent the Akhtyrsk Hussars, Sievers' cavalry and the 2 regiments of Douka's cuirassiers who managed to get the 57th to fall back. They even captured 2 cannon and the artillerymen, but not for long, because the 1st Corps cavalry and those of Bruyères, Mourier and Beurmann charged, freed the artillerymen and forced the cuirassiers to retire. Dessaix who was following was wounded, General Romoeuf, Chief of Staff, was killed; Davout's horse was killed under him. Seeing him fall thus, Sorbier's artillerymen warned Napoleon of the probable death of his Maréchal.

The Emperor sent Rapp to replace Compans and Murat to replace Davout but the Maréchal who was only suffering from bad bruising, told him he was going to keep his post. Poor Rapp, as usual, got wounded in turn.

Preceded by intense firing from Foucher's battery, Ney committed himself against the two outposts on the left. Sorbier's battery was shooting at the same time at Semenovskoi and thus all these artillery pieces ravaged the area of the outposts and their badly finished and vulnerable earthen ramparts.

Ermolov and Koutaissov at the head of the Russian counter-attack with a battalion from Oufa's Regiment which had two colour flags of the 1797 type (the artist has added the monogram of Alexander in the corners which is curious).

Ledru's and Marchand's soldiers on the left and the two Compans and Dessaix divisions finally took the outposts. Bagration was looking everywhere for reinforcements. He took eight Raïevski battalions and the second divsion of grenadiers from Toutchov coming from Konovnitzin and from Strogonov. It seems also that the Pavlovski Regiment's grenadiers were present for on the picture of the battle we can make out these grenadiers with their characteristic mitres at the defence of Semenovskoi. Bagration had all his army's artillery reserve brought up, but he also sent to Kutuzov for additional forces.

These were: Baggowout's 2nd Corps and a part of Korff's 2nd Cavalry Corps. Kutuzov ordered the Guard to advance progressively towards Semenovskoi with 3 regiments of cuirassiers of the 1st Division (the Guard) and

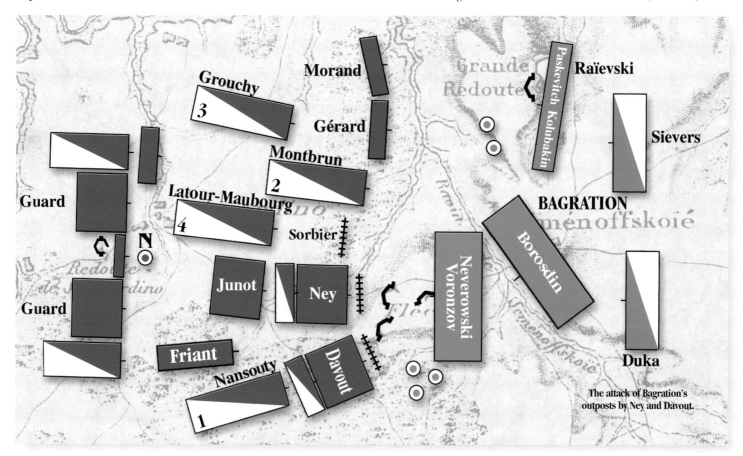

The attack of Bagration's outposts by Ney and Davout.

Re-inforcements coming from the Russian centre for Bagration.

100 cannon from the reserve, but this second group only arrived later having had to come from too far away.

Andreyev, an officer in the Neverovski Division, said that his division had been destroyed by the French artillery. Coming up towards Semenovskoi, he found his commander with 40 men. The infantrymen, the dismounted cavalry and the artillerymen were trying to resist, sometimes with only big sticks...

The Russian reinforcements went over to the attack, the cuirassiers charged and fell upon several cannon; they re-took the outpost after very hard fighting. Ney wanted reinforcements; Friant's division came up to help. Davout's and Ney's Light Horse together with that of Bruyère's Division all intervened in this *mêlée* which defied description; but the French finally overran and took the outposts which had now been all churned up. Murat cited Bruyères' and Beurmann's cavalrymen in particular. The outpost had been recaptured. The 24th was cited by Ney for this attack. Junot passing behind Nansouty's Corps, went up to support Poniatowsky.

BAGRATION WOUNDED

Towards midday, Bagration wanted to lead another attack on the outposts, but he fell seriously wounded; his chief of staff Saint Priest and Borosdin were also wounded. This dramatic loss stopped the Russian advance; it fell back. It was Dokhturov who came up to take command of the Semenovskoi line. Bagration died of his wounds on 24th September.

Friant's division started its march towards this village with General Dufour commanding the 15th Light and the 48th of the Line in the front.

THE RUSSIAN CAVALRY'S DIVERSIONARY ATTACK AGAINST PRINCE EUGENE

The Russians have greatly exaggerated its importance.

It only delayed operations and created a moment of worry. Kutuzov sent Platov with his Cossacks to try to overwhelm the French left, with his thousands of cavalry. At the same time, the Ouvarov cavalry corps attacked them directly. Prince Eugène who had kept the 106th in Boro-

dino had also installed a battery directed towards the north protected by the infantry of the 92nd and the Bavarian cavalry. In front of his reserves he only had Ornano's cavalry which was covering the 84th, the Croatian regiment, the 8th Light and the Italian Guard. Of course there was Broussier's division, and further to the right Morand's and Gérard's divisions from the 1st Corps. Since Morand had been wounded in the first attack of the great redoubt, he was replaced by Lanabère, from the Imperial Guard. Finally, even further on the right and behind this line Grouchy's cavalry was advancing progressively.

The brutal surprise attack of all this Russian cavalry repulsed Ornano's squadrons fairly quickly, but behind him, the intact regiments were formed up into squares and Ouvarov's onslaught was stopped by the batteries that had been set up and by the terrible firing from the squares. Platov's Cossacks, the dragoons, the hussars and the uhlans fell back.

Napolcon was about to go and see the size of the attack for himself and had directed the Vistula legion towards his threatened left. The failure of the Russian diversion freed him for an attack on the principal objective.

The only results were that Ornano's light cavalry came out very weakened, the cannon had been under a very grave threat for a moment, but the troops in the squares suffered almost no losses. However Kutuzov had a bit of respite before the French attacks. The death of Koutaïssov had greatly disturbed the operation of the Russian artillery which was less efficient than normal.

The action began towards three o'clock in the afternoon.

OPERATIONS ON THE FRENCH FAR RIGHT

After Outitsa, Poniatowski was confronted with a hillock where Toutchov had installed the Strogonov Division with 18 cannon. but it fell back and the support of the grenadiers of the division was needed to recapture this little hill. But Bagration took out some troops from this position for re-inforcements. Other troops came to fill up the gaps left by these troops, the 17th Division was directed towards them by Bagration, General Olsufiev in command, replaced Toutchov, who had been killed in this fight.

Above. Bagration wounded.
Below. Ouvarov's cavalry attack supported by Platov.

THE BIG FRENCH OFFENSIVE

ON THE LEFT, THE ATTACK OF THE GREAT REDOUBT

This time, Prince Eugène had the means.

Three columns of infantry were lined up with, to the north Broussier's division, with the 9th of the Line at its head; in the centre the Morand division, now commanded by Lanabère who marched with the 17th regiment. More to the south there was Gérard's division whose 21st of the Line was the first regiment to be committed.

Montbrun's 2nd Cavalry Corps had to charge to the right of the redoubt, but Montbrun who had gone off looking for a better position for his cavalry was killed by a cannonball in the chest. This legendary cavalryman, Lasalle's successor, had also had premonitions that this would be his last fight. Napoleon had him replaced by Auguste de Caulaincourt who took command of this historic charge. Behind this Corps, Groughy's 3rd was in battle order ready to charge.

The artillery was organised with 150 pieces which were formed into three batteries to fire on the great redoubt and its immediate surroundings from three sides.

The charge led by Caulaincourt had Watier de St Alphonse's division at its head. The 5th and 8th Cuirassier regiments were the first, following their new chief. This mass of cavalry gathered speed, galoped up the flank of the great redoubt, then turned abruptly to the left to fall upon the zone of the gorge where the support for the Russian battery were committed to the defence of the cannon and the artillerymen. It was the Russians of the 17th Division of Baggowouth's 2nd Corps, commanded by Likhatchev, who took the brunt of this avalanche of cuirassiers. The redoubt was effectively blocked up by cannon and caissons and the Russian infantry left by the little ravine which was just behind.

SECOND ATTACK OF THE GREAT REDOUBT

At the same time, on the front of the redoubt, the infantry of the three columns charged their objective. They climbed the earthen wall at the moment that the cuirassiers charged the Russian occupants.

The battery was definitely taken, General Likhatchev was captured, but General Lanabère who had replaced Morand was killed during the attack. The French artillery was able to set itself up on these heights and return the shooting from the Gorki redoubt and fire towards the east where the Russian reserves were grouped.

The French infantry moved up beyond the redoubt and as far as possible, protected he assault on this great Raïevski battery which became one of the symbols of this immense battle.

THE BIG CAVALRY FREE-FOR-ALL

The cavalry of the 2nd Corps continued their charge against the Russian infantry lined up on the plateau in the second line.

Behind the cuirassiers, Defrance's Carabiniers followed up the charge,

The second attack of the Great Redoubt

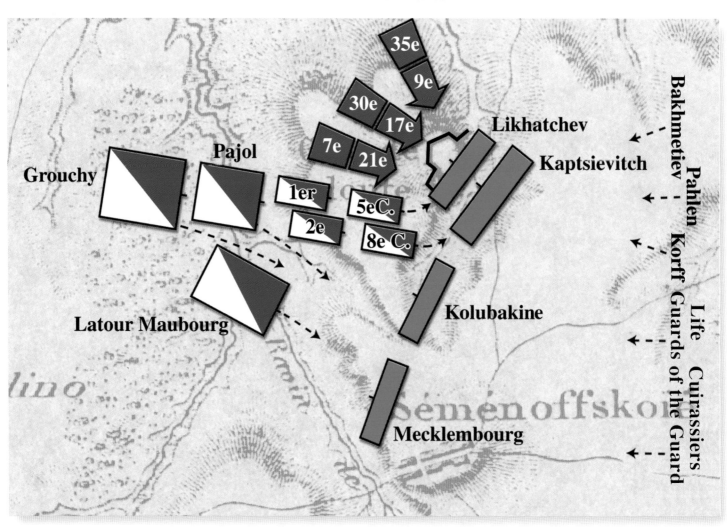

Above and below. Cuirassiers in the ditch in front of the great redoubt.

Cavalry of the Guard moving off into the attack (detail from the panorama)

supported by all the light cavalry of the corps. They attacked Kaptsevitch's men, the other division from Dokhtourov's corps who tried to resist, as well as elements from the Russian 4th Corps coming from Gorki. The Russian infantry tried to form up into squares and other soldiers lay down to allow this cavalry storm to pass. The carabiniers and the regiments following clashed with the Russian cavalry which arrived with the Horse Guards.

The Russians called on the Horse Guards helped by cavalry from Korf's and Pahlen's corps (2nd and 3rd cavalry Corps). Grouchy's intact cavalry came onto the scene into this formidable free-for-all which got mixed up with the one around the centre at Semenovskoi. The Cuirassiers of the 2nd Corps, which had been brought back were replaced by the carabiniers with their beautiful breastplates with golden reflections. Behind was the light cavalry of Pajol; the 11th and 12th Infantry were cited by Murat on this occasion.

Behind a new wave was following, Grouchy's cavalry. They made several charges against the Russian squares which were still badly formed and against the Horseguards. This was noted in the service records of several officers. The 6th and 25th Infantry breached the Russian battalions, charged against the cavalry and got through into a square. This general action of the cavalry joined that of Latour-Maubourg's corps which was more to the right, and freed the approaches to Semenovskoi. The Russian cavalry had no reserves left except bits of regiments which went to accompany the Foot Guards which had set off for Semenovskoi.

THE CAPTURE OF SEMENOVSKOI.

Latour-Maubourg's cavalry opened the way for Friant's division to capture Semenovskoi. They also took part in the great cavalry free-for-all but on the right. Latour-Maubourg placed the Saxon Life Guards at the head. He harangued them by telling them that they had not yet received their breastplates but that he was sure that this would not stop them showing off their worth. It was the first three squadrons who marched in the front line follo-

wed by Zastrov's cuirassiers and the 4th squadron of Guards. Zastrov's cuirassiers were wearing their black breastplates. The painter of the very beautiful panorama which can be admired in Moscow, has committed a double mistake: they are charging in front of the Life guards and without breastplates. Artists are permitted this sort of licence, because the onslaught has been very well rendered and has been placed at the right spot and at the right time. They can be seen over-running the last defenders of Semenovskiï at the moment that Friant's infantry attacked this capital spot on the battlefield.

The Westphalian cuirassiers and the cuirassiers of the 14th Polish Regiment took part in this charge which brought them up to the squares formed up by the regiments of the Russian Guard which were just like fortresses. They were just as impenetrable for the cavalry as those of Davout had been for the pretentious Prussian cavalry at Jena.

Latour-Maubourg's cavalry, disunited by the charge reformed to continue fighting against the Russian dragoons of the 2nd or 3rd Cavalry corps now reunited in one single unit. Friant's division took advantage of this charge to attack the village of Semenovskoi, crossing the little stream and chasing all the Russian infantry out of the ruins. The major objective had been reached, the French were on the plateau.

THE THREAT FROM THE RUSSIAN GUARD.

Murat seeing the mass of infantry of the Russian guard advancing had alerted all the artillery and put his batteries into place progressively in front of Friant's division, deployed inside Semenovskoi. They fired grapeshot which stopped then repelled the Russian Guard, which formed up into squares by regiments then stood up without flinching to the artillery fire from the French. Napoleon had got on his horse and rejoined Murat in order to get a good idea of the relative positions.

Thus towards four o'clock in the afternoon, the disposition was the following: On the extreme right of the French, Poniatowski supported by the

Dokhtorov has taken command of the defenders of Semenskoya (details from the panorama)

Saxon Guard of Honour.

Zastrov's Cuirassiers.

Westphalians finished by occupying a hillock situated near the old Smolensk to Moscow road. In front of him was Olsufiev with what was left of his division. He had replaced Tutchkov, who had been killed, and who only had the Karpov Cossacks and Stroganov's division left after Bagration had taken what he needed; behind him was the mass of the Moscow Militiamen. Apart from some action undertaken by Polish cavalry and the artillery, the battle stabilised around this point.

Just nearby, a little to the west, was Nansouty's 1st Cavalry Corps which included the Valence Division, intact, the Saint-Germain Division and especially Bruyère's Cavalry which was the most heavily committed.

This mass of cavalry had advanced towards the north, behind its 36 artillery pieces firing at the square bastions of Russian Guards. These battalions, very much weakened by the giant struggle for the capture of the outposts, the Compans and Dessaix's Divisions and those of Ney's 3rd Corps were used as support to the fantastic batteries which were put into place to fire on the Russian Guard.

Before Semenovskoi, it was Friant's Division which had advanced behind the cannon directed by Sorbier, who had the same objective: the Russian squares. Latour-Maubourg's Corps reformed in the little ravine of the stream, behind them. In front of the great redoubt, it was the same principle for the 4th Corps of Prince Eugène, together with another objective: to fire as much as possible on the Gorki battery and also on the squares. Grouchy's Corps and Montbrun's old Corps reformed on the plateau or were still fighting with the Russian cavalry. Several regiments of the 4th Corps, well sheltered and having only fought a little were almost intact, such as the 84th and the Italian Guard. Napoleon said to Murat: *"these Russians let themselves be killed like machines."*, then adressing Sorbier who was working to increase the central battery in front of Semenovskoi, *"...seeing as they want it, let them have it!"* and Sorbier let them have it.

THE ARTILLERY OF THE GRAND MASSACRE

After 4 p.m., the infantry and cavalry duels were beginning to run out of steam, the French had conquered all the strong points of the battlefield, after having beaten the occupants, but they no longer had the strength, nor the means to wage another battle against the Russian Foot Guards whose compact squares still blocked the road. Indeed, this guard, pushed back from its attempts to attack by the grapeshot from the cannon placed in front of Friant, had retreated to a position in front of Psarevo and remained there immobile, a last elite rampart; but it could not reasonably attack.

Kutuzov could have pulled back his army behind this last curtain, but the old general obstinately stayed in the same place, without having seen the least action. There now took place a strange and suicidal spectacle: the massacre of the Russian Guard. These compact and serried squares were made up of the elite soldiers of the Preobrajenski, Semenovski, Ismailovski, Finnish Regiments and the Battalion of the Marine Guards. On the flanks of the Guard, were the survivors from the other engaged divisions who were still valid together with the cavalry of the Guard and the other cavalrymen who had also taken part in the charges but who were now quite weak.

Such squares were practically invicible against cavalry charges, especially if the cavalry was exhausted. However the squares were extremely vulnerable to an artillery attack since each shot took out a great number of soldiers, tracing furrows with each cannonball. These reassembled cannon with all sorts of calibres took a very heavy toll for several hours on the compacted immobile masses. They only stopped at nightfall. Like the grenadiers at Waterloo, the Russian grenadiers showed that the Russian Guard died but did not surrender. The famous saying of the *Grande Armée* finds was most appropriate. They used to say: *"It is not enough to kill a Russian... you have to push him for him to fall"*.

The squares of the Russian Guard

The French Light Artillery of the French Guard manoeuvering.

THE FRENCH PRESENT AT THE MOSKOVA

In order to approach something like the truth amidst all the writings, memoirs and miscellaneous souvenirs, the most valuable method seemed to me to be a direct search in the archives containing the records of the officers having participated in the battle and in the 1812 campaign. I also consulted the registers of the soldiers, but only a few details about these soldiers are to be found.

The figures obtained for the officers are therefore precise and if I mention an officer as having been wounded at the Moskova, this means that he definitely survived the battle. Here is then the balance sheet of this Grande Armée but for the regiments, I have given only the figures and a few interesting detailed careers. I have finished this report with an overall evaluation of the officers during the whole campaign, with three groups, the killed, the missing and the prisoners who came back from the Russian prisons in 1814.

I will first give an example of the method which I used to obtain as complete a record as possible from the Vincennes Archives. I chose, for the presentation below, the 5th Cuirassier Regiment which formed the head of the 2nd Cavalry Corps column, led by Auguste de Caulaincourt in the attack the great redoubt.

THE 5th CUIRASSIERS

THE OFFICERS' ROLL

This document was established at Pont-à-Mousson, the depot of the regiment, and dated 1st November 1812.

There are **52 officers**.

Seven officers were at the depot, with the **Captain Quartermaster Cinglant** and the 5th squadron (2 captains, 2 lieutenants and two second-lieutenants). They all remained at Pont à Mousson. So only 45 officers left France with the war squadrons.

— **Captain Vast-Vimeux** was seconded as aide de camp.

— **Second-Lieutenant Muiron** with three other second-lieutenants led 106 cuirassiers. They went to Hannover where they remained until 2nd July 1812 when they moved up to Berlin. They were therefore not at the Moskova but went to Moscow once mounted. **Muiron**, born at Reims, LH in 1809, commissioned as a lieutenant in 1815.

— **Désarbres**, born in Chalons, lieutenant first with the Guards of Honour in 1813. LH in 1814, half-pay.

— **Cognail**, remained in Gumbinen, then disappeared.

— **Franquefort**, died 9th November 1812.

— At the crossing of the Niemen a figure of 34 officers and 649 men was recorded. 2 officers and 101 horsemen were in the rear or in the hospitals.

— At the Moskova, 33 officers and 533 men were present but there were only 487 horses left. One officer was killed: **Second-Lieutenant Johann** (born in Strasburg) and 4 were wounded. Among the men 11 were killed and 7 captured, one returned from captivity.

— On 20th September at Moscow, 28 officers and 406 cavalry were present, 4 officers wounded were at the hospitals but there were now only 286 horses.

THE PRIVATE FILES OF THE OFFICERS

— **Colonel Christophe**, born in Nancy in 1769, for a long time with the 8th Hussars, captured in Spain. It was he who organised the escape from the old hulk *Vieille Castille* on 16th May 1810. He joined the Gendarmerie and retired in 1830 with the rank of honorary brigadier. LH 26 Marsh 1804, OLH at Moscow, CrLH in 1814.

— **Squadron Commander Jeannot**, born in Besançon. Died 4th October 1812. LH 1808.

— **Squadron Commander Rondot**, born Montigny les Dames, wounded 18th October 1812, wounded in 1814, dismissed in 1815. OLH in 1814.

THE ADJUDANT-MAJORS

— **de Vergez**, born at Prichac (Htes-Pyrénées) with the 1st Regiment of the Guards of Honour in 1813. In the regiment in 1815, half-pay, taken back into the Gendarmerie in 1830, squadron commander in Alger where he died in 1839. LH in 1809.

— **Dubois**, born at Privat, wounded at Waterloo and dismissed in 1815. LH in 1809.

THE CAPTAINS

— **de Lampinet**, born in Navenne, emigrated to the army

of Condé then in Russian service until 1801; wounded at Austerlitz then at Wagram. Got a bayonet wound at the Moskova and 6 wounds on 18th October 1812 and taken prisoner. returned to France in 1814, served in 1815, squadron commander in 1820, retired in 1828.

— **Vernerey**, born in Baume (Doubs), wounded at the Moskova, then on 4th October 1812. Squadron commander in 1813, served in 1815, Lh at Moscow.

— **Rémy**, born at St Jean (Marne) volunteer in Year II, Sabre of Honour, heros of Hoff and Eylau; three horses killed. Knight in 1809, baron in 1813, served in 1815, then retired.

— **Count Montagu**, born in Paris, King's Guard in 1815, colonel in 1826, retired in 1830. LH in 1809, OLH in 1821.

— **Sestier**, born in Metz retired in 1815, LH in 1807.

— **de Jouvancourt**, Ordnance Gendarme in 1806, wounded at the Moskova where he captured General Likhatchev. Dismissed in 1815. Commanded the militia on Bourbon Island from 1819 to his death in 1826. LH at Moscow, OLH 1814.

— **de Beuvrand de la Loyère**, born in Dijon. St-Cyr in 1806, squadron commander, Nansouty's aide de camp in 1813, probably died at Leipzig, LH in 1809.

— **de Beurges**, born in Triment (Meuse), squadron commander, discharged in 1822, LH in 1809, OLH in 1815.

— **Lamothe**, born at Souillac, wounded at the Moskova by a bullet in the right wrist. He was in fact a lieutenant but was promoted at Moscow. Wounded at Waterloo, dismissed but re-instated in 1831. LH in 1807.

— **Foirquignon**, born in Heudicourt, wounded at the Moskova by a lance in the right arm. Wounded at Waterloo and retired afterwards. Lh in Year XII.

THE LIEUTENANTS

— **Perrin** (des Isles), died in battle in 1813

— **de Paix de Cœur**, born in Dugleville, captured in the Gumbinen hospital, disappeared.

— **de Mulder**, born at Nivelles, wounded at Hanau, died at Waterloo, LH in 1813.

— **de Mercey**, born at Vesoul, had his right thumb frozen, dismissed in 1815. LH in 1814.

— **Soubdès**, born in St Puy (Gers), inactive in 1814, LH in 1809, Knight.

— **de Sambuy**, on leave in Turin in 1813.

THE SECOND-LIEUTENANTS.

— **Joham**, died at the Moskova, already mentioned.

— **Grenier**, captured on 10th December 1812, missing (?).

— **Toutain**, captured (?) had the same name as an officer with the 1st Chevau-Légers Lancers, captured and returned. LH in 1807.

— **Collet**, Lasalle's *protégé*, treated for severe ophthalmia, at the very beginning of 1812.

A homonym returned with Aubry from the Russian prisons in 1816 and is mentioned in the memoirs of this man.

— **Blanchard**, disappeared in Russia, LH in 1807.

— **Dereims**, captured in July 1813.

— **Guinegagne**, in the regiment since Year XI, escaped from the hulks with the colonel, retired on 5th August 1813.

— **Piognand**, born in Pennesières, lieutenant in 1813, dismissed in 1815, reinstated 1824, left in 1834. LH in 1813, Croix of St Ferdinand. 1823.

— **Lebas**, born in Bléville, dismissed as a lieutenant in 1815, LH in 1807.

— **Astruc**, born in Geneva, lieutenant in 1813, dismissed in 1815, re-instated in 1821, discharged captain in 1828. LH in 1813.

— **Dupré**, born in Namur, two horses killed and wounded at the Moskova, resigned since he was a Belgian General-Major. LH in 1814, OLH in 1837.

— **Brouville**, born in Clermont (Hte Marne), wounded at Waterloo, then dismissed. LH in 1814.

— **Luchapt** or **Luchat**, died 16 June 1815. LH in 1814.

— **Petit**, born in Braban, dismissed in 1815, LH in 1814.

— **Audry**, born in Aix-en-Provence, wounded at the Moskova. Lieutenant in 1813.

To these officers must be added Muiron and his three comrades who were in Berlin and Vast-Vimeux, aide de camp. This then is the roll of the officers and all their adventures. The small number of casualties for this regiment which was in the heart of the battle is surprising. For the whole of the campaign, 4 officers were killed, 5 disappeared during the retreat and two prisoners who returned.

Maréchal-des-logis-chef Mouffet is to be mentioned apart. Born in Pont sur Saône, wounded at the Moskova several times by bayonets and sabres. Remained in the hands of the Russians, did not return until 8th January 1815.

He was promoted to second-lieutenant immediately. He served at Waterloo and was dismissed afterwards. He wore the LH during the Hundred Days; on half-pay, he reclaimed his decoration in 1830. He lived in Mailleroncourt-Charette in Haute-Saône.

THE MEN

It is very much more difficult to keep tracks of them than the officers. The 11 killed and the 7 prisoners are verified.

Their origins have been checked and a large number have been found to come from conquered departments, especially German and Belgians and Italians (73 came from Marengo). They were 33% of the strength in Russia.

For the whole of the campaign more than 400 cavalrymen were captured or were listed as missing and on the registers only 18 were listed as having returned from Russian captivity. It is also certain that those from the conquered territories returned home.

These complete details are given to illustrate the complex research involved which was only possible for the French regiments.

During the course of the text, simplified figures will be given corresponding to each section comparable with this one.

THE EMPEROR'S HOUSEHOLD

It was quite sizeable for this campaign, which is in contrast to its small size before 1810. In this country without ressources, it needed a lot for all its horses and its employees.

THE CIVILIAN HOUSEHOLD
— **Duroc,** Duc de Frioul, Grand Marshall of the Palace.
— **Caulaincourt**, Duc de Vicence, Grand Equerry.
— the **Comte de Turenne**, Chamberlain, Master of the Wardrobe, left his job in 1815.

THE MARECHAL DES LOGIS OF THE PALACE
— The **Comte de Ségur**, Academician in 1830, Lieutenant-General in 1831. He brought out a book on the 1812 campaign. GdCxLH in 1843.
— The **Baron de Canouville,** brother of Pauline's lover who was squadron commander with the 10th Chasseurs, killed at the Moscova. Peer in 1832.

THE EQUERRIES
— The **Baron de Saluces**, died in 1852.
— The **Baron de Lambertye**, only arrived on 8th November and was not therefore at the Moskova.
— The **Baron de Mesrigny**, served in 1815, dismissed, deputy for the Aube in 1834, inspector of the stud farms.

THE QUARTERMASTER CAPTAINS
— **Raillon**, went to Elba, arrested in 1815 and tracked until 1830. Colonel in 1831.
— **Emery** dismissed in 1814, in the Gendarmerie in 1822.

THE PAGES
— **Duval-Dumanoir**, LH in 1814, OLH in 1821.

Caulaincourt

The Comte de Ségur

Bacler d'Albe

— **Hennequin de Frenel**, resigned in 1818, LH in 1814.

With the EMPEROR

— **Constant** and **Roustan**, who abandonned him in 1814.

— **St-Denis**, called "Ali", died in 1856.

THE CABINET SERVICE

— **Baron Bacler d'Albe**, died in 1824.

THE SECRETARIES

— **Baron Fain**, who was taken back by Louis-Philippe.

— **Baron Meneval**, died in 1850

— **Baron Mounier**, son of the convention member, died in 1843.

— **Colonel Deponthon**, Egyptian Campaign, Lieutenant-General in 1838.

THE INTERPRETERS

— **Wonzowitch**, **Tillet de Mautort** and **de Belabre** brought up in Russia were nominated later.

— **Lelorge d'Iderville**, baron in 1813, exiled 1815, Deputy in 1837, LH.

CARTOGRAPHERS

— **Laneau** and **Duvivier**, returned form Russia.

— **Peyrusse**, paymaster, author of souvenirs.

— **Burthui**, captured, returned in 1814.

THE HEALTH SERVICE

— **Yvan**, Baron, came back with Napoleon.

— **Lerminier**, the Emperor's doctor, doctor at the Charité.

— **Jouan**, Deputy-Surgeon, retired in 1835.

— **Rouyer**, Napoleon's pharmacist, decorated in 1813 with the Réunion.

Rapp

Lauriston

THE MILITARY HOUSEHOLD
THE EMPEROR'S AIDES DE CAMP

— **Count Rapp**. Peer in 1819, died in 1835. His private aides - de -camp were **Waldener de Freudenstein**, sacked in 1815, Major-General in 1853; **Turkheim**, returned from Moscow. LH at Moscow.

— **Lauriston**, followed the King to Gand, voted for the death of Ney, died in 1828.

— **Longuerne**, Brigadier in 1834.

— **Hammer de Clairbooke**, in the King's Household. OLH 1814.

— **Lebrun**, Duke of Plaisance in 1824 (he had with him the Count of Briqueville), Deputy in 1827, conspired against the Bourbons, fought against the son of Soult in 1830. Died in 1844. GCLH in 1853, Military Medal.

— **Moutin**, Comte de Lobau, captured at Waterloo, Brigadier in 1831, Peer (he had with him Perrin, Baron at Moscow, Colonel at Waterloo and de Castellane, Peer in 1837, Brigadier, died in 1862).

— **Durosnel**, Count, *Commandant d'Armes* at Moscow, retired in 1816; aide de camp to Louis-Philippe in 1832, Peer (with him were La Bretonnièère, Baron in 1813, Brigadier, retired in 1827; and Picot de Dampierre, Brigadier in 1822).

— **de Narbonne**, Count, died in November 1813. Minister of War in 1792, then emigrated (aides de camp: Ruelle, non-active in 1815, taken back as Colonel in 1830 and Chabot, the future Duc de Rohan, discharged in 1830).

— **van Hogendorp**, Governor of Lithuania 8 July 1812. Died in Brazil in 1822.

— **Comte de Pac**, future member of the Polish government in 1830, emigrated to Smyrna.

— **Prince Sanguzko**, Polish general.

NAPOLEON'S ORDERLY OFFICERS

— **Gourgaud**, Baron at Moscow, went to St Helena for three years, was then exiled. Aide de Camp to Louis-Philippe in 1832, Peer of France, died in 1852.

— Count **Montesquiou-Fézensac**, Anatolian, Peer in 1841, died in 1846.

— The **Duke of Montmorency**, died in 1846.

— The **Count of Montaigu**.

— **Christin**, Baron in 1813.

— **Clément deTeintegnies**.

— **Baron Desaix**, dismissed in 1815, Colonel in 1830, Brigadier in 1835.

— **De Caraman**, killed at Constantine in 1837.

— **Count Moreton de Chabrilland**, Commander of the squadrons in 1813.

— **Baron de Mortemart de Rochechouart**, future Duke, followed the King in 1815. His cousin de Rochechouart was in the service of the Tsar. It seems they met for dinner during the campaign?!

— **Baron Athalin**, aide de camp to Louis -Philippe in 1830, Lieutenant-General, retired in 1848.

— **D'Hautpoul**, Baron at Moscow.

— **Galz de Malvirade**, baron in 1826.

— **Lauriston**, Baron, Peer in 1828.

— **Prince d'Arenberg**, died in 1877.

All these men of the world returned from Moscow, often writing memoirs. They replaced Bonaparte's companions, which caused a bad atmosphere in this army. Napoleon thought that he could mix with these old families, but he was mistaken.

Auguste de Caulaincourt

THE INNER IMPERIAL STAFF

— **Auguste de Caulaincourt**, brother of the Duke of Vicence, killed whilst entering the great Rayevski Redoubt. He had as aides de camp: Cham, discharged in 1814; Chasteigner, a relation of the general whose brother was with the Duke. Retired in 1814; Wolbert, non active in 1815, taken back in 1830 as Commander of the Squadrons.

— **Sokolicki**, French general, died at Warsaw in 1816. His aide de camp, Soltyk, a future polish general, wrote memoirs.

COMMANDANT D'ARMES

— **Darriule**, commanded the Kremlin, General in 1813, Baron in 1814, Lieutenant-General in 1832. Pair de France. Died in 1840. With him were

IMPERIAL HOUSEHOLD AND HEADQUARTERS
GENERAL STAFF OFFICERS

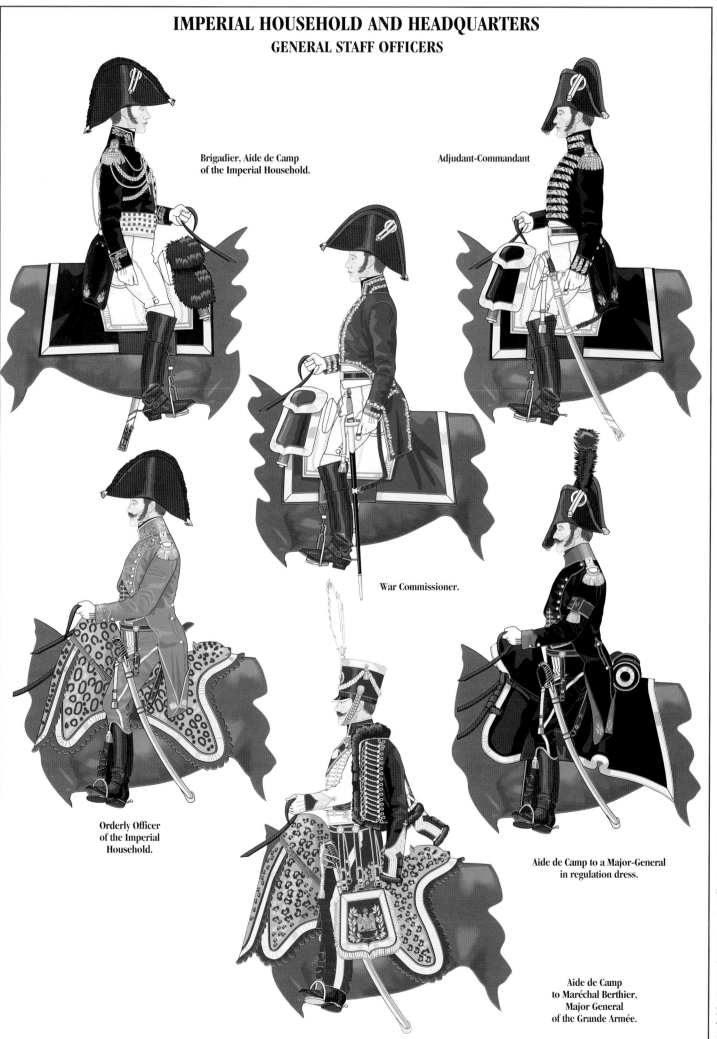

Brigadier, Aide de Camp
of the Imperial Household.

Adjudant-Commandant

War Commissioner.

Orderly Officer
of the Imperial
Household.

Aide de Camp to a Major-General
in regulation dress.

Aide de Camp
to Maréchal Berthier,
Major General
of the Grande Armée.

André Jouineau © Histoire & Collections 2000

Colonel Leroy, captured with frozen hands and feet, returned to France in 1814 and retired. LH in Year XII; and Coquel, Egyptian Campaign, retired in 1816.

HEADQUARTERS ADMINISTRATION
— **Joinville**, Chief Ordnance Officer, died in 1849.
— **Burthin**, book-keeper, captured in December, but returned.
— **Chastel de Boinville**, Supplies Officer, died at Vilna.
— **Bourgeois**, Chief-Surgeon, served at Waterloo. Decorated with the Réunion in 1813.

Berthier

Lejeune

THE GENERAL STAFF OF THE *GRANDE ARMEE*
Under the orders of **Berthier**, Prince de Neuchatel, Aides de Camp:
— **Baron Lejeune**, Colonel in the Engineers, General at Moscow, a very talented painter. He got through with Oudinot, had his face frozen. Left his post without leave, arrested in 1813, then released. Married Marie Clary. Died in 1848 at Toulouse. Gd OLH in 1841.
— **Comte de Flahaut**, son of Talleyrand, Grand Equerry to Queen Hortense with whom he had a son, the future Duke of Morny. Exiled in 1815, returned in 1830. Peer of France, made to retire in 1848, died in 1870. GdCx Lh in 1838, Grand Chancelier of the LH in 1865, Military Medal in 1866.
— **Baron Pernet**, volunteer in 1792, Squadron Commander, in charge of detailing, Honorary Brigadier, died in 1846.
— **de Noailles**, died 28th November at Beresina.
— **Lecoulteux de Canteleu**, wounded leaving Moscow, mistaken for a Cossack. Colonel, died in 1844.
— **Aimery de Montesquiou-Fézensac**, future Colonel of the 4th of the Line. Clarke's son-in-law, General in 1813, Lieutenant-General in 1823, Duke and Peer of France in 1832, GdCx LH in 1845.

WORKING WITH MARECHAL BERTHIER
— **Baron Dufresne**, review inspector, Italian campaign, returned from Russia, LH in Year XII.
— **Leduc**, Berthier's private secretary, returned from Russia.
— **Coutant**, Postmaster, Captain in 1813, served in 1815, dismissed. OLH.

GENERALS WORKING WITH BERTHIER
— **Count Bailly de Monthion**, Divisional General in December, replaced Berthier. Wounded at Waterloo, died 1840. GdCx LH, GdCx de St-Ferdinand and St-Louis.
— **Jomini**, theoretician, soon-to-be-traitor, responsible for histrorical matters.
— **Bertrand** went with Ney on 10th September. Retired in 1815 (his aide de camp Prues received a Sabre of Honour, Colonel in the 13th Chas-

seurs and the heros of Belfort in 1815. Served in Belgium in 1831, OLH in Year XII).
— **Tarayre**, left as commander at Kovno. Went over to the 1st Corps on 15th Seprember.
— **Franceschi**, baron commanded an infantry brigade at Vilna, responsible to Gouvion St-Cyr. Died of typhus in January 1813 at Danzig.
— **Baraguey d'Hilliers**, commander at Smolensk, suffered a severe setback on 9th November, arrested, sent back for inquiry, died of grief.

the others were:
— **Barthier de St Hilaire** who was with Doumerc. **Roch-Godart**, Governor of Vilna 4th October. **Lambet**, ill, allowed to return home.
— **Baron Fabre**, went to the 1st Corps at Moscow on 17th September, wounded at Viasma, died in 1858.
— **Normand**, died at Vilna.
— **Lanchantin**, reported missing at Krasnoi.
— **Corsin**, passed over to the 1st Corps at Moscow, captured, returned, served in 1815.
— **Evers**, in the cavalry reserve at Moscow, captured, returned to Holland.

Other generals commanded different places, two died at the end of the retreat. The list of the adjudant commanders is also available, but they were not at the Moskova, like a lot of adjudant officers. On these lists, certain did not rejoin their regiments for diverse reasons, like Brunet who died in Catalonia.

Guilleminot

One adjudant commander was present at the battle:
— **Pariset**, sailor at 13, gentleman-cadet with the colonial battalions in 1782, took part in the Cochinchina Expedition in 1788, Captain at the Siege of Pondichéry in 1792, taken prisoner and released only in 1798. Considered as an *émigré*, did 11 months' prison. With Decaen in Egypt and India. Adjutant-Commandant 10th August 1812, seconded to the 1st Corps, wounded three times at the Moskova. Left with the convoy of wounded escorted by 1 000 men, served in 1815, Chief of Staff of the 4th Military Division, retired in 1817.

Among these officers with Berthier there were a large number of young noblemen, former *émigrés*. The majority of these officers returned from Russia, only 2 being posted missing and one captured, who returned in 1814.

ARTILLERY GENERAL STAFF
— **Count de Lariboisière**, born at Fougères. With Bonaparte in the regiment at la Fère. Major-General in 1807, died 21st December 1812 at Koenigsberg, exhausted by the retreat. His son, Lieutenant in the 1st Carabiniers was killed at the Moskova. GdOLH and GdCX de la Couronne de Fer.

His aides de camp:
— **Planat de la Faye**, author of memoirs, was with Drouot in 1813.
— **Duchesné**, born at Vire in 1802, decorated at Moscow, retired in 1844 with the rank of Lieutenant Colonel.

CHIEF OF STAFF
— **Charbonnel**, Italian and Egyptian Campaigns, General in 1809 and Baron. Major-General in 1813, Count in 1814, Peer of France in 1841. Died 1846, GdCxLH in 1824.

Lariboisière and his son

ASSISTANT-CHIEF OF STAFF

— **Marion**, Colonel, wounded and captured at Krasnoi, returned in 1814. Brigadier in 1825, died in 1847, OLM at Moscow.

Assistants:

— **Poirel**, captured at Vilna, returned 1814. Retired with the rank of Brigadier in 1825.

— **Saint-Cyr**, colonel in 1814, died in 1829.

— **Paixhans**, captain, Lieutenant-General in 1845.

Among the other officers of the General staff, several became generals, such as:

— **Caraman**, Brigadier in 1823, died of cholera at Constantine in 1837.

— **Bouteiller**, Brigadier in 1848.

— **de la Place**, Lieutenant-General in 1843, Senator in 1852.

GENERAL STAFF OF THE ENGINEERS

— **General de Chasseloup-Laubat**, took part in numerous sieges in Italy, then that of Danzig. He was Counsellor of State, Senator in 1813. Did not follow Napoleon in 1815. Helped Eblé at the crossing of the Beresina, but the pontoneers were responsible to, and were to be so for many more years, the artillery and at Orcha, they had to abandon their equipment because the horses were needed to draw the remaining artillery pieces and caissons. Cr de la Couronne de Fer, GdOLH, GdCx LH in 1816.

Several engineer officers are mentioned as having worked on the bridges at the Beresina, entering the water several times.

THE CARTOGRAPHIC SERVICE

— Major-General, **Count Sanson**, commanded this service. Sabre of Honour in Egypt. Captured on the 23rd October but returned. Retired in 1815 (his aide de camp Theviotte died in February 1813).

— **the Surveyors**

Seven died in Russia, two were reported missing. Six were captured and returned, three with their general. Seven returned directly and were dismissed in 1815.

THE POLICE

This was commanded by **Lauer**, Provost Marshall. Returned with 185 out of 408 gendarmes that took part in the campaign, died in 1816.

THE GENERAL ADMINISTRATION

— **Count Mathieu-Dumas**, served in America as La Fayette's aide de camp. President of the the Assembly in 1792, went to Switzerland during the Reign of Terror. Peer in 1831, died in 1837.

HIS AIDES DE CAMP WERE:

— **Denayer**, died during the retreat and **Bernard**, Lieutenant-Colonel in 1825.

HIS PRIVATE SECRETARY:

— **Lanneau**, his friend, who was mayor of the 12th Arrondissement in Paris in 1824, Director of the Institute for Deaf-Mutes in 1851. On 5th November 1812, he was replaced by **Daru**, Count, Minister, served in 1815 which lost him all his posts except that of the Institute. Died in 1829, Gd Aigle de la LH.

Mathieu Dumas

— **Chambon** was responsible for the Territorial Service. Retired in 1816, LH in Year XII.

— **Saint Didier**, Dumas's son-in-law was secretary of the Intendance Générale.

THE SENIOR ORDNANCE OFFICERS

Seven returned directly among which **Sartelon**, Egyptian Campaign, who was Deputy for the Corrèze in 1815. Another was listed as missing.

THE ORDNANCE OFFICERS FIRST CLASS

All eight returned.

THE ORDNANCE OFFICERS SECOND CLASS

Six returned, one was reported missing and one was killed in a square at Krasnoi. For the 23 assistants, two were killed, one was missing and one taken prisoner but who returned.

THE STAFF RESPONSIBLE FOR SUPPLIES

Out of 16 one was killed at Vilna, the others returned. **Belangé**, the Director of the Warehouse Guards, lost his effects at Moscow. Dismissed in 1814, he became Mayor of Alger and served in 1838.

THE PRINTING

It was run by **Levrault**. All the staff disappeared at Beresina.

THE MEDICAL CORPS

— **Baron Desgenettes**, captured at Vilna on 10th December. Alexander sent him back with a Guard of Honour on 25th March 1813. He had not wanted to abandon the wounded and the sick. Mayor of the 10th Arrondissement in 1830, died in 1837.

— **Baron Larrey**, in 1832, left for Algeria, returned ill, died in Lyon.

—With them 15 doctors, one was lost, two were captured at Vil-

Desgenettes

na but returned. Out of four pharmacists, one was captured but returned. Two hospital employees died at Vilna, one was captured but returned.

— Of the health officers, 14 returned, one was lost and those captured returned.

"INSPECTION AUX REVUES"

— **Viénot-Vaublanc**, with Roichambeau in America, died at Gumbingen 19th December 1812. LH in Year XII.

— **General Lamer**, seconded to the cavalry reserve, missing at Beresina.

— **De Bélizal**, served in 1814.

Larrey

TROOPS ATTACHED TO HEADQUARTERS 1

Numerous detachments were attached to headquarters. A roll dated 21st September 1812 gives their status and their missions at Moscow, on that precise date:

● **1. The Elite Company.**

Commanded by Captain Faget, who was Squadron Commander in the 9th Hussars in 1813, on half pay in 1814. He had 5 officers and 37 cavalrymen, 33 of which were mounted. 35, all mounted were distributed thus:

On picket duty with the Emperor: 12
With Berthier: 13
With Monthion: 7
With Dufresne: 2
With Flahaut: 1
On their way to join up: 5 officers and 10 troopers.

● **2. The 2nd Baden Regiment of the Line.**

On the 21st September, there were 4 officers and 47 men available; the others were distributed thus:

Supply Headquarters: 7 officers and 255 men

The 2nd Baden Regiment of Line

With Joinville: 3 officers and 111 men
With Battalion Commander Schweisguth: 11 men
In the Gumginen Garrison, with the surveyors: 8 men
In the Ostrowno Garrison: 26 men
At Uschatz: 1 officer and 32 men
At Beschenkowski: 1 officer and 30 men
For transporting prisoners back to Vilna: 5 officers and 195 men.
For those supplied to Colonel Dentzel several times: 49 men.
Left at Vitebsk in safe-keeping: 36 men.
To which must be added 94 lost, 96 in the hospitals.
Total numbers: **31 officers and 1 081 men, without horses.**

● **3. The Dragoons, and Prince Albert's Saxon Light Horse**

The numbers of a squadron with 9 officers and 156 cavaliers.
Available 7 officers and 29 cavalrymen of which 23 mounted. 39 men distributed amongst the generals as orderlies, apparently; 8 cavalrymen with Berthier, 4 with Joinville, and 20 with Supply Headquarters. 25 got lost, 2 officers and 11 men in hospital.

● **4. 28th Cavalry**

Available: 5 officers and 10 cavalrymen of which 7 mounted.
With Dumas: 1 officer and 34 cavalrymen all mounted.
With Joinville: 12 men
With Mortier: 10 men
83 were seconded to various tasks in the rear. 2 officers and 21 men were affected to escort duties, Murat's coach, the money casket, or prisoner escort. 1 officer and 61 men were sent to the depot. 2 officers were in hospital. Total: **13 officers and 258 cavalrymen.**

● **5. The Polish Cavalry.**

Numbers: 2 officers and 10 mounted men who were with Berthier and Joinville. 26 cavalrymen were affected to various liaison tasks.

● **6. The Portuguese cavalry.**

They were to be found at Moscow at headquarters. They were 33 officers and 308 troopers of which 244 were mounted.

SPECIAL CASES

Two special cases have to be mentioned concerning units which were more or less attached to headquarters or the Guard, but which were not at the Moskova.

● **1. The Neuchatel Battalion**

This was Berthier's personal battalion. It was *en route* to join up, but only reached Smolensk on the 10th October and was therefore not at the Moskova. It was at Smolensk, where de Bosset had just died from an infection due to the corpses of men and beasts rotting there, that Berthier rejoined his battalion nicknamed *les Canaris*. He also discovered the organisational deficiencies in the depots set up along the route.

● **2. The Hessian Light Battalion.**

At the beginning there were two regiments of fusiliers and they had been regrouped into one regiment of the Corps. Alone the 1st battalion reached Borodino after the battle and for the following three days it took part in the recuperation of weapons on the battlefield. It was joined later by the 2nd Battalion and the Guards regiment, towards Moscow. There Napoleon attached them to the Guard.

They were only 1 300. The Prince of Hess for his part had followed the Emperor and had taken part in the great battle.

---

(1) I have included these details to show that the scope of the operations meant that the troops were widely dispersed in numerous garrisons which reduced the number of soldiers available for the army itself.

FRENCH IMPERIAL GUARD
GRENADIERS and *CHASSEURS A PIED*

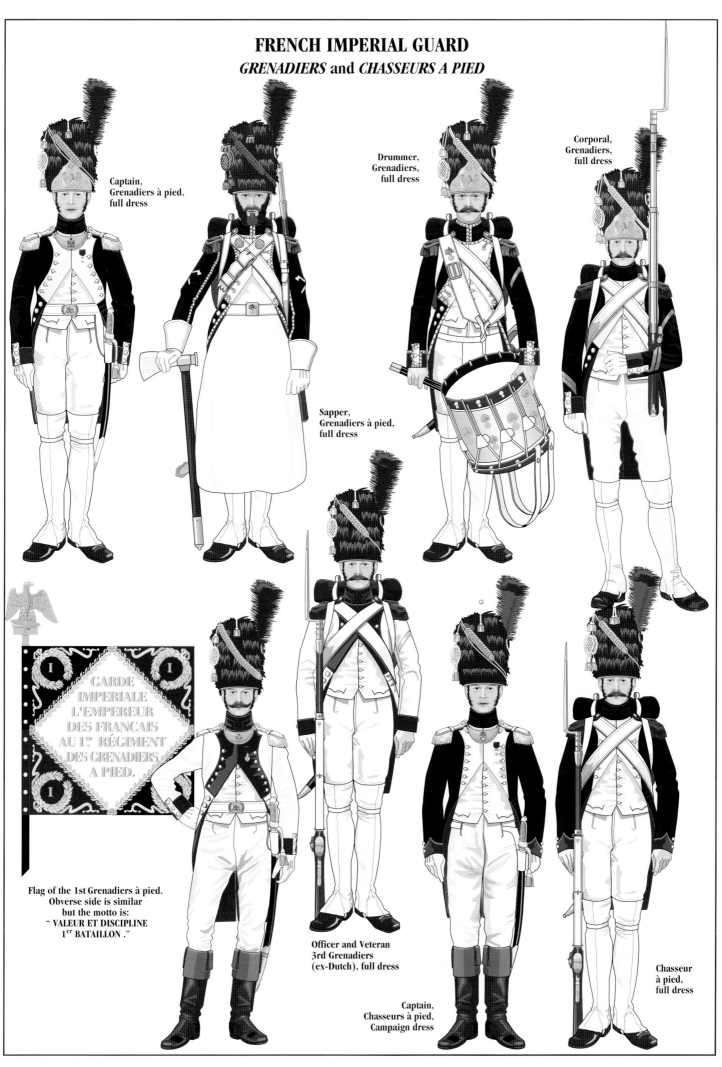

Captain,
Grenadiers à pied,
full dress

Sapper,
Grenadiers à pied,
full dress

Drummer,
Grenadiers,
full dress

Corporal,
Grenadiers,
full dress

GARDE
IMPERIALE
L'EMPEREUR
DES FRANCAIS
AU I.er RÉGIMENT
DES GRENADIERS
A PIED.

Flag of the 1st Grenadiers à pied.
Obverse side is similar
but the motto is:
" VALEUR ET DISCIPLINE
1er BATAILLON ."

Officer and Veteran
3rd Grenadiers
(ex-Dutch), full dress

Captain,
Chasseurs à pied,
Campaign dress

Chasseur
à pied,
full dress

FRENCH IMPERIAL GUARD
FUSILIERS-GRENADIERS and FUSILIERS-CHASSEURS

Lieutenant,
Fusiliers-Grenadiers,
full dress

Sapper,
Fusiliers-Grenadiers,
full dress

Drummer
Fusiliers-Grenadiers,
full dress

Corporal
Fusiliers-Grenadiers,
full dress

Lieutenant,
Fusiliers-Chasseurs,
full dress

Fusiliers-chasseurs,
full dress

André Jouineau © Histoire & Collections 1999

FRENCH IMPERIAL GUARD
TIRAILLEURS-GRENADIERS and VOLTIGEURS REGIMENTS

Lieutenant,
Tirailleurs-Grenadiers,
full dress

Drummer
Tirailleurs-Grenadiers,
full dress

Sergeant,
Tirailleurs-Grenadiers,
full dress

Tirailleur-grenadier,
full dress

Sapper,
Voltigeurs,
full dress

Voltigeurs,
full dress

André Jouineau © Histoire & Collections 1999

FRENCH IMPERIAL GUARD
CAVALRY

St Sulpice's Brigade

L'EMPEREUR DES FRANCAIS AU RÉGIMENT DE DRAGONS DE L'IMPERATRICE

Cavalryman, Dragoons of the Guard,
Full dress

Officer, Dragoons of the Guard

Brigadier (Corporal),
Mounted Grenadiers
of the Guard,
full dress

Krasinski
and de Colbert's Brigade

Officers, 1st Chevau-Légers
of the Guard (Polish).
This campaign dress (above) was worn
by an unknown officer during the Battle.

Officer, 2nd Chevau-Légers of the Guard,
campaign dress, summer 1812.

André Jouineau © Histoire & Collections 1999

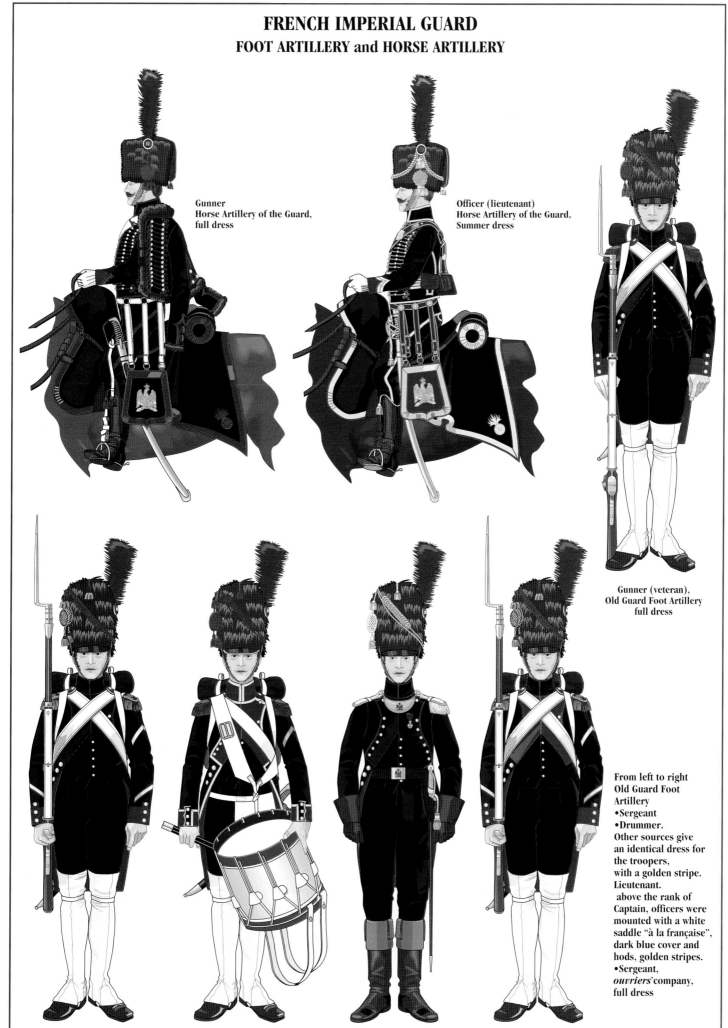

FRENCH IMPERIAL GUARD
FOOT ARTILLERY and HORSE ARTILLERY

Gunner
Horse Artillery of the Guard,
full dress

Officer (lieutenant)
Horse Artillery of the Guard,
Summer dress

Gunner (veteran),
Old Guard Foot Artillery
full dress

From left to right
Old Guard Foot
Artillery
•Sergeant
•Drummer.
Other sources give
an identical dress for
the troopers,
with a golden stripe.
Lieutenant.
 above the rank of
Captain, officers were
mounted with a white
saddle "à la française",
dark blue cover and
hods, golden stripes.
•Sergeant,
ouvriers'company,
full dress

André Jouineau © Histoire & Collections 1999

THE IMPERIAL GUARD

The Imperial Guard was above all a spectator and did not take part in the battle; it remained grouped around the Emperor. However its artillery played an essential role at the Moskova.

There was a particular problem concerning the Young Guard. In the march towards Borodino, the Young Guard had been left behind at Smolensk, waiting for the marching battalions of the Guard coming up from Vitebsk. Berthézène who commanded the 1st Brigade of the Young Guard specified that it was Lanusse's 2nd Brigade which had been left behind at Smolensk.

As soon as this brigade was freed, it moved up by the Moscow road, but it is not certain whether it reached the field in time for the battle. At any rate it would have remained in reserve.

The numbers of the Guard, at this moment were very much lower than those given by many famous historians. Roguet's Division was missing 1 200 men from the flanking regiments, which had remained at Vilna and Vitebsk.

Berthézène gave the following figures for the Guard:

— **Infantry:** 15 500 men plus 7 companies of marines

— **Cavalry:** 5 000 cavalrymen plus the artillery, a total of less than 25 000 men.

The infantry regiments only had 2 battalions and the 4th Skirmishers of Berthézène's brigade could only field 400 men.

At the Moskova, the numbers were even lower, for the cavalry as well. This elite phalanx could not have tipped the scales of the battle against an army still in reasonably good order with the massive squares that made up the Russian Guard; only the artillery could inflict severe losses on the enemy by firing into these compacted masses where each shot took a terrible toll.

The discussions around the myth of the Guard which should have participated are not realistic. Making cavalry attacks against these squares was suicidal and the infantry battalions would have exhausted themselves without affecting the final outcome. Napoleon, seeing his troops exhausted, knew how to keep a reserve by destroying a static enemy, who was indifferent to death coming from French cannon.

THE ARTILLERY OF THE GUARD AT THE MOSKOVA

This was the only unit committed. It was commanded by

— **General Count Sorbier**. Born 1762, Lieutenant in 1782, promoted general by Hoche on the battlefield of Neuwied. Major-General in 1800, Deputy during the 100 days, exiled in 1815. Died in 1827. Gd Cordon de la Couronne de Fer in 1809, Gd Cordon de la LH in 1814.

His aides de camp were

— **Hatry**, Baron in 1827, Colonel in 1830, Brigadier in 1839, Major-General in 1848, CrLH.

— **de Laboulaye**, captain and LH in 1813.

Sorbier

SECOND-IN-COMMAND

— **Noury**, Baron. Italian Campaign. Major-General in 1813. Served at Waterloo, died in 1839. LH in Year XII, CRLH, GdOLH. His aide de camp was de Lagrange. Battalion commander in the Royal Guard.

CHIEF OF STAFF

— **Lallemand**, Egyptian campaign, General in 1814, Lieutenant-General in 1815, wounded at Waterloo, condemned to death his absence with his brother, exiled to Texas where he died in 1823.

His deputies were:

— **Pailhou**, colonel in 1814, Brigadier in 1819, Lieutenant-General in 1841. On 1st September 1812, he was with the 6th Company of the Foot Guards. GdOLH in 1847.

— **Lavilette**, captured in November, died in captivity at Kaluga.

— **Laporte**, Squadron Commander in 1813, served in 1815, Colonel and Baron in the same year. OLH in 1813, CrLH in 1815.

— **Sautereau**, Colonel, Baron in 1813, retired in 1829, Brigadier. OLH in 1813.

LIGHT ARTILLERY

Commanded by **Baron Drouot**. Served at Trafalgar, he was Major-General, aide de camp to Napoleon in 1813, went to Elba; Peer of France in 1815, served at Waterloo. Exiled returned to be judged, acquitted. Half pay. Died blind in Nancy in 1847. GdCxLH in 1830.

— **Boulart**, Italian Campaign. Baron then General in 1813, commanded at Strasburg in 1815. He was the son of the Master of the Chapel at the Cathedral at Reims. Died in 1842, LH in Year XII, CrLH in 1813.

— **Cottin**, heros of St Domingo, Colonel in December, died in 1827.

— **Boileau**, health officer decorated at Moscow, retired in 1834.

THE ADJUDANT-MAJORS

— **Evain**, Colonel in 1822, CrLH in 1831.

— **Hortet**, Colonel in 1832, CrLH in 1843.

Two others died at Vilna and one was reported missing.

THE CAPTAINS IN THE 1st AND THE 2nd

One died and ten returned, amongst whom:

— **Couin**, Italian and Egyptian Campaigns, in Lyon during the 100 days, retired Colonel in 1824. LH in Year XII.

— **Pion des Loches**, author of memoirs, pursued as a seminarist, engaged in 1793. Colonel in 1815, died in 1819. LH in Year XII.

— **Cuny**, Italian and Egyptian Campaigns. Returned with frozen feet. Retired in 1824. LH in Year XII.

— **Leclerc**, Brigadier in 1835.

THE LIEUTENANTS IN THE 1st AND THE 2nd

Two died at the Moskova, one at Kovno and one in captivity. One lieutenant decorated at Moscow was killed at Lutzen. Ten returned. One returned with Drouot bringing with him 173 artillerymen.

HEAVY ARTILLERY

— **Desvaux de St Maurice**, Italian Campaign, OLH Year XII, Major-General in 1813, killed at Waterloo.

— **Dubuard**, called "Marin", in the artillery of Napoleon's guides in Egypt, wounded twice, received a Grenade d'Honneur. Wounded in Italy, at Eylau, in Russia on 24.10.1812 and at Waterloo as Colonel. Retired in 1815, taken back in 1830. CTLH.

— **Chauveau**, in the artillery of the guides in Italy. Horse killed under him at the Moskova. Killed by the Saxon artillerymen during their defection. LH in Year XII.

— **Thérin**, Surgeon-Major, served in 1815, OLH.

Three adjudant majors returned.

THE CAPTAINS

— **Georges Delemud**, Squadron Commander, Baron at Moscow, retired in 1815, OLH October 1812.

— **Sandras**, Italian Camapaign. Bayonne, Major in 1815, LH in XII.

— **Boisellier**, Italian and Egyptian Campaigns in the guides, killed at Reims in 1814, LH in Year XII.

— **Lafont**, Italian and Egyptian Campaigns, Colonel in 1813, resigned during the 100 days, Brigadier in 1817, deputy in 1830. LH in Year XII, GdOLH in 1825.

— **Chambray**, captured in December, returned, Brigadier in 1830.

— **Savarin**, Standard-Bearer and Squadron Commander in 1813, LH

FRENCH IMPERIAL GUARD
DEPOT, ARTILLERY TRAIN, ENGINEERS

Driver, 1st Guard Artillery Train, full dress

Captain 1st Guard Artillery Train, full dress
He has been given a sack *à la Soubise* like the non-commissioned officers although there is no known illustration of this.

Lieutenant, Imperial Guard Engineers. All the officers of the Engineers wore an "aiguillette".

Drummer Imperial Guard Engineers.

Sergeant Imperial Guard Engineers, Campaign dress

Corporal Imperial Guard Engineers, full dress

André Jouineau © Histoire & Collections 1999

in Year XII, OLH in 1813.

THE LIEUTENANTS

— **Devries**, wounded twice at the Moskova, decorated at Moscow, disappeared at Kovno, but as he was Dutch he may have returned home.

— **De Marcilly**, decorated at Moscow, Colonel in 1836.

— **Lyautey**, decorated at Moscow, uncle of the future marshall. He was Brigadier in Africa in 1840. Major-General in 1848, GdOLH in 1852, Senator in 1854.

— **Massias**, returned in a sledge with Boulart, served in the colonies in 1824.

— **Deniset**, captured but returned.

— **Delabogne**, captured, but probably returned as he was required to be an aide de camp later.

THE ARTILLERY OF THE MIDDLE AND YOUNG GUARD

— **Henrion**, came from Spain. Holder of a Grenade d'Honneur, Major in 1813, Baron , retired in 18232, Honorary Brigadier, CtLH.

— **Charpentier**, served in 1815, Colonel in 1830, CrLH in 1845.

THE CAPTAINS

One died during the retreat, one captured but returned.

— **Framery**, retired in 1826, Brigadier, CrLH in 1856.

— **Faivre**, Egyptian Campaign, Honorary Colonel in 1824.

— **Lefrançais**, Colonel in 1823, CrLH in 1831.

— **Euvrard**, wounded at Lodi, Major in 1813, LH in Year XIII.

— **Bitsch**, wounded before Paris, served in 1815.

— **Maillard de Liscourt** "taking the waters" on 1st September, writing from Moscow on 10th September, Colonel in 1823.

THE LIEUTENANTS

— **Munéraut,** Italian and Egyptian Campaigns, Grenade d'Honneur, Captain in 1813, re-engaged in 1831.

— **Dumont**, part of the guard of the Consuls, discharged in 1814.

— **Demetz**, Colonel in 1830, CrLH in 1837.

— **Zerlaut**, present at Marengo, decorated at Moscow, retired in 1814.

— **Cornuel**, decorated at Moscow, went to Elba.

— **Delasarras**, came from the Dutch Guard, resigned in 1814.

Two lost, one disappeared and one left dying at Vilna: **Merville, de Mauroy** and **Lesueur**.

THE DEPOT

— **Pellegrin de Millon**, General in 1813, served in 1815, retired.

— **Bergier**, Colonel in 1823, retired in 1832.

— **Marilhac**, Colonel in the reserves of the Guards, Italian and Egyptian Campaigns, Brigadier in 1825, died in 1832.

— **Bosquette**, Lieutenant in charge of workmen, Honorary Colonel in 1830.

— **Guettemann**, formerly of the Guards of the Consuls, retired in 1813. Suffered from frostbite. LH in Year XIII.

TRANSPORT

Principal Battalion and secondary Battalion.

— **Leroy**, Italian and Egyptian Campaigns, LH in Year XII, Colonel in 1813, commanded the regiment, retired in 1816.

— **Desmaidy** commanded the secondary battalion.

One killed and one captured, but returned.

Six officers escaped from the hulk *Vieille Castille* in Spain and were there together; they were

— **Colomb**, Egyptian campaign, wounded at the Moskova, Squadron Commander in 1813.

— **Baron**, died at Dresden.

— **Brenier**, retired in 1815.

— **Fillon,** dismissed in 1815.

— **Bulotte**, retired in 1823 after a period of inactivity. LH in Year XIII.

— **Monin**, died at the end of the retreat.

At Moscow, the Artillery received 10 Legion d'Honneurs and the Transport Corps 21.

STRENGTH OF THE GUARD AT MOSCOW

In the report drawn up on 15th October 1812, the following figures are available:

1. THE INFANTRY

— the **Old Guard** had 206 officers and 6 500 men including those who had been detached.

— **Roguet's division** numbered 52 officers and 3 570 men of whom 30 were administrative staff (including those detached). The regiment of flankers was detached as a whole, 32 officers and 1 178 men remained at Vitebsk and Vilna and therefore did not take part in the Moskova.

— **Delaborde's Division**. It consisted of 170 officers and 3 540 men of which 40 were administrative staff. 1 628 were detached, though where is not mentioned. They were possibly at Smolensk. On the spot there were less than 500 men per regiment. This brings us back to the figure that Berthézène gave us, stating that the 4th Skirmishers had 400 soldiers. On the roll, there were in fact 463 men. Even exaggerating the numbers, the clerks only gave about 15 000 infantrymen as not having already been engaged [1].

2. THE CAVALRY

At Moscow, it had:

— 11 officers and 77 Elite Gendarmes, of which 5 were mounted.

— the mounted grenadiers of which 67 officers and 1 020 men

— the dragoons had 61 officers and 848 men (798 mounted)

— the mounted infantry had 62 officers and 980 men of which 923 were mounted.

— the Mameluks had 6 officers and 57 men of which 50 were mounted.

— the two regiments of lancers were not at Moscow but with Murat. No figures are available for them. Lachouque says they were 1 400. So according to the roll 3 170 cavalry of the Guard including the officers, though not all mounted, together with the lancers with Murat. For the whole of the cavalry, they were about 5 000 men.

They were not engaged and arrived in the best conditions, with the entourage of the Emperor. A certain number of conclusions useful for the approximate total of combattants at the Moskova can be drawn.

3. THE ARTILLERY AND THE TRANSPORT

At Moscow they were 35 officers and 964 men. They had 644 draught horses. They should have had 39 4-pounders and 32 6-pounders. But as at the 11th October, Mortier gave the numbers as follows: 16 4-poun-

---

1. THE RETURN AND THEIR LOSSES.

I have chosen the example of a solid regiment to give as precise an idea as possible of their odyssey. It concerns the Fusilier-Grendiers of Roguet's Division, making up the medium guard. As young veterans they had reached Moscow with their numbers almost intact, i.e. 32 officers and 1 352 men. They were engaged at Krasnoi in a terrible night attack which annihilated the Vanguard of the Russian General Ojarowski, who had tried to pass by the french columns and had set up his camp to the south of the French but at the same level. This night attack by Roguet's Division was a complete success, though 2 officers and 36 men were killed. There were also 181 men who were listed as missing during this combat. On the total in the retreat, 30 returned though 5 were killed on the way, this being explained by the fact that 7 officers were picked up on the way from the little depots at Vilna, for example.

As far as the soldiers were concerned, it was more difficult and I studied the registers of the regiment and found that 172 soldiers returned directly from Russia and some were noted as having rejoined in the first months of 1813. There were 42 who returned and who had become officers since. Also, 5 men had been detached in Germany once they had returned. So 219 men out of 1352 men came back directly from Russia. 6 prisoners returned in 1814, but for this group, a lot must have been missing for the regiment was disbanded at the end of 1814 and 1815. This is the case of my direct ancestor, listed as missing in Russia, but who returned form the Sarapol salt mines in the Urals after a 7-month walk. Even if this group is evaluated at 41, that only leaves 260 men returned out of 1 352, or 16.27%.

I also considered the origins of the men in this regiment and I counted 301 men from occupied countries: 101 Italians, 113 Belgian / Dutch, 72 Germans and 15 miscellaneous. 35 returned. This shows that even in the Guard, more than 20% of the soldiers came from occupied countries.

ders,10 6-pounders, 6 3-pounders and 4 24-pound howitzers. All the others like the caissons were horseless. All the French heavy artillery together with that recovered from the redoubts, could not follow as there were no horses.

4. CLAPAREDE'S DIVISION

This was attached to the Guard without being really part of it. On the roll there were 110 officers and about 2 300 men including the eternal 'detached soldiers'. Lachouque only accounts for 87 officers and 1 683 men at that date. In a roll of the Young and the Middle Guard as at the date of 11 October 1812, Mortier claims that there were 7 officers and 921 men in the rear without permission, 21 officers and 4 431 men in the hospitals - had they not fought then? - together with 67 officers and 4 245 men detached between Koenigsberg and Moscow.

This appears quite considerable, even though the soldiers detached were here justified (flankers, men from the Young Guard and from the lancers).

For the Army corps things must have been worse.

DAVOUT'S FIRST CORPS

This corps was the former Army of Germany, constituted by Davout. It was the most solid kernel with its five divisions. They were involved in the whole campaign.

The French regiments had 6 battalions of which the 5th remained at the depot, under the command of the first Major, the so-called "Gros-Major". These regiments were considered as brigades and were therefore commanded by a general, the titular Colonel was seconded by the second Major. This is one of the explanations of the high numbers of Generals present at the Moskova.

The divisions played an essential role, for Napoleon was conscious of the 4th Corps' weakness and reinforced it with Morand's and Gérard's Divisions. Similarly, Ney received the timely support of Friant's Division and Maréchal Davout only had the Compans and Dessaix Divisions with him while his men guaranteed the glory of others. This relative disgrace was due to his critical attitude since Smolensk.

GENERAL STAFF

THE MARÉCHAL'S AIDES DE CAMP

— **Colonel Kobilinski**, lost a leg at Malojaroslawetz, survived and died a Préfet in 1860.

— **Major Brosset**, not active in 1815.

— **Squadron Commander de Castres**, cadet in 1784, émigré in 1792, returned in 1802, served Davout in 1815, retired, taken back in 1818 with the rank of Colonel. Died in 1832, LH in 1809, CrLH in 1823.

— **Squadron Commander Hervo**, OLH in 1828.

— **Lieutenant de Castries**, Marquis and future Duke. Colonel with the 4th Chasseurs in 1815, Brigadier in 1828, died in 1866. LH 10th August 1812, CrLH and St Ferdinand in 1823.

— **Captain de Beaumont**, Squadron commander in 1813.

— **Captain de Fayet**, St Cyr in 1804, squadron Commander at Moscow, not active in 1821, LH 10th August 1812, OLH in 1820.

— the Chief of Staff was **Baron Romeuf**. He arrested the King at Varennes, was at Malta. With Davout in 1803, killed at the Moskova.

His assistants:

— **Captain Laloy**, Davout's aide camp in 1813, died in 1816.

— **Lieutenant Despréaux** went over to the 17th of the Line at Moscow.

— **Captain Thomas**, Squadron commander, was at Moscow.

— **Captain Tartarat**, serving in 1824.

— **Captain Chauvin**, on Davout's staff in 1815.

In his suite were:

— **General Beaupré**, Madame Davout's uncle, died 26th February 1813 in Berlin.

— **General Pamplona**, left at Mohilev with his aide de camp Pereira.

— **Adjudant Commander Pariset**. Formerly of India, Egyptian Campaign, wounded at the Moskova, returned.

— **Captain Lacger**, wounded at the Moskova, LH at Moscow, commanded the Gendarmerie.

— **General Saunier**, with Davout since 1803, served in 1815, Lieutenant-General in 1820, CrLH 1813.

THE COMMISSAIRES-ORDONNATEURS,

two died during the campaign.

— **De Beauvollier**, former Vendéen, captured and exiled, served here; in 1815 returned to the Vendéen side, Intendant-General.

— **Servan**, postmaster in the Guard in 1813, colonel in 1818.

— **Albitt**e, in the 4th Division died near Moscow. He was a Conventionnel and Regicide.

— **Berlié**, decorated in 1834 in Africa, but was heavily in debt.

— **Blanchot**, born at Colmar, with the 3rd Division, served in 1815, then was tax-collector at Molsheim until 1858.

In the health service of the General Staff there was certain **Delaunay** who was captured, but chose to remain in Russia. He wrote a letter in 1860 and his descendant was among the dissidents who followed Solzhenitsyn out of the Soviet Union.

ARTILLERY OF THE 1st CORPS

It was commanded by

— **Pernetty**, Major-General, Conseiller d'Etat in 1817, Senator then Pair de France in 1835 in 1856. GdCx de la Réunion in 1813, GdCx Lh in 1821.

His aides de camp were

— **Captain de Bérauvi**, commanded Morand's artillery at Borodino, where he was wounded, colonel in 1826, LH in 1807.

— **Captain Moret**, wounded at Mohilev and at the Moskova, Lieutenant-Colonel in 1830, retired in 1837.

The second in command was

— **General Baltus de Pouilly**, Lieutenant-General in 1827, died in 1845, CtLH 1807.

— **Dauty**, his aide de camp died in February 1814.

— **Gay de Verdon** died in Russia.

— **General Jouffroy** supervised the last three divisions. He had served since 1781 and was a lieutenant in 1792. Took part in the defence pf Paris in 1815 and was retired. Re-engaged in 1831, died in 1846.

His aide de camp was

— **Brussel de Brulart**, decorated at Moscow, served in Hamburg.

THE GENERAL STAFF

Its Chief was **Colonel Gerdy**, captured in Poland, was listed as missing. His assistants were

— **Captain Mazerat** killed at Leipzig.

— **Captain Prévost**, Battalion Commander in 1823, LH at Moscow. The Reserve.

— **Colonel Bode**, Dutch, wounded at the Moskova and disappeared in Russia.

The Main Pool was directed by

— **Colonel Saint-Vincent,** killed at the Moskova.

— **Major François**, who was at Danzig, besieged.

— **De Vésian**, born at Crest, colonel in 1840. and CrLH in 1843.

— **Bubarry de Lesqueron**, Colonel in 1840 retired in 1845.

Distribution amongst the divisions.

1. MORAND'S ARTILLERY DIVISION

Battalion Commander Raindre who was in command, was wounded at Smolensk where he remained.

— **1st Company, 7th Heavy Artillery regiment:** one officer killed at the Moskova and one died during the retreat.

— **7th Company , 1st Light Artillery regiment:** the captain was killed at the Moskova, his second in command was wounded and captured later. Returned.

— **1st and 2nd Companies, 1st Transport Battalion.**

— **1st Company of the 12th Equipment Battalion,** officer disappeared in October. To be mentioned:

— **Muller**, holder of a Sabre of Honour was wounded 25th October 1812 whi-

le killing a Russian baron, a Cossack chief. In 1814, captured and wounded, he freed 100 prisoners. Retired in 1816.

— **6th Company, 3rd Sappers** with the **battalion commander Girardin**, Lieutenant-Colonel in 1829, and **Captain Lieutaud,** holder of a Sabre of Honour, wounded at the Moskova and retired in 1815.

2. FRIANT'S ARTILLERY DIVISION

— **2nd Company, 7th Heavy Artillery Regiment:** two officers wounded at the Moskova, both returned.

— **5th Company, 3rd Light Artillery Regiment:** all returned.

— **the 4th and 6th of the 9/2 Transport,** returned except one disappeared during the retreat.

— **the 4th of the 12th section.**

— **5th Company, 5th Sapper Battalion.**

3. GÉRARD'S ARTILLERY DIVISION

— **3rd Company, 7th Heavy Artillery Regiment:** one officer wounded at the Moskova then disappeared.

— **4th Company, 3rd Light Artillery Regiment:** three wounded at the Moskova of whom one died during the retreat.

— **1st and 4th Companies, 1st Transport Regiment.**

— **1st and 3rd Companies, 12th section.**

— **9th Company, 5th Battalion of Sappers** with **Captain Teissier**. Lieutenant-Colonel in 1826, retired in 1830, OLH 1814.

4. DESSAIX'S ARTILLERY DIVISION

— **9th Company, 7th Heavy Artillery Regiment,** all returned.

— **3rd and 6th Companies, 1st Transport Battalion.** The commander of the 3rd was wounded at the Moskova and died at Bérésina.

— **4th Company, 12th Section.**

— **3rd Company, 2nd Sapper Battalion:** Captain **Mittifot,** died at Danzig.

5. COMPANS' ARTILLERY DIVISION

— **16th Company, 7th Heavy Artillery Regiment: Labbé**, decorated at Moscow, captured and returned. **Tardu**, presumed dead but captured during the battle and returned in 1814. Served in 1815.

— **2nd and 4th Companies, 9th Transport Battalion:** one officer died during the retreat. One wounded at the Moskova.

— **5th Company, 3rd battalion of Sappers: Captain Finot**, Colonel in 1828, LH at Moscow, CrLH and Retired in 1831.

THE RESERVES AND THE POOL

— **3rd and 17th Companies, 1st Heavy Artillery Regiment: Captain de Mouchy**, Battalion Commander in 1813, LH at Moscow.

— **Lévy-Feistel**, squadron Commander in 1835.   LH at Moscow.

— **6th Company, 7 Heavy Artillery Regiment: Richard**, Lieutenant-Colonel in 1826.

— **1st, 5th and 6th Companies, 1st Transport Battalion.**

— **6th Company, 3rd Transport Battalion.**

— **Companies 1-5, 9th Transport Battalion.**

— **5 Companies from the 12th Sections.**

— **8th Company, 5th Sapper Battalion.** One ambulance and the mounted Gendarmes.

1st CORPS ARTILLERY PIECES

There were 12 12-pounders, 50 6-pounders, 64 3-pounders, called "regimental" and 24 howitzers of which 4 were heavy.

THE PERSONNEL

At the beginning, on 15th June, the following figures can be given:

— a heavy artillery company included about 3 officers and 100 men.

— a light artillery company included 3 officers and 90 men.

— an artillery transport company had one officer, 75 men and about 125 draught horses.

— a section transport company had 1 officer, 50-70 men and about 70 draught horses.

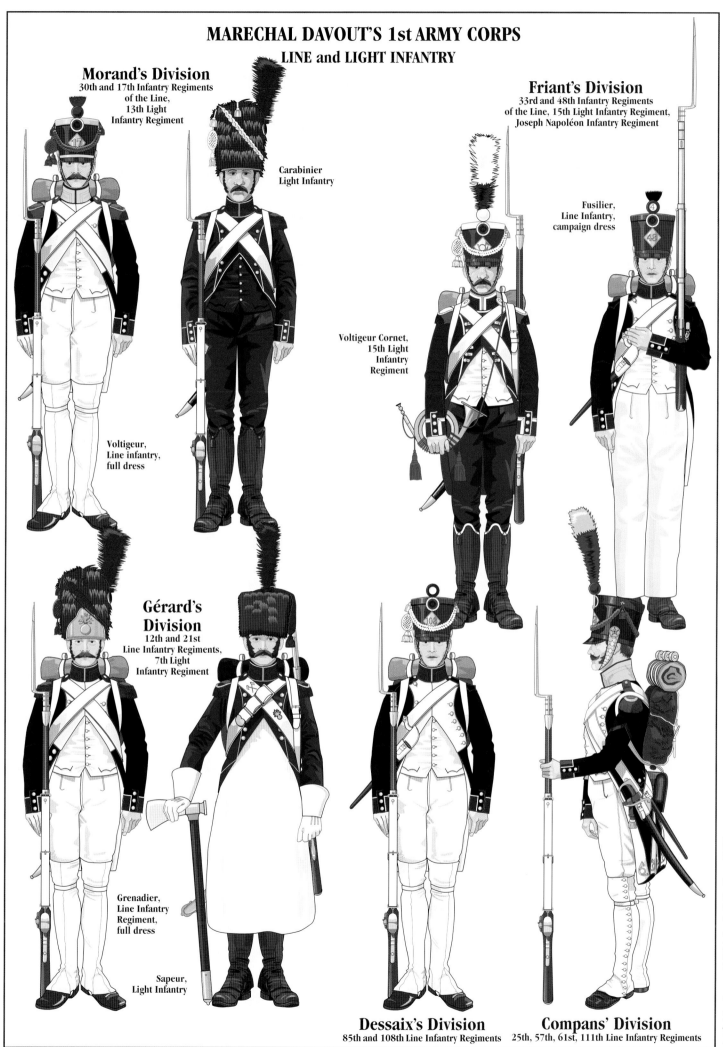

MARECHAL DAVOUT'S 1st ARMY CORPS
LINE and LIGHT INFANTRY

Morand's Division
30th and 17th Infantry Regiments of the Line, 13th Light Infantry Regiment

Voltigeur, Line infantry, full dress

Carabinier Light Infantry

Friant's Division
33rd and 48th Infantry Regiments of the Line, 15th Light Infantry Regiment, Joseph Napoléon Infantry Regiment

Fusilier, Line Infantry, campaign dress

Voltigeur Cornet, 15th Light Infantry Regiment

Gérard's Division
12th and 21st Line Infantry Regiments, 7th Light Infantry Regiment

Grenadier, Line Infantry Regiment, full dress

Sapeur, Light Infantry

Dessaix's Division
85th and 108th Line Infantry Regiments

Compans' Division
25th, 57th, 61st, 111th Line Infantry Regiments

MARÉCHAL DAVOUT'S 1st ARMY CORPS
ARTILLERY, ENGINEERS, ARTILLERY TRAIN

Corporal
Foot Artillery, full dress

Lieutenant
Foot Artillery

Driver,
Artillery Train

Brigadier ,
Horse Artillery,
campaign dress

Driver
Equipment Train

Driver
Engineer Train
Campaign dress

Engineer (Sapper)
(First Class), full dress.
He is wearing
Corporal's chevrons
on left arm only.

André Jouineau © Histoire & Collections 2000

— About ten artillery workers in a division.

— the Sappers had two officers and 100 men per company.

THE ENGINEERS OF THE 1ST CORPS

Commanded by **General Haxo**, Italian Campaign, Major-General in 1813, died in 1838. His aide de camp was killed at Mohilev. LH in Year XII, GdOLH in 1821.

CHIEF OF STAFF

— **Prévost de Vernois**, on the Rhine in 1815, Brigadier in 1831, Lieutenant-General in 1840, GdOLH in 1846.

His second :

— **Battalion Commander Emy**, Colonel in 1822. OLH 1814.

— **Speelweldt**, Dutch, left very ill at Dubrovna.

Deputies:

— **Cocconceli**, captured 9th September 1812, returned. Battalion Commander in 1831. LH in 1815.

— **Kool and Everes,** returned to Holland in 1814.

— **Jacques de Cassières**, wounded at Fleurus, decorated in 1815, colonel in1843.

— **Vuilleret,** discharged in 1830, LH 1814.

POOL

— **Battalion Commander Prost**, Colonel at Moscow, discharged 1829.

— **Captain Lagrange,** disappeared, LH at Moscow.

RESERVE

— 8th Company, 5th Sappers of **Captain Brignon** who was discharged in 1826.

TRANSPORT

— **Hottelard,** died in Russia, and **Cercelet** who swam across the Beresina, saving the money of his company.

Morand

I. MORAND'S DIVISION

The General, Egyptian Campaign, Count in 1808, was wounded in the jaw during the first attack of the great redoubt and replaced by Lanabère of the Guard. He was Napoleon's aide de camp, exiled to Poland, condemned to death in his absence, he was allowed to return in 1819, aquitted. Pair de France in 1832, GdCxLH 1830.

His aides de camp were

— His brother from the 15th Light

— **Parguez**, Colonel at Moscow, Honorary Brigadier, died in 1829.

— **Despans de Cubières**, Squadron Commander at Moscow, colonel in 1813. Wounded at "Quatre Bras" and at Waterloo. Brigadier in 1829. Lieutenant-General in 1835, Minister of War, compromised in the Teste Affair. This brother of the general, then President of the Court of Cassation received a large sum of money for granting a rock salt concession. Cubières was rehabilitated in 1852. OLH 1813.

— **Fourier D'Hincourt**, colonel in 1821, brigadier in 1829, died in 1840.

— **General Lanabère**, Marengo, went over to the Guard, commanded the Fusilier-Chasseurs. At the Moskova, replaced the wounded Morand and was himself mortally wounded leading the attack of the great redoubt at the head of the 17th.

CHIEF OF STAFF

— **Delort de Glion**, named general at Moscow, died at Vilna.

Deputies:

— **de Pouilly**, disappeared during the retreat.

— **Vignon**, disappeared in Russia.

The Morand's division attacks the Great Redoubt during the second assault of the day. French Cuirassiers' regiment are on the right wing. (Lejeune)

DALTON'S BRIGADE

The general, wounded at Smolensk, was allowed to return, and was thus not at the Moskova. Lieutenant-General in 1815, demoted after Waterloo; re-instated in 1821.

THE 13th LIGHT INFANTRY REGIMENT.

Colonel d'Argence, General at Moscow, captured at Beresina, returned and retired in 1815.

The regiment suffered large losses at Smolensk. At the outset there were 102 officers and 3 480 men. At the Moskova, 6 officers were killed and 14 wounded. At Moscow, 71 officers and 921 men were present. Three officers and 392 men were detached and 2 134 were in hospital. The total for the campaign: 21 officers dead, 13 missing and 13 prisoners returned.

Special cases:

— **Captain Hurault de Sorbée**. He joined the Guard and went to Elba. Wounded at Waterloo, inactive until 1823, colonel in 1830. Brigadier in 1833, retired 1848.

— **Lieutenant Mauduit**, captain at Moscow, captured at Waterloo, served in Spain then Belgium, brigadier in 1846, died in 1875.

GRATIEN'S BRIGADE

The general served in 1787, then was promoted lieutenant in the *Enfants Rouges* Battalion in 1789. In the service of Holland in 1807, returned to French service, wounded at Smolensk. Major-General at Moscow, in Italy in 1813 and 1814 the year of his death.

His aides de camp were

— **De Castel Laboulbène**, former émigré, in Italy after 1812.

— **Belle**, was wtih the 14th Cuirassiers in 1814, in Alsace with Lecourbe in 1815.

THE 17TH INFANTRY REGIMENT OF THE LINE

— **Colonel Vasserot**, wounded at Smolensk and at Beresina, general in 1813, Viscount in 1823, GdOLH.

At the beginning, the regiment included 96 officers and 3 498 men in theory. At the Moskova, 26 officers were killed of whom 3 on the 5th September and 43 were wounded (certain several times). At Moscow, 58 officers and 1 281 menwere present. On 12th October, the regiment received 41 LH, of which 20 for the officers. For the campaign as a whole, 37 officers died, 30 listed missing and 15 prisoners who returned. More than 30 2nd-Lieutenants were appointed in Russia. Except for one officer killed at Dresden, all officers who returned survived the Empire.

Special cases

— **Captain Lamarque**, called the "Hero of the Moskova". Wounded, he rallied his fleeing men and stopped the flight of the 2nd Battalion. Promoted Battalion Commander at Moscow, aide de camp to Ricard in 1813.

— **Battalion-Commander Levasseur**, wounded twice on 5th September, wounded on the 7th, he was the first to enter the redoubt. LH in 1813, OLH in 1815.

— **Captain Locqueneux**, captured at Dresden, reached the rank of general.

— **Captain Herbin**, received three shots and a bayonet wound at the Moskova, dismissed in 1815, LH 1813.

— **Captain Feisthamel**, wounded at Smolensk nand twice at the Moskova, colonel in 1830, brigadier in 1839, died in 1851.

— **Alaume**, promoted second-lieutenant at Moscow, 13 bayonet wounds at the Moskova, wounded at Viasna, captured and returned.

— **Battalion Commander Barriès** wrote to his wife on 24th September, celebrating the victory and the merits of the Emperor. Told of the fire at Moscow and that 3 out of 5 battalion commanders were killed during the battle. Captured on 19th December, escaped but died at Gumbinen in January 1813 in the house of a cabinet maker and buried in the protestant cemetery of the town.

BONNAMY'S BRIGADE

The general was captured covered in bayonet wounds during the first attack of the great redoubt. Returned from Russia in 1814, lieutenant-general in 1815.

His aides de camp were:

— **Walsh,** received the LH on the battlefield at Wagram, retired in August 1812, for reasons of ill-health, was not therefore at the Moskova.

— **Veranneman**, replaced Walsh, retired in 1814.

— Solirène, wounded at the Moskova and Hamburg, dismissed in 1815.

THE 30th OF THE LINE

— **Colonel Buquet**, escaped from Cadiz, wounded at the Moskova, general at Moscow, inactive in 1815, retired in 1825, taken back in 1830 and 1831, CtLH 1813.

At the beginning the regiment had 93 officers and 3 715 men. At the Moskova, 19 officers were killed and 32 wounded. At Moscow, 37 officers and 917 men were present on 15th September. On 12th October, the regiment received 38 LH of which 22 for the officers and one for Drum-Major Garon. In all in Russia, 35 officers died of whom 4 were at Smolensk before the Moskova, the others during the retreat or at the very beginning of 1813. 27 were listed as missing, 13 prisoners returned of whom 5 had been wounded at the Moskova by bullet or bayonet in the great redoubt. 25 were promoted second-lieutenant in Russia, 75 officers returned directly and the regiment returned to Hamburg with Davout. The majority of the officers survived Napoleon's campaigns except for 3, killed at Ligny.

Special cases:

— **Ramand**, came to replace the wounded colonel from the Fusiliers Grenadiers of the Guard. Received a Sabre of Honour at Arcoli, promoted Colonel at Moscow, received the Couronne de Fer in 1813. Wounded at Hamburg, dismissed in 1815.

— **Major Hervé**, one of the first to enter the redoubt, gave the figure of 19 cannon. Colonel in 1813, retired in 1815.

— **de Rascas**, colonel in 1819, serving in 1823.

---

1. In his souvenirs, Captain François tells that he received a bullet in his leg and that he lost three men skirmishing supporting the Compans Division, on 5th September.
He also talks about the assault on the great redoubt and the first fight with the Russians placed in front and crushed by the regiment's fire. Men fell into the wolf's holes with the Russians. The Captain penetrated into the redoubt through a breach at the moment that the cannon had just fired, the Russians received the French with levers and *refouloirs* and were very redoutable in hand to hand fighting. They got 50 yards into the redout but did not get enough support. Only one battalion of the 13th Light was following and they were forced to retreat with 11 officers and 257 men surviving. General Bonnamy received 14 wounds and was captured by the enemy.
François' wound in the leg re-opened and he received a lot of bruising. Lead to the ambulance by a light infantryman, he saw Morand wounded in the jaw.
In the ambulance he rejoined 27 other officers of the regiment of among which 5 amputees. There were more than 10 000 wounded in the ambulances and the neighbouring houses. His batman found him, brought his horses and found food for him at a very heavy price (15 francs the loaf of bread, 4 francs an egg and a half pound of meat 6 francs). Some lightly wounded soldiers of the regiment came to see them and announced that 67 men of the company were dead. The regiment was reduced to 300 men. In the night, 7 out of 9 officers died. On 28th September, the captain walking with a crutch got hold of a horse, reached Moscow with a convoy of 700 men led by Poniatowski. He rejoined his company to find only 7 men who brought him presents found in the town.

— **Captain Richard**, wounded at the Moskova, promoted Battalion-Commander at Moscow, killed at Ligny. OLH in 1814 at Hambureg.

— **Captain François** [1], Egyptian Campaign, wounded at the Moskova, decorated at Moscow then wounded at Krasnoi, dismissed in 1815.

— **Battalion-Commander Witas**, wounded in the thigh and a bullet wound in the right arm rejoined Moscow on 21st September. In a letter to his wife, dated 23rd September, he told how he is with several others from the regiment in this very beautiful and very clean but disorganised hospital. He returned, Major, retired, died in 1835.

THE BADEN 2nd OF THE LINE

There were only two battalions. One was with the headquarters of Berthier, the second joined the Daendels Division at Smolensk. The regiment had 25 officers and 888 soldiers at the beginning .

II. FRIANT'S DIVISION

The General, Count, Egyptian Campaign with Davout, Major-General in 1799. Nominated Commandant of the Foot Grenadiers on 7th August 1812, wounded at the Moskova. Chamberlain in 1813, wounded at Waterloo, retired 1815. After his wounds at the Moskova replaced by Ricard, Grand Aigle of the LH 1805.

His aides de camp:

— **His son Jean-François**, Napoleon's page, Captain, wounded at the Moskova. General of the National Guard in 1830, aide de camp to the King. He returned to France with his father, wounded.

Friant

Chief of Staff:

— **Galichet**, Baron and Adjudant Commandant, wounded 10th September. His first deputy, the Count of Marquessac was Lieutenant-Colonel in 1814, with the General Staff in 1821. The second deputy was Fongy who was killed at the Moskova.

GRANDEAU'S BRIGADE

The general was not at the Moskova. Appointed major-general after his wound at Smolensk. At Besançon in 1815, retired in 1825, GdOLH in 1814.

THE 15th LIGHT.

–– **Colonel Noos**, ill, was sent back to convalesce at Danzig where the general wrote him a letter intercepted by the Cossacks. He was not at the battle.

— **Brice**, major when wounded at the Moskova, appointed colonel at Moscow. Retired in 1816, LH in Year XIII, CtLH in 1814.

At the beginning the regiment had 113 officers in theory and sufferd severe losses at Smolensk. At the Moskova, 9 officers were killed and 21 wounded; the regiment also suffered heavy losses on 10th September at Mojaisk. At the end of the campaign there were 25 officers killed, 25 missing and 27 returned prisoners.

Special case:

— **Saint Marcellin**, attached to Prince Eugène, had a horse killed under him and received three sabre wounds in the redoubt. Appointed lieutenant and decorated at Moscow. Retired in 1813.

VAN DEDEM'S BRIGADE

The general, the author of memoirs, served Holland, then France. Wounded at Smolensk, argued with Friant at Moscow. Resigned in 1814, Honorary lieutenant-general. Taken back by the King after Waterloo and naturalised.

His aide de camp, de Kervyn de Volkaersbeke died in 1831.

THE 33rd OF THE LINE.

— **Colonel Pouchelon**, Italian Campaign, wounded at St John of Acre, wounded twice at the Moskova, general at Moscow, retired in October 1816. Taken back in183 died in 1831.

At the begining there were 102 officers and 3 372 men. This was an exaggerated figure and the regiment only had 2 500 men (van Dedem) on the 15th August. At the Moskova, 6 officers were killed and 15 wounded. In all in Russia 12 officers died, 35 were listed as missing and 12 captured returned.

Special case.

— **Second-Lieutenant Aubry**. Saint-Cyr in 1809, wounded at the Moskova and captured in December 1812. He returned 12th August 1814 after two years spent in the Tambov prisons.[2]

DUFOUR'S BRIGADE

The general was a volunteer in 1792, baron, wounded at the Moskova where he led the attack on Semenovskoi with the 48th and the 15th Light. Major-General in 1813, died of illness, 14th April 1815. CtLH.

THE 48th OF THE LINE.

The colonel appointed at Moscow died during the retreat.

On 15th June, the regiment had 97 officers and 3 476 men. At the Moskova, 4 officers were killed, (4 others were listed as dead by mistake). 18 officers were wounded. In all in Russia, 21 officers died, 33 were missing and 12 prisoners returned.

Special cases

— **Pelet**, appointed colonel at Moscow, wounded three times at Krasnoi. General in 1813, in the Guard at Plancenoit, 18th June 1815. GdCxLH in 1849.

— **Langlois**, military painter, Pelet's aide de camp in 1813. Dismissed in 1815, LH.

THE 2nd AND 3rd BATTALIONS, JOSEPH NAPOLEON REGIMENT

The other two were with Broussier's Division in the 4th Corps.

The battalions had an officer killed at the Moskova and two wounded. However, their losses were heavier on 10th September when they were committed directly. After this fight, one of the two battalions only had 14 officers and 96 men remaining.

III. GERARD'S DIVISION

This was formerly Gudin's Division, which had lost its remarkable commander at Valoutina. It suffered heavy losses in this fight.

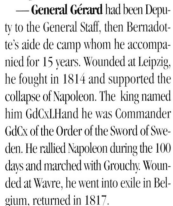

— **General Gérard** had been Deputy to the General Staff, then Bernadotte's aide de camp whom he accompanied for 15 years. Wounded at Leipzig, he fought in 1814 and supported the collapse of Napoleon. The king named him GdCxLHand he was Commander GdCx of the Order of the Sword of Sweden. He rallied Napoleon during the 100 days and marched with Grouchy. Wounded at Wavre, he went into exile in Belgium, returned in 1817.

Gérard

Several times Liberal deputy , Maréchal de France and Minister of War in August 1830. He led the Belgium Campaign in 1832. Pair de France. President of the Counsel in the place of Soult. Grand Chancelier of the LH, died in 1852; he married the daughter of General Valence.

LECLERC DES ESSARTS' BRIGADE

The General was the brother of Pauline Bonaparte's husband who took her to St Dominga. Wounded at Wagram, CtLH, brother in law of Davout, he married General d'Hautpoul's widow. Served at Hamburg then non-active in 1815.

THE 7th LIGHT

— **Colonel Rome**, mentioned at Valoutina, wounded at the Moskova, Cheva-

lier and general in 1813. Served at Hamburg then in 1815 with Gerard and Grouchy. CtLH Moscow.

At the outset, the regiment had 107 officers and 3 604 men.At the Moskova 8 officers were killed and 15 wounded. Before the battle, the regiment had already lost 14 officers killed and 19 wounded. Losses mainly at Valoutina where the regiment received 32 decorations. At Moscow on 15th September, there were 65 officersand 1 444 men. The regiment received 28 Croix de la LH of which 17 for the officers. On the 1st October there were 78 officers and 1 555 men remaining of whom certain had just rejoined. in all in Russia, there were 32 officers killed, 33 missing and 15 prisoners returned.

Special cases:

— **Captain Comte de Moncey**, wounded at Valoutina, colonel of the 3rd Hussars in 1814, wounded at Montmirail. In 1815, wounded at Belfort. Died in 1817. LH in Russia.

— **Sergeant Bertrand** stated in his memoirs that on the 2nd January1813, at the end of the retreat, there remained a kernel of the regiment with 47 officers, 34 non-commissioned officers and 111 men without counting those who managed to return more or less alone.

DESAILLY'S BRIGADE.

The general got his thigh smashed at Valoutina, so he was not present at the Moskova. Retired in 1813, he died in 1830. Was replaced on 17th September, at moscow by General Fabre who was later at Headquarters.

THE 12th OF THE LINE

Started off with 108 officers and 3 683 men. On 15th September there were only 69 officers and 1 216 men left, but the regiment received 5 officers and 200 men in reinforcement. The losses sufffered on 19th August at Valoutina, were already quite considerable. Colonel Thoulouse had been killed as well as 11 other officers, 23 wounded on the same day. 213 men were killed and there were more than 1 000 wounded. Some soldiers wounded at Valoutina were also wounded at the Moskova, like one of their officers. Thirty decorations were awarded to the regiment for this very hard battle. At the Moskova, 7 officers were killed and 121 wounded. They received 35 crosses of which 15 were for officers. In all for the campaign, 26 officers were killed, 232 were missing and 19 captured and returned.

Special cases:

— **Captain Mounier** who was with the 7th Light came to the 12th of the Line at Moscow. Colonel in 1826, he was wounded in Africa and died in Lyons during the insurrection of 1834. CrLH 1830.

— **Captain Thiery**, wounded at Valoutina, decorated at Moscow, colonel in 1838, general in 1843, in Africa. Major-General in 1848, died in 1864.

— **Second-Lieutenant Lafontaine**, lieutenant at Moscow, aide de camp to Gérard in 1813 and saved Gérard at Ligny. We meet him again in 1830. Mentioned at Antwerp, colonel in Africa in 1837, Brigadier. Deputy in 1848, major-general. He was born in Moscow in 1792. LH 1813.

— **de Rumigny**, author of memoirs.

GERARD'S OLD BRIGADE

The general succeeded Gudin at the head of the division.

THE 21st OF THE LINE

— **Colonel Teullé**, wounded at the Moskova, retired in 1813, CtLH at Moscow.

At the beginning theorectically, the regiment had 11 officers and 3 582 men. At Valoutina, the 21st had 7 officers killed, 3 captured and 27 wounded of which 3 were also wounded at the Moskova. On the 20th August, the regiment received 25

2. Dismissed in 1815, he had trouble with the Royalists in Lorient were he lived. In 1820 a report from the Commandant of the Departement told that he was a drunkard, had disgusting morals and awful principles. He was a great enemy of the Bourbons and his father who was a *Bonnet Rouge*, hanged himself in 1810 because Napoleon had allied himself with the family of the King. The ministry asked Lieutenant-General Coutard, commanding the region, for further information. It was learned that he lived with a prostitute suffering, as he was, from a shameful illness, which *"made him dangerous."* He had a further period of 6 year's inactivity. Conclusion, he was discharged according to normal procedures.

Colonel Teullé

Capitaine Guilmard

Lieutenant Doignon

Lieutenant Oustin

Survivors of 1812 (History of the 21st, General Bertin)

— **Captain du Bourget**, a Savoyard, killed at the Moskova.

Chief of Staff:

— **Couture**, general in 1813, wounded at the Moskova, captured at Dresden, died in 1841, CrLH in 1825.

— **Captain Herdebondt** his deputy, a Belgian. Captured but returned.

— **General Barbanègre** with the 33rd Light.

This regiment of Dutch origin did not have the same discipline as a Davout style regiment. So on 10th July, the Maréchal had them file past, barrel downwards. At any rate, the 33rd, badly appreciated by the Maréchal was left behind at Smolensk and in Minsk. They did not get to the Moskova.

Dessaix

decorations for the Battle of Valoutina. at the Moskova, 5 officers were killed and 25 wounded. The regiment received 31 crosses of the LH at Moscow of which 18 were for the officers. At Moscow there remained 58 officers and 1 060 men. In all in Russia, 25 officers died, 22 disappeared and 8 returned from the prisons.

THE 127th OF THE LINE

Made up of men coming from the German conquered departments, there were only two battalions which left with 46 officers and 1 415 men. At Moscow there were only 38 officers and 460 men left. There were heavy losses at Smolensk and at Valoutina: 10 officers killed and 21 wounded. It was without doubt left near Smolensk and was engaged during the retreat at Krasnoi. It probably was not at the Moskova. Forgotten for the decorations after Valoutina, it got 11 crosses, of which 6 were for the officers.

IV. DESSAIX'S DIVISION

The general was a doctor, a revolutionary in 1789, he was condemned by the Senate in Savoie, and fled to Paris, joining up with the Allobroges. He was one of the attackers of the Palais des Tuileries. Replaced Doppet at the head of the Allobroges (27th Lights). Wounded at the siege of Toulon. Italian Campaign, wounded and captured at Rivoli. Elected to the Council of the Five Hundred and opposed the 18th Brumaire coup d'état. Returned to command the 27th Light. Wounded at Wagram, appointed major-general. He had an arm smashed at the Moskova. Hero of the Alps in 1814, he was at Lyons in 1815, emprisonned for 4 months in 1816, he retired to Ferney-Voltaire then Marclaz where he died in 1834. GdOLH 1811.

His aides de camps:

— his brother, nicknamed **Fanfette**, very strong at chess. Another brother, a doctor, and their cousin who had accompanied them returned. The Surgeon-major of the regiment returned with them and the wounded general. They had a Russian cook who was a spy in the pay of the Tsar.

— **Girod** (from the Ain), colonel in1832, brigadier in 1842, CtLH in 1838.

FRIEDERICH'S BRIGADE

The general, born in Montmartre, soldier in 1791, went into the Guard where he commanded the Fusilier-Chasseurs. General in 1809, he was appointed major-general at Moscow. Replaced Dessaix who returned home wounded. Killed at Leipzig. CtLH in 1809.

His aide de camp **Lieutenant de Villeneuve** joined the 1st Corps General Staff in August 1812. Commandant until 1843 when he was discharged for his unbearable character and his debts.

THE 85th OF THE LINE

— **Colonel Piat**, wounded three times in Egypt, Baron in 1810, general in 1813, wounded at Ligny. Took part in the revolution of 1848 and was a fervent bonapartiste propagandist. GdOLH in 1850.

On the 15th June, the regiment had 105 officers and 3 796 men. For the Battalion Commander Leroy, there were not more than 2 400 men present on that date; at Moscow there were only 89 officers and 2 060 men. At the Moskova 4 officers were killed and 9 wounded. The regiment's losses were relatively low because two battalions had been used to support the artillery of the Guard. In all, 18 officers were lost, 38 were missing and 6 prisoners returned. 19 second-lieutenants were appointed in Russia.

Special Cases:

There were 23 officers who were present during the Egyptian Campaign; they all returned except one. Two received a Sabre of Honour.

— 41 Non-commissioned officers returned were commissioned before 1815.

— **Leroy**, Battalioin Commander, author of memoirs. Major and dismissed in 1815. He lost his son, a sergeant during the retreat. LH in Year XII, OLH 1813.

— **Lieutenant Loubers** received a bullet, two lance and two sabre wounds at Viasma. Left for dead and captured, he returned in 1814. Affected to the Guard he was sent to Amiens where the 6th Light Infantry was to be formed up, although there was not enough time for this to take place. Dismissed in 1815, he left for Toulouse.

LEGUAY'S BRIGADE

The general was a former aide de camp to Moreau, died of exhaustion at the end of the retreat.

THE 108th OF THE LINE

— **Colonel Achard**, born in the Antilles, captured twice by the English, returned in 1804. Wounded at Mohilev, two horses killed under him, mentioned at Hamburg, Brigadier 5th June 1815, cancelled, re-appointed 1823, then Lieutenant-general in 1830; served in Africa then in Belgium. GdCxLH 1846.

103 officers and 3 700 men were at the start. At Moscow 91 officers and 2 246 men remained. Like the 85th, this regiment was heavily committed at Mohilev. At the Moskova, one officer was killed and 11 wounded. In all for the campaign, 23 officers dead, 43 missing and 12 captured and returned.

THE 2ND HESSIAN REGIMENT

It had 2 battalions but the 1st remained at Kovno and the second was attached to Berthier's Headquarters but left in the rear and so did not take part in the battle.

V. COMPAN'S DIVISION

The general began with the 3rd Battalion of Haut-Garonne in 1791, was at Toulon. Chief of staff to Lannes and then to Soult. Wounded at the Moskova, refused to serve Napoleon and dismissed 7th June 1815. The King appointed him Pair de France 17th August. Voted the death of Ney. GdCxLH in February 1815.

His aides de camp were

Compans

— **Captain Provana de Vilar**, born in Turin. Served with the Pô Sharpshooters. At the Moskova, was wounded and had a horse killed under him. Retired in 1819, OLH at Moscow.

— **Captain Baron de Chamouin**, served in 1804. Brigadier in 1830, retired in 1837, died in 1865. CrLH 1820.

— **Lieutenant de Quelen**, Ordnance Gendarme in 1806, had a horse killed at the Moskova Colonel in 1828, retired in 1830. LH at Moscow

— **Colonel Simmer** was the chief of staff. Baron in 1809, wounded twice 5th September at Schwardino. General at Moscow, major-general in 1815, served at Waterloo. Demoted. Exiled to le Mans, he was elected deputy for the Puy de Dôme in 1828, defeated in 1834, re-elected in 1837 and defeated in 1842. Died in 1847.

Two deputies, **Périer** and **Clary**, were killed on 5th September.

DUPPELIN'S BRIGADE

The general died at Thorn on 25th january 1813, at the end of the retreat.

— **Captain Seghino** of the 25th, his first aide de camp, was wounded at the Moskova, at Viasma and at Krasnoi. He had a frozen foot and was dismissed in1814.

— his aide de camp **Mazure** was awarded the LH in June 1812. Served in 1815.

THE 25th OF THE LINE.

— **Colonel Dunesme**, a volunteer from the Ardennes, served in Vendée then at Genoa with Masséna. General in 1813, killed at Kulm. OLH and Baron.

The regiment is marked on the 15th June, as having 70 officers and 1 949 men. It is also known that two battalions joined up by forced march and that on the 5th July they reached Vilna where they were given three days of bread. At the Moskova, 8 officers were killed, one on 5th september, and 6 were wounded. At Moscow there were 83 officers and 1 638 men. In all for the campaign, 15 officers were lost, 19 disappeared and 14 captured but returned in 1814. Twenty second-lieutenants were commissioned at Moscow.

Special cases:

In this regiment there were 11 from the Egyptian Campaign. All returned directly.

— **Lieutenant Lapeyre**, born at Poitiers. Colonel in 1840, brigadier in 1847. Died in 1868, LH at Moscow, CrLH.

— **Diettmann**, born at Lunéville, Saint-Cyr in 1816, colonel in 1834, brigadier in 1844, died in 1854, CrLH.

— **Lieutenant Paradis**, three of his letters were intercepted, in which he said that he counted 20 Russians dead for one Frenchman. He said also that he found himself in front of 500 Russians who let themselves be massacred without moving. According to him, they were all drunk. He got a bullet in the chest but it was stopped by his rolled-up riding coat and the shock only threw him over. Captain in 1813, wounded and captured at Waterloo, died in 1855.

TESTE'S BRIGADE

The general was a volunteer from the Gard, was wounded at the Moskova, major-

general in 1813, served in 1815 with Grouchy. Made inactive but took up service again for the Belgium Campaign. Peer of France in 1839, died in 1862. GdCxLH 1849.

His aide de camp **Mouchon** was killed at the Moskova.

THE 57th OF THE LINE

— **Colonel Charrière**, Italian Campaign, Baron, had a horse killed at the Moskova, 5th September; general at Moscow, he commanded a brigade of dismounted cavalry. Couronne de Fer. Commanded Calais during the Hundred Days. Retired in 1815. Taken back in 1831, retired in 1832, LH in Year XII, CtLH in 1813.

The regiment had 97 officers and 3 485 men on 15th June 1812. At the Moskova, 6 officers were killed, 11 wounded and about 20 men out of action. On 7th September, 15 officers were killed and 29 wounded. For the men, 108 were killed, 867 wounded and 236 disappeared. This count is a precious example. At Moscow there were 54 officers and 1 389 men.There were 1 800 men in the hospitals of which 1 202 at Mojaisk, 195 in Germany and 100 prisoners. For the whole campaign, 32 officers dead, 35 missing and 8 captured and returned. 32 second-lieutenants were commissioned.

Special cases:

— **Major Duchesne** commanded the combined light infantrymen on the 5th September. He was promoted colonel at Moscow. Captured at Kulm in 1813 and retired in 1822.

— **Battalion Commander Boyer**, wounded and lost a horse at the Moskova. With an agile manoeuvre, he succeeded in repelling the Russian Cavalry which was trying to turn the division. Captured at Beresina, stripped by the Cossacks and left naked in the snow. Returned in 1814, LH at Moscow.

— **Laffont**, Battalion Commander on 25th September at Moscow. Mentioned on 5th August, at Viasma and at Krasnoi where he was wounded. Mentioned at Kulm in 1813, and appointed colonel, mentioned at Strasburg in 1814, dismissed in 1815, died in 1841, LH in Year XII.

— **Sauret**, born at Arles, his letters were published in the "Sabretache". Wounded at the Moskova, he left Moscow before the others with the last three companies of the 6th Battalion, to go and fetch re-inforcements at the depot and to take charge of them. This early departure was applicable to the 1st and the 4th Corps. Colonel in 1840 and died in 1871. OLH.

GUYARDET'S BRIGADE

The general died at Thorn just before Duppelin, on 5th January 1813.

— **Sommelier**, his aide de camp, was wounded on 23rd July, then on 7th September and finally 24th October 1812. Wounded at Dresden in 1813. He was in the Guard and was dismissed in 1815.

THE 61st OF THE LINE.

— **Colonel Bouge**, born at Toulon, mentioned on 5th September, horse killed under him on the 7th. Prisoner during the retreat, returned and retired in 1815.LH in Year XII, CtLH at Moscow.

On 15th July, there were 98 officers and 3 022 men; at the Moskova,on 5th September, 2 officers were killed and 4 wounded. It must be noted that in the officers' files there were 19 special citations, which was not very frequent at that period. On 7th September, there were 5 officers killed and 15 wounded there again with several citations. At Moscow on 15th september, there were only 54 officers left and 1 366 men. In all for the campaign, 19 officers were killed and 32 missing, with 6 captured and returned. 20 second-lieutenants were commissioned at Moscow.

There were 10 former Egyptian Campaigners and a Hero of Italy, called Molière or "Alexis", holder of a Rifle of Honour; all but two returned.

LONCHAMP'S BRIGADE

The general had just arrived at the division in June. Egyptian and Italian Campaigns, in the Grenadier Guards. Baron, fortress commander from May 1813. Commandant of the Basses Alpes during the 100 Days. Inactive following this. CtLH.

— **Ballon**, his aide de camp, decorated on 5th May 1812, mentioned on 5th

September, dismissed in 1815, Brigadier in 1839, major-general in 1848. Died in 1859. CrLH.

THE 111th OF THE LINE.

— **Colonel Juillet** lost a horse at the Moskova, wounded at Viasma and died at Kovno on 10th December. OLH at Moscow.

The regiment started off with 85 officers and 3 768 men; it was mainly made up of Piemontese. At Moscow, on 15th September, there were only 53 officers and 1 651 men left. At the Moskova, detailed losses are available concerning the soldiers also. On 5th September, 4 officers and 82 men were killed. 15 officers and 540 men were wounded. 33 were captured and 138 were missing or lost.

On 7th September 1 officer and 38 men were killed. Six officers and 270 men wounded. That day, two battalions were placed in support of the artillery; the rest of the regiment repelling skirmishers towards the right, on the side of the wood. In all, in Russia, 26 officers died, 51 were listed as missing and 12 captured but returned. 27 second-lieutenants were commissioned.

Special cases:

— **Adjudant-Major Gardier** wrote a diary which is preserved in a library at Macon. He says that in July the division left about 4 000 laggards on the Ochmiana road. At Minsk a rest camp was set up and he confirms the episode of the punishing of the 33rd Light by Davout on 10th July. He quotes Adjudant Druet (or Druez) from Tournai who distinguished himself in the capture of the first redoubt and was commissioned at Moscow. He was at Hamburg, dismissed in 1815, he finished as a colonel. LH 5th September 1812.

— **Captain Legros**, mentioned at Viasma, at Orcha. He was in the Guard in 1815, dismissed the same year.

— **General Penne**, Baron, was called from Headquarters on 1st August 1812, he was sent to Compans' division. He was killed by a cannonball on the day following Waterloo.

— His aide de camp, **Comte de Sainte-Marie**, lieutenant-colonel in 1818, LH in 1813, OLH in December 1815.

THE COMPANS DIVISION ON PARADE AT MOSCOW

Several officers recount that they took part in this parade of the Compans Division on 10th October past Napoleon in Moscow, where the LH was awarded to the regiments. 28 were for the officers. The 61st received 26 of which 18 for the officers. For the 111th, 27 of which 18 for the officers, the Drum-Major Biglin was one of those decorated. For the 57th, there were 38 decorations, of which 3 for the officers. 6 officers and men of the artillery and transport train of the division were also decorated.

VI. THE LIGHT CAVALRY OF THE 1st CORPS

Originally commanded by Pajol, who had to replace Sebastiani, the *"surprise"* general, and command the light cavalry of the 2nd Cavalry Corps. Replaced at the Moskova by General Girardin, commanding one of the brigades, with his colleague Bordessoulle commanding the other.

GIRARDIN'S BRIGADE

— **General Count de Girardin d'Ermenonville**, born in 1776, Berthier's aide de camp in 1803. General 4th january 1812, major-general in 1814, died in 1855, GdOLH 1825.

— **Mercy d'Argenteau**, his aide de camp, was later Bishop of Namur then Archbishop of Tyre and Napoleon III promoted him GdCxLH.

THE 2nd CHASSEURS.

— **Colonel Mathis**, heros of Santo Domingo was a general in June 1815, revoked then taken back. On the 15th July the regiment numbered 40 officers and 699 men. A detachment arrived at Moscow with the 6th Battalion. At the Moskova, Pauline Bonaparte's lover, Baron Canouville, was killed; two officers were wounded. In all, in Russia, 6 officers died, 6 disappeared and 7 were captured but returned in 1814.

Special Cases:

— **Lieutenant Imbert de St Amand** was brigadier.

— **Major Lacroix**, colonel in 1813, was killed at Waterloo.

— **Squadron Commander Dukermont**, wounded twice in August before the Moskova, was brigadier in 1821.

THE 9th POLISH LANCERS

On 15th June there were 34 officers and 683 men. At the Moskova, 7 officers were wounded.

BORDESSOULLE'S BRIGADE

The general received a Sabre of Honour in 1802; had his jaw shattered at the Moskova. Major-general on 4th December 1812. Brilliant in 1814, he followed the King to Gand. Deputy, he illustrated himself in Spain. Pair de France, retired in 1832. Died in 1837. GdCxLH in August 1815, GdCXSL 1821.

THE 1st CHASSEURS.

Colonel Meda has remained famous for his attempt on the life of Robespierre. Killed by a cannonball at the Moskova. LH in Year XII. OLH and Baron in 1807.

Bordessoulle

On 15th July the regiment numbered 40 officers and 699 men; at the Moskova, 1 officer was killed and 9 wounded, especially by the artillery. In all 4 dead, 1 missing and 2 captured but returned.

Special cases:

— **Colonel Hubert** former aide de camp to Montbrun who replaced Méda, was a general in 1814, with Piré in 1815, then lieutenant-general in 1823, GdOLH.

— **de Vence**, colonel in 1813, revoked in 1815, brigadier in 1817. Died in 1834. GdOLH 1825.

— **Buzen**, general in 1831, aide de camp to the King of the Belgians, minister, committed suicide.

THE 3rd CHASSEURS

— **Colonel Saint-Mars**. Baron, he was wounded 5 times on 21st July near Mohilev where his regiment was ambushed. Captured, he returned to the Royal Guard and was dismissed in 1815. OLH He was replaced by Dejean, former aide de camp to Lasalle, escaped from English prisons. Wounded the 21st July and the 5th September at Schwardino. It was Cap-

Colonel-baron Méda
commanding the 1st chasseurs.

tain Martin who commanded the regiment on 7th September. Major in 1813, served in 1821.

The regiment had 30 officers and 686 mounted chasseurs. At the Moskova, 2 officers were killed, 3 wounded. In all for the campaign, 5 officers died, 3 disappeared and 16 officers were taken then returned.

Special Case:

— **de la Malle**, mentioned at Krasnoi on 14th August, wounded at the Moskova. Regimental Colonel in 1823, brigadier in 1830, CrLH. Retired in 1836 and died at Chaulgues in 1863, Nièvre.

AN ASSESSMENT OF THE 1st CORPS

In the official strength, the corps was supposed to have 35 000 men — a figure that was certainly exaggerated — 3 000 artillerymen (and trans-

MARECHAL DAVOUT'S 1st ARMY CORPS
CAVALRY

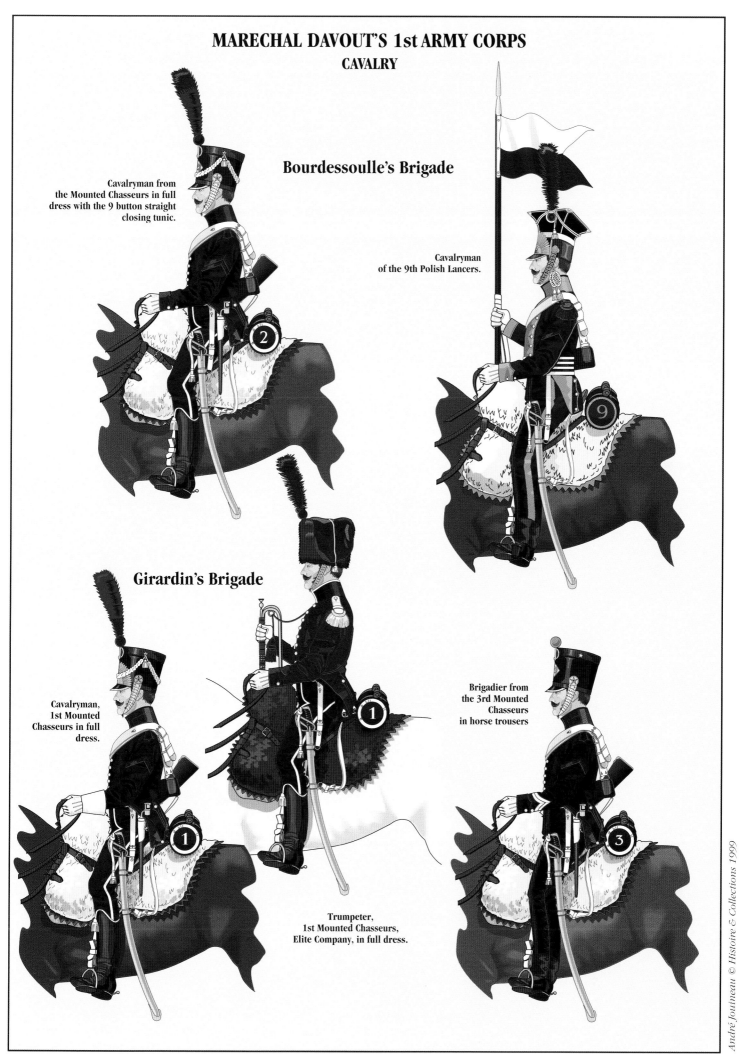

Bourdessoulle's Brigade

Cavalryman from the Mounted Chasseurs in full dress with the 9 button straight closing tunic.

Cavalryman of the 9th Polish Lancers.

Girardin's Brigade

Cavalryman, 1st Mounted Chasseurs in full dress.

Brigadier from the 3rd Mounted Chasseurs in horse trousers

Trumpeter, 1st Mounted Chasseurs, Elite Company, in full dress.

André Joutineau © Histoire & Collections 1999

port) and 1 000 cavalrymen. We know that a number of regiments were left behind along the road, like the 2nd Baden (at HQ to the rear), the 33rd Light, the 2nd Hessian and the 127th.

Many men remained at the rear in the hospitals because the corps had been engaged in a lot of fighting: Dessaix's Division at Mohilev (Solta-novka) against Bagration, the whole corps at Smolensk and Gudin's Division at Valoutina where it gave the French their victory, but at the same time losing its commander and numerous soldiers.

Nevertheless, this corps was the armature of the *Grande Armée*, it was the best disciplined, the best led. It was the one which arrived in the best condition for this battle.

In his Russian report, Boutourlin estimated the number of men at 48 000, of which 40 000 were present at the battle. These estimates are a bit high, considering it was the corps that made the principal effort under three different commanders, with only 30 000 to 35 000 men on the basis of 400 to 500 men per battalion for its big regiments, the only ones to have 5 battalions in the army; the regiments who were absent from the Moskova have to be subtracted, which means eleven battalions less than the official strength.

Eugène particularly used the Morand and Gérard divisions at the points which were the hardest, preserving his own forces. Ney would have liked

to use the Friant division at Semenovskoi, having tired out what was left of his 3rd Corps on the fighting for the three outposts. Davout only had the already weakened Dessaix Division and the Compans Division to use for the capture of the outposts. Napoleon did not spoil him.

At Moscow the parade gave the roll for the 15th September, with for the 1st Corps, about 21 000 infantrymen. So almost 14 000 men are missing, but many returned later, in particular the lightly wounded, like for the other corps.

For a casualty estimate, based on the figures of the officers killed and applying an approximate co-efficient, guided by the few cases where the number of troops lossed had been registered, this co-efficient can be fixed at between 10 and 20 men killed for each officer, taking into account the effort made by each unit.

Starting with these figures, for the 1st Corps we have 148 officers killed — this figure is precise — thus a figure of 2 200 to 2 500 killed for the five exposed divisions.

The corps had 150 officers killed and 348 wounded at the Moskova. Its total losses for the campaign were 394 officers killed, without counting a Polish cavalry regiment and the 2 Joseph Napoleon battalions ; so there were about 400 officers killed, about 410 officers missing and about 222 captured but returned.

NEY'S 3rd CORPS

His aides de camp:

— **Bresson de Valmabelle**, born in 1772, in Nîmes, cadet in 1787, appointed general at Mocsow, died at Koenigsberg of exhaustion from the retreat.

— **Laboissière**, general in 1813, died of his wounds on 15th September 1813.

— **Saint-Charles**, commanded the headquarters, retired with the rank of colonel in 1833.

— **Count of Bourgoing**, title received in 1830, captured at the end of the retreat, returned and served as squadron commander in 1815; re-integrated in 1817, lieutenant-colonel in Spain in 1823.

— **d'Albignac**, son of the general, appointed squadron commander.

— **Marchant-Billet** (from the 11th Hussars), killed at the Moskova.

— **Macors**, from the 7th Equipment Battalion. Egyptian Campaign, served at Waterloo, retired in 1836, OLH in 1831.

Chief of Staff:

— **General Gouré**, Killed at Lutzen. His aided de camp was Cavaignac who was brigadier in 1844 and died 1867. GdOLH 1852. The deputy was Count of Danzig, son of Lefebvre, died at Vilna on 15th December.

— **Dubreuil**, adjudant-officer, killed at the Moskova.

— **Ybry**, decorated at Moscow, wounded at Waterloo, colonel of the 10th Chasseurs in 1830.

— **Breton**, who had just arrived and was captured, returned and wrote his memoirs.

THE ARTILLERY OF THE 3rd CORPS

Commanded by **Major-General Foucher du Careil**. At the Metz School in 1781, retired in 1818. GdOLH 1813. His aide de camp was **Reguis**, first-lieutenant, LH in 1814.

Second in command:

— **General Martuschewitz**, came from serving in Holland. His aides de camp were his son and **Captain de Sainte-Marie**, polytechician, lieutenant-colonel in 1831. OLH in the same year. The artillery consisted of 7 Heavy Artillery Companies plus one of pontooneers and workers. Finally there was the Wurtemberger artille-

MARÉCHAL NEY'S 3rd ARMY CORPS
LINE and LIGHT INFANTRY

General Ledru's Division (10th)

Flag model 1812 of the 72nd of the Line.

General Razout's Division (11th)

Above, from left to right
— **Sergeant-major, 24th Light Infantry Regiment**
— **Grenadier, 1st Portugese Infantry Regiment**
— **Officer, Grenadiers' Company of**
the 46th or 72nd Line Infantry Regiment.

From left to right
— **Fusilier, 2nd Portugese Infantry Regiment**
— **Voltigeur, 18th Line Infantry Regiment, full dress**
— **Voltigeur wearing the overcoat of the infantryman,**
4th or 93rd Line Infantry Regiment

André Jouineau © Histoire & Collections 1990

Foucher du Careil

by **Germain**, died in Russia. 4 officers were killed and one captured but returned. There were 5 companies of the 6th Battalion and the 14th ex-Dutch. Each division will be considered separately.

ENGINEERS

— **General Dode de la Brunerie** arrived with Gouvion-St-Cyr in August. The Engineers had 3 companies with in all 9 officers, plus two appointed in Russia, 4 were listed as missing, 3 captured and returned. It was **Martin-Campredon** who was in command at the Moskova; he died at Vilna.

There was also the 6th company of the Transport Engineers. Out of the three officers, one died in December and one disappeared.

I. LEDRU'S DIVISION (10th)

— **General Ledru des Essarts**, volunteer in 1792, general after Austerlitz. Wounded 4 times. Major-general in 1811, served in 1815 (Army of the Alps). Reinstated 1817, GdCxLH in 1827.

His aides de camp were **Murphy**, a naturalised Irishman, colonel in 1813, he finished as brigadier.

— The chief of staff was **Delage**. Mentioned at Marengo, Baron de St-Cyr in 1808, CLH in 1815, reinstated in 1830.

The artillery was commanded by **Ragmey** who served at Besançon in 1814.

GENGOULT'S BRIGADE

The general was decorated in the Year XII. Seriously wounded at the Moskova, appointed major-general during the 100 days, dismissed and reinstated in 1831.

THE 24th LIGHT

— **Colonel de Bellair**, Baron, GdOLH in 1813, served at Waterloo. Retired then reinstated in 1831.

At the beginning the regiment numbered 84 officers and 3 020 men. 9 officers were killed at the Moskova and 7 wounded. A Moscow, the regiment received 18 LH of which 9 for the officers and the regiment was mentioned by Ney in his despatch. It had already received 30 decorations as at 2nd September. In total for the the campaign, 29 officers were killed, 37 disappeared and 6 were captured but returned among whom Pomailly, who was brigadier in 1846.

THE 1st PORTUGUESE

— the colonel was **Freyre-Pégo**, who was made prisoner in November

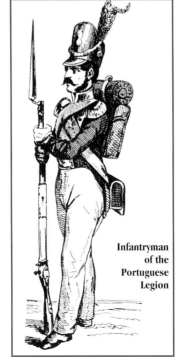

Infantryman of the Portuguese Legion

ry. Among the French there were 7 officers killed during the campaign of which 2 were wounded and one killed at the Moskova. One officer was listed as missing and 7 prisoners returned. The others returned directly.

The commandant of the pool was **Colonel Mangin**, brigadier in 1823. His deputy was **Captain Forestier de Villeneuve**, CSL in 1820. The commandant of the reserve was **Major Matieu**, colonel of the 2nd Artillery in 1820, his deputy was **Delesvaux**, wounded when battalion commander in 1814.

The artillery train was commanded

1812. Appointed general , he was retired in January 1815. His son who was with the regiment, was killed at the Moskova; his son-in-law was captured.

— **Battalion Commander Caldeiro**, commanded the 1st Battalion and **Treinté** the second (colonel in 1815).

8 CxLH were awarded at Smolensk where they suffered heavy losses as well as at Valoutina. This regiment was a so-called elite regiment, being made up of only grenadiers and voltigeurs. It had theoretically 36 officers and 1 150 men to start with. At the Moskova, 4 officers were killed or died as a result of their wounds and 9 were wounded. At Moscow on the 1st October, there were only 32 officers and 206 men left. Moreover, witnesses said that the regiment had left more than 2/3rds of its strength in the rear.

MARION'S BRIGADE

The general was killed at the Moskova.

THE 46th OF THE LINE

At the Moskova , 2 officers were killed and 19 wounded. 31 LH were awarded to the regiment on 2nd September. At Moscow it received a further 19.

In all in Russia, the regiment sufferd heavy losses at Smolensk, then on the return at Krasnoi. 23 officers died, 44 were missing and 17 prisoners returned, of which 10 from the 6th Battalion which rejoined the regiment and had all been captured at Minsk on 15th November 1812.

BRUNY'S BRIGADE

The general had been promoted colonel by Rochambeau. Wounded at the Moskova, retired in 1832; his aide de camp, **Descombes** was captured and returned.

THE 72nd OF THE LINE

— **Colonel Baron Lafitte** was a general in 1813, then wounded and captured at Leipzig, died in 1839.

At the Moskova, 12 officers died (Martinien gave 15 which have not all been accounted for) and 15 wounded of whom one died on 11th December. At Moscow, 15 CxLH were awarded on top of the 32 given on 2nd September. In all in Russia, 29 officers died, 25 were missing and 15 captured and returned. 5 officers arrived at Moscow on the 22nd September as reinforcements.

THE 129th OF THE LINE.

This very much weakened regiment was not present at the Moskova.

II. RAZOUT'S DIVISION (11th)

The general, Count in 1813 was a member of the court-martial which aquitted Morand in 1819. GdLOH in 1813.

His aides de camp were **Goguillot** who served in 1814 and **Dufey** wounded at Arcola, retired in 1814. The chief of staff was **Montbrun**, brother of the cavalryman. CtLH and General in 1812, demoted then aquitted in 1814 for having abandonned Moret. Served in 1815. The deputy was **Prevost de Gagemont** who was dismissed in 1815.

— The artillery was commanded by **Battalion Commander Bernard** of the 1st Heavy. Colonel in 1814, then Honorary Brigadier in 1827.

On the 15th July, the division had 319 officers and 8 119 men. 5 officers and 705 men were declared to be in the rear and 8 officers with 1 260 men were in the hospitals. The 1st October, at Moscow, there were only 204 officers and 3 120 men left.

COMPERE'S BRIGADE

The general was killed at the Moskova.

THE 2nd PORTUGUESE

The regiment was commanded by **Major Xavier** who was wounded at Wagram and at the Moskova. OLH.

They only had a third of their strength before the battle. At Moscow, the regiment only had 32 officers and 184 soldiers left. At the Moskova, 8 officers were killed and 6 wounded. In all, 12 officers were killed in Russia, 19 wounded, 18 captured and 12 missing. This regiment only had 84 Portuguese. The soldiers had been recruited amongst Spanish prisoners and there were also 77 Frenchmen, one German and one Napolitan. Major Xavier had asked for permission to create elite companies. Finally this regiment left Moscow on 19 th October to escort 1 400 Russian prisoners. They left their baggage in the care of the 3rd Corps; it was looted by the Cossacks. Moreover, in 1813, when the officers in charge of organising this legion made their request, they met with "irritable" resistance from Napoleon who did not want to hear about these foreign corps formed from recruited prisoners any longer, especially Spaniards.

THE ILLYRIAN REGIMENT

Sent to the rear, it was not present at the Moskova.

JOUBERT'S BRIGADE

The general was a former member of the Dromadarians in Egypt, Viscount in 1822, retired in 1825. OLH.

— His aides de camp were **Comte du Rocheret** (he began in the Navy). Wounded at the Moskova. On Davout's staff in 1815, brigadier in 1832, lieutenant-general in 1841. GdOLH in 1844, the year of his death; and **D'Audéric**, retired in 1814 to Narbonne. LH in 1813.

THE 4th OF THE LINE

— **Colonel Massy**, was killed at the Moskova and replaced by de **Fézensac** at Moscow.

On the 15th August at Smolensk, before the fighting, there were 68 officers and 1 892 men. After the Moskova, there were 43 officers and 726 men. At the Moskova there were 9 officers killed and 19 wounded. In all in Russia, 7 officers died and 24 disappeared. 21 were captured and returned. De Fézensac says that three convoys with reinforcements rejoined the regiment in Russia, but he only brought back 200 men. Others returned in little groups. 100 returned from the prisons, among them the officers. At Moscow, there were numerous promotions and decorations: 42 CLHs were awarded. Among them the Drum-Major Lefebvre and Drum-Master Pomelet. A figure dated 27 September gave 20 officers and 1 012 men present including the re-inforcements.

Special cases:

— **Colomb d'Arcins**, wounded at the Moskova, followed the King in 1815. Brigadier in Algeria in 1830.

— **Astre** who received a Rifle of Honour in Italy was wounded at the Moskova and retired at Moscow, returning to Clermont-Ferrand.

— **Sire**, wounded 8 times, retired in 1814 to Nancy, LH in Year XII.

— **Captain Tierce**, wounded at Moskova, decorated at Moscow, he lost his right arm at Leipzig. He continued fighting, brandishing his sabre with his left hand. He was killed the same day.

THE 18th OF THE LINE

— **Colonel Pelleport**, Egyptian Campaign and Syria. Lost a horse under him at the Moskova. General in 1813. Lieutenant-General and Viscount in 1823. Peer of France in 1841. Died in 1853, LH in Year XII.

The regiment had about 3 000 men at the beginning but only had 1 600 men at Moscow according to the memoirs which were no doubt optimistic, but nevertheless took into account the reinforcements that joined up. The total casualties was about 600. At the Moskova, 12 officers were killed, 26 wounded. At Moscow, the regiment received 28 CLH. For the whole of the campaign, 19 officers died, 20 missing and 32 captured and returned in 1814 or 1815.

Special Cases:

— **Major Materre**, mentioned at Rivoli, wounded at St John of Acre. General in 1814.

— **Battalion Commander Bonnet**, author of memoirs, born in Geneva, naturalised in 1824. Brigadier in 1839. He says he lost 36 men from his company at the end of the battle. How many returned?

— **Lamarre**, wounded at the Moskova, appointed Battalion Commander at Moscow, brigadier in 1835.

— **Captain Berchet**, wounded 23 times at Eylau, served at Waterloo, disappeared afterwards.

— **Captain Charon**, wounded at the Moskova. Brigadier in 1845. LH at Moscow.

— **Dervieux**, was the first to enter the outposts of the redoubt, retired in 1827.

— **Boudousquié**, wounded several times at the Moskova, captured at Krasnoi, returned. On half pay, studied law and became "procureur" in 1830. Deputy for the Lot in 1834, his letters were published at Cahors.

D'HENIN'S BRIGADE

The general, captured by the English at Santo Domingo, returned in 1811. Wounded twice at the Moskova. Lieutenant-general on 1st July 1815. Viscount in 1829. Reservist in 1839.

THE 93rd OF THE LINE.

— **Colonel Baudouin**, wounded at the Moskova, appointed general in 1813, killed at Waterloo.

On the 15th August, there were 1 918 in the regiment, 757 in the hospitals and 467 said to be "lost". At the Moskova, 4 officers were killed and 21 wounded. After the Moskova the numbers at Moscow were 64 officers and 755 men, then on the 1st October there were 92 officers, some of whom must have come back from the hospitals. In the hospitals there were 18 officers and 1 557 men. The figure for the "lost" had dropped to 429. In all for the campaign, 20 officers were killed, 8 disappeared and 13 were captured but returned. The regiment was reinforced twice, once at Moscow and then at Smolensk. 36 decorations were awarded at Moscow to the 93rd which had already received 19 for Valoutina.

Special Cases:

— **Major Marchal**, future colonel of the regiment, wounded at the Moskova. Served in 1815 with the 7th Light Infantry of the Guard. Dismissed. LH in Year XII, CtLH in 1813.

The Colonel who had two wounds and the Major returned together to France. On 8th November, they were at Smolensk each with his own carriage.

Marchand

III. THE WURTEMBERGER DIVISION (25th)

— **H.R.H Prince of Wurtemberg** was accompanied by **General von Scheler** who commanded the division until the 9th August. At that date, Marchand came to take over. According to Pelleport, on the 10th August there were only 1 800 men left.

— **General Marchand** was born in 1765, Italian Campaign with Joubert. Major-general in 1805, he followed Ney at Jena then to Spain. In command at Grenoble, he was accused of letting Napoleon enter, judged and aquitted. He was Peer of France in 1837 and died in 1851.

The division included: the **1st** and **2nd Battalions of Chasseurs**, the **1st** and **2nd Light Regiments**, the **1st of the Line** with 2 battalions, the **2nd of the**

Wurtemberger infantry at rest in Russia (Drawing by Faber du Faur).

Wurtemberg artillery in Russia (Drawing by Faber du Faur).

Line with 2 battalions, the 4th of the line with 2 battalions, two companies of Heavy Artillery, two companies of mounted artillery and one battalion in action.

At Moscow, 33 CLH were awarded to this infantry, the artillerymen received 12 crosses. Faber du Faur said that when the regiments were reconstituted, before the Moskova, there was only a fraction of this corps left, supplying only one light battalion and two of the Line. He states that it was the same thing for the two Portuguese regiments reduced to a third of their number. For the Wurtembergers, their strength in infantry can be estimated at less than 1 800 men (figure for the 20th August) present for the 7th September. These troops fought very well for possession of Bagration's outposts. Faber du Faur showed them closing round Murat coming to shelter in their midst when he was being chased by Russians. At Moscow for Chuquet, they numbered 1 197 infantry, 444 cavalry and 385 artillerymen. On the roll of 1st October there were 67 officers and 1 102 men. In the hospitals or elsewhere, there were 5 289 men and officers at the rear.

IV. THE 3rd CORP'S LIGHT CAVALRY

It included three brigades without a major-general.

MOURIER'S BRIGADE (9th)

The general, Italian Campaign, wounded at the Moskova, was commander of the Creuse, Cavalry Inspector and retired in 1832. CtLH. His aide de camp was **Prévost**, from the 15th Chasseurs. Colonel of the 1st Chasseurs in 1830, general in 1840, major-general in 1848, died in

On the 15th July 1812, the brigade numbered 79 officers and 1 700 men. At Moscow there were only 56 officers and 500 cavalrymen left. This includes the 4 Wurtemberg Chasseurs attached to this brigade.

THE 11th HUSSARS.

This regiment was formed with Dutch cavalrymen and lost a lot of its strength and horses from Vitebsk onwards.

— **Colonel Baron de Collaert**, brother of the general, was born in 1758. Had a horse killed at the Moskova, retired at Moscow, replaced by Liègeard who had just arrived.

At the Moskova, five officers died, two more the 5th, one on the 7th and two at the Moscow hospital where they had been left, among whom **Captain Huber**, who had received 14 wounds during the battle and died on 29th September. In Russia in all, 7 officers died, 8 disappeared and three prisoners returned, among whom **de Croy**, Colonel of the 5th Dragoons at Waterloo; and **Geiswert van der Netten**, who retired with the rank of general in Holland in 1835. The regiment only had 122 cavalrymen left at Moscow and 79 crossed back over the Niemen, joining up with 160 others from the regiment who had been evacuated before, wounded or ill.

THE 6th CHEVAU-LÉGERS LANCERS.

This regiment coming from the 29th dragoons and formed at Turin was commanded by **de Marbeuf** who was mortally wounded on 14th August 1812. Replaced at the Moskova by **Jacob**. Died 31st January 1813. LH in Year XII, OLH at Moscow. At the start there were 26 officers and 547 cavalrymen. At the Moskova, 3 officers were killed, 5 wounded. **De la Barre** was listed as killed on this day though he

really was on 18th October 1813. In all in Russia, 8 officers died, 6 disappeared and 3 were captured but returned. 25 officers returned directly of whom 2 were promoted at Moscow and 7 came from Germany (with 264 cavalrymen) in support. On the way to Russia, the regiment was engaged at Krasnoi, on 14th August losing one officer and 34 men killed and 5 officers and 49 men wounded. At Moscow before the arrival of the re-inforcements, there were only 19 officers and 154 men.

BEURMANN'S BRIGADE

The general was reared by the army in 1784, he was Kléber's aide de camp. Wounded at Austerlitz, general in 1811. Retired in January 1815, committed suicide at Metz on 13th April 1815. CtLH after Winkovo, 2nd September 1812. His aide de camp was **de Reiset**, a cousin of the general. decorated at Moscow, squadron commander, he helped Ney in 1815 by giving him his passport so that he could go and shelter in Bassanis Castle, near Aurillac. Another aide de camp **Lambrechts** arrived on 4th September, from the 11th Hussars, was killed at the Moskova on the 5th.

The brigade included, together with the two Wurtemberger Chevau-Léger regiments on 15th July, 78 officers and 1 712 cavalrymen. At Moscow, there were only 44 officers and 321 men left.

THE 4th CHASSEURS À CHEVAL.

— **Colonel Boulois**, wounded on 14th August 1812 and at Valoutina where he was thought to be dead. He lost three horses at the Moskova. General in 1813, lieutenant-general in January 1815. Retired in 1816, CtLH.

On 15th July, the strength was 34 officers and 669 men. At the Moskova, one officer killed and 12 wounded. In all in Russia, 12 officers dead, 3 missing and 32 returned directly of whom 8 were commissioned in Russia. The regiment suffered heavy losses before the Moskova, engaged on 27th July, the 14th and 19th August (5 officers dead and 7 wounded).

Special cases:

— **Pernet**, squadron commander. Mentioned four times and decorated on 2nd September 1812. One horse killed at the Moskova. Major in 1813, served in 1814.

— **Robert**, captain, charged 6 times at Valoutina and two horses killed. Decorated on 2nd September. He was squadron commander in 1813. At the Moskova the regiment, having being disunited by three charges against a redoubt, Robert rallied thirty-odd men and charged two Russian cuirassier platoons which had taken a light battery. He re-captured the cannon and the artillerymen, captured and killed all the Russians. His horse was killed under him in this action.

— **de Jarnac**, lieutenant, wounded on 14th August then twice at the Moskova (a bullet wound and a lance wound). Aide de camp of de Bousnois in 1813, wounded in 1814.

— **Suremain de Flamerans**, lieutenant, aide de camp to Beurmann on 19th September. Wounded at the Moskova. Followed the King in 1815. With the 1st Hussars in 1827. LH in 1812 and OLH in 1823.

THE 28th CHASSEURS

— Colonel was listed as "on a mission". He was replaced by **Major de Quinto d'Avogrado**, who was captured dying at Koenigsberg. This regiment formed from a provisional regiment, numbered a lot of Piemontese and was reduced to about 200 cavalrymen at the beginning of the campaign. A squadron was at Imperial headquarters.

At the Moskova, 3 officers were killed and 3 wounded. In all 7 officers died.

— **Lieutenant d'André**, the son of the deputy for Aix, can be mentioned; he represented the nobility at the States-General. Emigrated to Vienna, he was in the service of Austria until 1810, when he returned to France. He was at Hamburg with Davout. In 1823 he was a colonel in the Gendarmerie. *Grand Prévôt* with the Duke of Angoulême. He was appointed brigadier by Charles X. Dismissed in 1830.

— **Captain de Bonnaire** was also an *émigré* in the service of Austria until 1811. He was with the 11th Chasseurs in 1814 and dismissed in 1815.

The WURTEMBERG CAVALRY

At the beginning they formed a brigade, but were quickly spread out among the

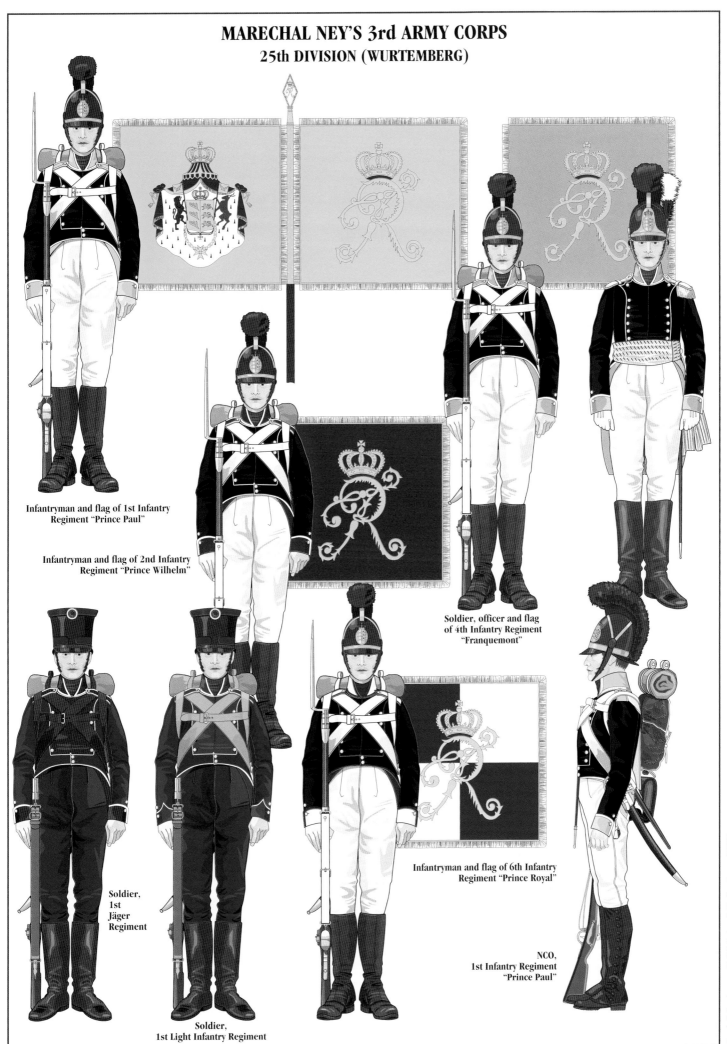

MARECHAL NEY'S 3rd ARMY CORPS
25th DIVISION (WURTEMBERG)

Infantryman and flag of 1st Infantry Regiment "Prince Paul"

Infantryman and flag of 2nd Infantry Regiment "Prince Wilhelm"

Soldier, officer and flag of 4th Infantry Regiment "Franquemont"

Soldier, 1st Jäger Regiment

Soldier, 1st Light Infantry Regiment

Infantryman and flag of 6th Infantry Regiment "Prince Royal"

NCO, 1st Infantry Regiment "Prince Paul"

MARECHAL NEY'S 3rd ARMY CORPS
CAVALRY

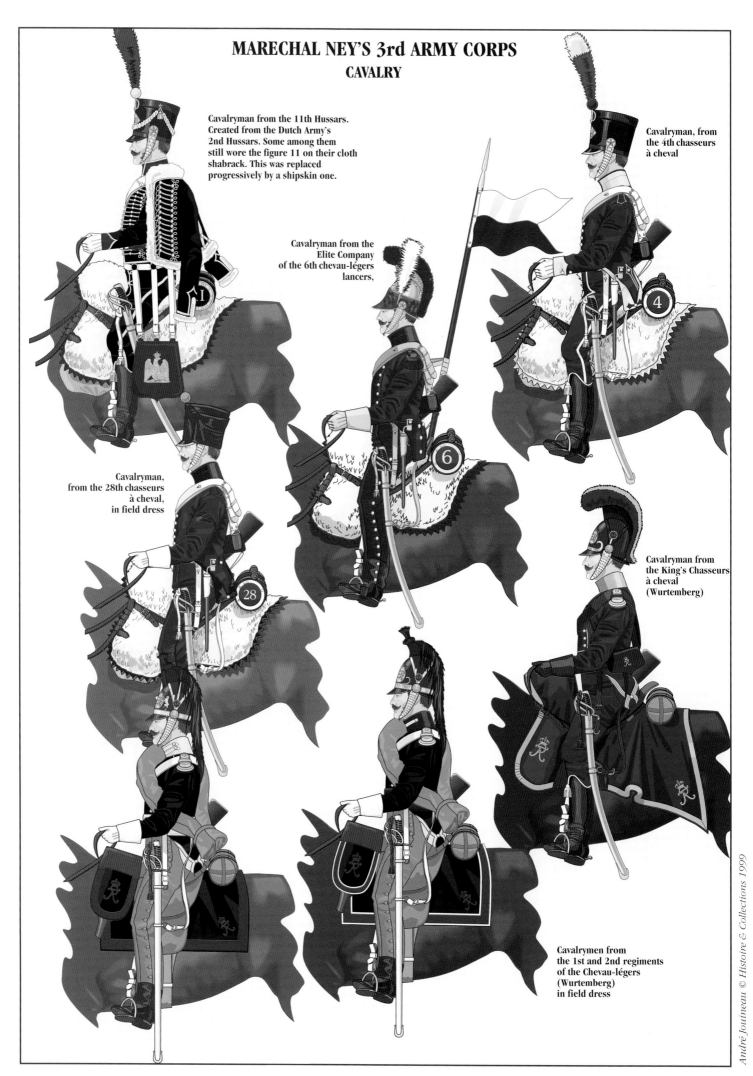

Cavalryman from the 11th Hussars.
Created from the Dutch Army's
2nd Hussars. Some among them
still wore the figure 11 on their cloth
shabrack. This was replaced
progressively by a shipskin one.

Cavalryman, from
the 4th chasseurs
à cheval

Cavalryman from the
Elite Company
of the 6th chevau-légers
lancers,

Cavalryman,
from the 28th chasseurs
à cheval,
in field dress

Cavalryman from
the King's Chasseurs
à cheval
(Wurtemberg)

Cavalrymen from
the 1st and 2nd regiments
of the Chevau-légers
(Wurtemberg)
in field dress

André Jouineau © Histoire & Collections 1999

two above brigades. There were three regiments of cavalry. Some were engaged on the 14th , the 19th August and the 1st September and in this fighting 151 officers were wounded.

THE KING'S 4th CHASSEURS

This regiment was joined to Mourier's brigade. At the Moskova, **Colonel von Salm** was killed as well as a cadet. Six officers were wounded.

THE 1st *CHEVAU-LÉGERS* OF DUKE HENRY

This was with Beurmann's Brigade and at the Moskova, one officer was killed and 8 wounded.

The regiment received 17 LH at Moscow including one for **First-Lieutenant von Bulow**.

THE KING'S 2nd *CHEVAU-LÉGERS*

This was also with Beurmann's Brigade. Two officers were killed and one wounded before the Moskova where one was killed and five wounded.

The integration of this cavalry within French brigades shows how little confidence Ney had in them and their dwindling numbers on the way.

The appointment of Marchal at the head of the 25th Division was for the same reason. However those who followed all the way to Moscow were mentioned by Murat, particularly for their involvement in the second attack of the outposts. For all this cavalry, the total figure on the 1st October, at Moscow was 921 horsemen, almost all of them mounted.

ASSESSMENT of the 3rd CORPS

For those present at the Moskova, Bourtoulin fixed the number at 18 000. In fact it was even lower, more likely 15 000 infantry and cavalrymen.

At the Moskova, there were 80 officers killed and 168 wounded. For the infantry there were between 700 and 800 dead. For the cavalry about 120, a total of 920 dead for the 3rd Corps. The number of wounded will be treated later.

All the officers who were wounded continued the campaign after care at Moscow. For the whole of the campaign, there were, without counting the Wurtembergers for whom no real figures are available: 207 officers killed, 204 missing and 149 returned from captivity.

THE 4TH CORPS OF EUGENE, VICEROY OF ITALY

The Viceroy within the 84th's square at the Moskova (Lejeune).

His aides de camp were:

— **Triaire**, who received 12 wounds before being appointed captain with the *Chasseurs à Cheval* of the Consular Guard and receiving a Sabre of Honour. Promoted general on 2nd May 1812. Wounded by a lance at the Moskova, retired in 1815, he went to Bavaria, then to Portugal, returning to France in 1830.

— **Count de Gisslenga**, mentioned at the Moskova, he was an general on 15th August 1812, lieutenant-general to the King of Sardinia in 1814. Exiled to Dover in 1821.

— **Delacroix**, relation of the painter (born 1798), captured 10th November, he returned from captivity and was retired in March 1815, with the rank of Honorary Brigadier.

— **Bataille**, Colonel at Moscow, retired in January 1815, went to join Eugène at Luchtenberg in 1817.

— **De la Bedoyère**, Charles, mentioned at the Moskova, Colonel of the 7th at Grenoble, when Napoleon returned in 1815, he went over to the Emperor with his regiment. Promoted to rank of general. After Waterloo, outlawed, but returned to France, denounced and arrested, tried and executed on 19th August 1815.

— **de Sayve**, had a brother with the 9th Cuirassiers who wrote his memoirs; returned from Russia.

— **Tascher de la Pagerie**, went into the service of the King of Bavaria.

— **Méjean**, son of the count who was counsellor to the Viceroy and went with him to Russia.

GENERAL STAFF

The Chief of the General Staff was **Dessolle**, former chief of staff to and friend of Moreau, was inactive until 1808. Ill at Smolensk, he was not present at the Moskova. Retired 19th August. Minister, Count and Peer of France of the King in 1814, followed him in 1815. Voted the death of Ney.

— **Guilleminot**, replaced the former before the Moskova and was wounded at the battle. General in 1813, died in 1840, GdCxLH and GdCx of St Ferdinand in 1823.

The deputy chiefs of staff were

— **Durrieu**, Egyptian Campaign. General in 1813, wounded at Waterloo. Lieutenant-General in 1829, Baron in 1830, deputy in 1834, Peer of France in 1845, died in 1862, GdCxLH in 1859.

— **Asselin de Williencourt**, brigadier in 1815 by Napoleon, revoked, re-instated in 1831, died in 1835.

— **de Bourmont**, conspired with Cadoudal, traitor at Waterloo, condemned to death in 1833, pardoned in 1840.

The deputies were **Martin,** colonel in 1830, **Caminade**, brigadier in 1840, **Girard**, who was captured and served at Waterloo, **Landvoisin** captured but returned and was adjutant commanding in 1815; **del Fante**, captain mentioned by **Césare de Laugier** as having gone up to the redoubt at the head of the 9th and the 35th. **Colonel Klicki** commnded the 1st Lancers of the Vistula Legion. He had just been appointed the commander of the Intelligence services of the 4th Corps. General in 1813, retired in 1814, he was commander of the Polish Army in 1831 and dictator, but had to emigrate.

— The Chief Ordonnateur **Joubert**, died in December 1812, LH inYear XII.

— The Supply Inspector **Rivet de la Thibeaudière** was captured but returned in January 1814.

THE 4th CORPS ARTILLERY

Was commanded by **General d'Anthouard** (de Vraincourt), born in 1773, died in 1852. At Toulon, Italian and Egyptian Campaigns where he was wounded 5 times. In the service of Eugène until 1814, Peer of France in 1831, retired in 1848, GdCxLH in 1831.

— The second-in-command was **General Couin** (1763-1834), in Vendée, Italian Campaign, wounded at Arcola. Captain of Bonaparte's Guides in Egypt. retired in 1814. His **aide de camp Mangin** was killed at the Moskova.

— The chief of staff was **Battalion Commander Berthier**, brigadier in 1831. His deputies were **Foux**, died in Russia,

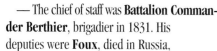

General D'Anthouard

Pron (brigadier in 1841, died in 1866, LH in Moscow, GdOLH in 1847.) **Duchemin**, brigadier in 1843, died in 1859, LH on 24th August 1812, CrLH.

The Reserve artillery.

— **Colonel Mongenet**, Knight of Malta, Egyptian Campaign, general in 1813, retired in 1816, CtLH in 1813. His deputies were **Major Vives**, served in 1815, retired in 1822 and **Pingenot**, wounded at Rivoli, recevied a Sabre of Honour in Egypt for his action against the English, amputated in 1813 and retired as Colonel-directeur.

— The Pool was commnded by **Colonel Fierck**, died in 1817, LH in Year XII, OLH in 1813, the deputy was **Mouchel**, served in 1815. In the National Guard in 1838.

Distribution of the companies.

In the Reserve, the 5th and 12th companies of the 2nd Heavy Artillery. with the Pool, the 8th,10th and 20th companies of the 2nd Heavy Artillery. With Broussier, the 7th Company of the 2nd Heavy Artillery and the 3rd Company of the 4th Light Artillery. With Delzons, the 9th Company of the 2nd Heavy Artillery and the 2nd of the 4th Heavy artillery.

With the Italian guard, its artillery company, commanded by **Battalion Commander Clément**, Major at Moscow, died at Limoges in 1815. With the French Chasseurs à cheval, the 1st Company of the 4th light Artillery.

The artilery was composed of 24 12-pounders, 46 6-pounders, 24 3-pounders and 22 howitzers. The train was the responsibility of 7 companies of the 7bis, together with the workers. At the Moskova, there were at least 6 officers killed.

The ENGINEERS

Commanded by **Poitevin**, Egyptian Campaign, general in 1805, lieutenant-general in 1814, served in 1815, viscount in 1822. With him was **Daullé**, colonel at Moscow, brigadier in 1835, lieutenant-general in 1843, retired in 1848. GdOLH.

At the Moskova there were about 300 sappers. Pino's Division was elsewhere and therefore was not at the battle, which reduced the numbers of the 4th Corps present at the battle.

I. DELZON'S 13th DIVISION

The general was wounded at Dego and Rivoli. during the Egyptian Campaign promoted to brigadier on the battlefield at the Pyramides.

— **Doté**, Baron, killed at Malojaroslawetz. Couronne de Fer, his brother born also at Aurillac was his aide de camp. Went through the Fontainebleau School. Battalion Commander 31st July 1812. Killed also at Marojaroslawetz. **Captain Duhot** was his second aide de camp, brigadier in 1841, LH at Moscow, OLH in 1814.

HUARD de ST-AUBIN's BRIGADE

The general was killed at the Moskova, commanding the 8th Light and the 84th and 92nd of the Line.

The chief of staff was **Boisserolle-Boisvilliers**, general in 1813. He replaced **Plauzonne** killed in Borodino and held the village with the 106th. The artillery commander was **Colonel Demay**, killed at the Moskova.

THE 8th LIGHT.

— **Colonel Serrant**, general at Moscow, captured in December, escaped and rejoined 2nd April 1813. Non active in 1815. At the beginning there were 44 officers and 1 409 men. At Moscow there were 44 officers and 984 men. They received 14 CxLH of which 8 for the officers.

The regiment suffered heavy losses on the 25th July, and, like the 84th, poses a problem: it suffered very few losses at the Moskova. As it is known that the Viceroy sought refuge within the square formed by the 84th, it must be supposed that these two regiments forming a brigade must have been in the second line and just had to fight off Ouvarov's assault which could not penetrate their squares.

THE 84th OF THE LINE.

— **Colonel Pégot**, general in 1814.

At the beginning there were 81 officers and 2 555 men; on 1st September there were 81 officers and 2 184 men. At Moscow, 79 men and 1 909 men. They received 21 CLHs of which 12 for the officers. Like the 8th Light, this regiment had hardly any losses during the battle. Sheltering in the second line, it formed its square against the Russian cavalry and repelled them without loss. For the whole campaign, the regiment lost 17 officers killed, 26 missing and 10 prisoners returned in 1814.

— **Lieutenant Guinguené** was a brigadier in 1843.

THE 92nd OF THE LINE.

— **Colonel Tissot** replaced **Colonel Lanier**, wounded and decorated on the 26th July, then evacuated towards the depot. Tissot was captured in Syria, dismissed in 1815, re-instated in 1821. LH in Year XII, OLH at Moscow.

The regiment started off with 83 officers and 2 591 men. At Smolensk, there were 66 officers and 1 904 men. at the Moskova, one officer and 67 men were killed. 8 officers were wounded. At Moscow they received 17 CLHs of which 9 for the officers. For the whole campaign there were only 17 officers killed and 47 disappeared. No prisoners returned in this regiment.

PLAUZONNE'S BRIGADE.

The general had come to replace **General Roussel**, killed 26th July by a scout who had mistaken him for a Russian. **Plauzonne** was killed at the Moskova.

THE 106th OF THE LINE.

— **Colonel Bertrand**, baron, wounded at the Moskova, retired in January 1813.

At the beginning the regiment had 80 officers and 2 717 men. On 1st August there were 73 officers and 2 285 men. One month later there were 85 officers and 2 174 men. at the Moskova 18 officers and 72 men were killed, 20 officers wounded. At Moscow, 42 officers and 1 284 men were present. 14 were decorated of which 8 officers. In all in Russia, the regiment lost 3 officers dead, 41 missing and 8 prisoners returned.

THE 1st CROATIAN PROVISIONAL REGIMENT (2 Battalions)

— **Colonel Slivaritch**, wounded at Ostrovno. General in February 1813. Captured at Leipzig, returned and he retired at the beginning of 1815.

On the 30th Jine 1812, the regiment numbered 44 officers and 1 329 men. On 17th August there were only 34 officers and 904 men left because of the

Delzons

PRINCE EUGENE'S 4th ARMY CORPS
LINE and LIGHT INFANTRY

General Delzons' Brigade
(13th)

From left to right.
— Light Infantrtyman of the 18th
Light.
— Captain, Light Infantry Company
wearing a greatcoat, 84th, 92nd
and 106th of the Line.
— Light Infantryman from the
1st Provisional Croat Regiment.
— Grenadier from the 1st
Provisional Croat Regiment.

General Broussier's
Division (14ᵗʰ)

From left to right.
— Captain from a Light Infantry
Regiment wearing an overcoat,
18th Light.
— Captain in full service dress, 9th,
35th and 53rd of the Line.
— Grenadier from
the "Joseph Napoleon" Regiment.

General Lecchi's
Italian Guard Division

From left to right
— Velite Grenadier.
— Conscript.
— Grenadier of the Guard
and 5 Companies of the Guard
of Honour.

L'EMPEREUR
ET ROI,
AU Bᴸᴼᴺ DE GRENADIERS
A PIED DE LA GARDE
ROIALE

André Jouineau © Histoire & Collections 1999

losses at Ostrovna — 1 officer killed and 9 wounded. At the Moskova, practically no losses; drawn up into a square next to the 84th, it simply repulsed the last attempted charge by Platov and Ouvarov. At Moscow there were indeed 34 officers and 897 men. They received 6 CLH of which 2 for the non-commissioned officers.

II. BROUSSIER'S 14th DIVISION

The general, Count, died of illness in 1814. GdOLH. **Battalion Commander Hermann**, commanding the artillery was killed at the Moskova.

Broussier

BERTRAND DE SIVRAY'S BRIGADE

The general was retired in 1815, he was with the 18th Light and the 9th of the Line.

His chief of staff was **Forestier**, the brother of a general, was wounded at the Siege of Toulon, Italian Campaign. General in 1813, died at Brienne in 1814.

THE 18th LIGHT

— **Colonel Gaussart** was a general in 1813, GdCxLH in 1831.

The regiment had 2 battalions to begin with and 36 officers and 1 401 soldiers. There were only 2 officers wounded at the Moskova because it was kept in reserve. At Moscow the Emperor awarded 12 CLH of which 7 for the officers. For the whole campaign, the regiment lost 11 officers killed, 18 missing and 4 captured but returned.

The 9th of the Line attacking.
(Picture hanging in the Regimental Mess)

THE 9th OF THE LINE *(the Heros of Ostrovno)*[1]

— **Colonel Vautré**, wounded at the Moskova, captured in December, he returned in 1814. Brigadier in 1816, retired 1831.

The regiment included 86 officers and 2 561 men. The 1st September, there were 91 officers and 1 949 men. At the Moskova, taking part in the capture of the Great Redoubt, it lost 8 officers, 4 dying of their wounds. The account gives 73 men killed, 717 wounded or ill of which 49 quickly rejoined. At Moscow there were 57 officers and 1 024 men left, they received 12 LHs of which 8 for the officers and for the whole of the campaign, 19 offciers died, 24 were missing and 6 were captured but returned.

Special cases:

— **Colonel Vautré**, the brother of the colonel, Battalion Commander, was lieutenant-colonel in 1821, 12 old Egyptian Campaigners returned directly.

ALMERAS' BRIGADE

The general was wounded at the Moskova, captured in November, returned but inactive in 1815.

---

1. A lot of regiments claimed that they were the first to enter this famous redoudt; for the cavalry, the priority seems to go without any doubt to the 5th and 8th Cuirassiers for this was marked on the service records of the officers. The claim by the Saxons of Zastrov's regiment was incompatible with their position on the battlefield and with the precise facts. Among the officers of the 5th Hussars, there was one mentioned as having captured a cannon inside the redoubt.

For the infantry regiments, several regiments must have entered at the same time: Broussier's 9th of the Line, Gérard's 21st and Morand's 17th. They formed the heads of the three assault columns which had left at the same time. In the service records of the officers, it was an officer of the 17th who arrived first.

In Charpentier's picture which is at the Musée de l'Armée, showing the death of Caulaincourt and the great confusion: the cavalry crosses the parapet between two artillery pieces, there are carabiniers mixed up with the cuirassiers and cuirassiers are seen arriving from the other direction. For the French infantry, the light infantry is mixed up with that of the Line and the very nice cornet is clearly from a light regiment. Among the Russians, artillerymen with bizarre dress, grenadiers wearing mitres, etc. Just so many fantasies with no relation to reality.

Le Blanc's picture presented in the official account of the 9th and hung in the mess of Honour of the RCP is much more reasonable. It is not impossible that the choice of the 9th be true, but it could be that this regiment at the head of the columns was chosen from among the three to please Prince Eugène for it was the only one belonging to the 4th Corps, the others coming from the 1st and lent to the Viceroy for the battle only. In favour of the 9th, there is its subsequent behaviour. It was mentioned as having fired upon the cavalry of the Russian Guard several times during the course of the cavalry free-for-all protecting the ground that had been won.

PRINCE EUGENE'S 4th ARMY CORPS
CAVALRY

Cavalryman from
Honour Guard
Regiment
from Bologna

Cavalryman from
Queens' Dragoons
(Italian Royal
Guard)

Corporal from
19th Mounted Chasseurs

Cavalryman from
2nd Italian Mounted
Chasseurs

Cavalryman from
9th Mounted
Chasseurs

Cavalryman from
3rd Italian Mounted
Chasseurs

Cavalryman from
3rd Bavarian Chevau-Légers
"Kronprinz"

Cavalryman from 5th
Bavarian Chevau-Légers
"Leiningen"

Cavalryman from
4th Bavarian
Chevau-Légers
"King"

Cavalryman from
6th Bavarian
Chevau-Légers
"Bubenhofen"

André Joutineau © Histoire & Collections 1999

THE 53rd OF THE LINE

— **Colonel de Grobon**, died in 1815, LH in Year XII.

At the outset, the regiment had 78 officers and 2 442 men. At the Moskova, 4 officers were killed and 9 wounded. At Moscow they received 14 decorations of which 9 for the officers. In all the campaign, 14 officers died, 40 disappeared and 8 prisoners returned.

THE 35th OF THE LINE

— **Colonel Penant**, killed at Malojaroslawetz, LH in Year XII.

On 15th June, the regiment had 74 officers and 2 225 men. On 1st September, before the battle there were 86 officers and 1 954 men. No doubt it had received reinforcements unless a mistake has been made concerning the numbers of the officers. At the Moskova, 4 officers were killed, 10 wounded. At Moscow, there were 73 officers and 1 422 men. For the whole the campaign, there were 16 officers killed, 27 disappeared and 8 prisoners returned.

— **Pierre Mayer**, from Geneva, who came as a replacement, wrote his memoirs.

THE JOSEPH NAPOLEON REGIMENT.

Only the 1st and 4th Battalions were present. The other two were with Friant. On the 15th June there were 21 officers and 606 men in the 1st Battalion and 15 officers and 671 men with the 4th. On 1st September, there were 459 men in the rear. At Moscow there remained 35 officers and 482 men for both battalions. They received 7 decorations of which 5 for the officers. One wounded at the Moskova; for the whole of the campaign, 5 officers killed, 1 missing and 1 prisoner returned.

III. THE ITALIAN ROYAL GUARD

Commanded by *Lecchi*, it included:

— **The Guards of Honour** consisting of the 1st from Milan, 2nd from Bologna, 3rd from Brescia, 4th from Romagna, 5th from Venice. They were 30 at the beginning. The corps commander was killed at Smolensk and there were only 198 left at Moscow. For the whole campaign, 19 officers were listed as missing.

The following were not engaged:

— **the Velites** (2 battalions), the infantry regiment with 2 battalions, the grenadiers and the conscripts with 2 battalions, the Dragoons of the Guard (2 squadrons) and the Queen's Dragoons (2 squadrons). They are illustrated on page 89.

IV. THE 4th CORPS 'LIGHT CAVALRY

Commanded by **Ornano**. This general, a cousin of Bonaparte was a count in 1808. Promoted to general on the battlefield of Fuentès de Onoro. He replaced Bessières in 1813, remained in the Guard. Exiled to Liège in1815, returned 1818,

Peer of France in 1832. Deputy and Senator, Governor of the Invalides, Maréchal de France in 1861, died in 1863, GdCxLH 1850, Grand Chancelier of the LH.

With him was **General Ferrière**, but he was left behind as commandant at Bialystok. There were **General Guyon** and the Italian General **Villata** who was at the Moskova commanding the Italian Brigade.

Ornano

GUYON'S BRIGADE (12th)

The general was present in the Italian and Egyptian campaigns where he won a Sabre of Honour. Colonel of the 12th Chasseurs at Auerstadt. Baron. With Lecourbe in 1815. Commandant at Tours in 1832, died in 1834, GdOLH in 1825.

THE 9th CHASSEURS

— **Colonel de Sainte-Suzanne**, died at the end of the retreat.

On 15th June, the regiment had 27 officers and 510 cavalrymen. At the Moskova,1 officer was killed, 9 wounded and 2 were especially mentioned in despatches. On 1st September, there were 31 officers and 468 men. At Moscow, 30 officers and 383 men were left. In all in Russia, 4 officers died, 7 went missing and 2 prisoners returned.

THE 19th CHASSEURS

— **Colonel Vincent** was a general in 1813, lieutenant-general in 1825.

On 15th June, the regiment had 23 officers and 511 cavalrymen. On 15th July, there were 27 officers and 468 men and at Moscow, 30 officers and 378 men. Certain elements joined up coming from Hannover. At the Moskova, 1 officer was killed and 7 wounded. In all for the campaign, 2 officers died, 4 disappeared and 2 prisoners returned.

Special cases:

— **Squadron Commander Alphonse de Frouchy**, wounded at the Moskova and at Viasma. Brigadier in 1831. Lieutenat-General in 1842, Senator in 1852. Died 1864, OLH in 1813, GdCxLH in 1862.

— **Bougenel**, came from Berthier on 9th June. Colonel in 1830, brigadier in 1838. Lieutenat-general in 1846. Died in 1865.

— **van Remoortère**, served as a Belgian in 1815, was wounded at the

I have reproduced here a period painting from the collection of my friend, P. Brétégnier, representing a review in 1812 before the departure for Russia. Behind the Viceroy there are cavalrymen wearing a helmet bearing an "N" who are Guards of Honour. Their helmet is of the French carabinier type but with a top representing the eagle with folded wings on each side. On the front of the helmet is the big "N" topped with a crown. On the right , they wear the silver aiguillettes of the Guard, as well as the lapel buttonholes. Their coat is green, but on the lapels on the facing and on the collar there is a distinctive marking their town of origin; pink for Milan, chamois for Brescia, scarlet for Romagna and orange for Venice.There was a trumpeter per company, with a coat of the colour of the distinctive, and the collar, facings and the retroussis sky blue like the trumpeter's flame with silver ornaments. The horse's harness was sky-blue edged with white also. The helmet had white chenille and plume. Variations of detail were given also for these trumpeters.

Quatre-Bras by a non-commissioned officer of the 19th Chasseurs. Belgian Major-General , he died in 1855.

— **Lebon Desmottes**, lieutenant, wounded 3 times at the Moskova, served at Waterloo. Brigadier, CrLH in 1846.

— Two captains were holders of the Sabre of Honour: **de Bree**, retired in 1813 and **Couillez**, retired in 1815.

VILLATA'S BRIGADE (13th)
THE 2nd ITALIAN CHASSEURS

39 officers and 608 cavalrymen at the beginning. Two at least wounded at the Moskova.

—**Second Lieutenant le Pays de Bourjolly** was a colonel in 1836, then brigadier in 1846.

THE 3rd ITALIAN CHASSEURS

33 officers and 601 cavalrymen. 1 officer wounded at the Moskova: **Lieutenant Haon**, born at Libourne, wounded four times on the 7th September. Back in French service, he was a captain in 1815. LH 1809.

They were put at the disposition of the 4th Corps under the command of Ornano. This brigade with the 106th, was thought to have been left behind at Borodino, with Junot's Corps, to guard and protect the ambulances. After the battle, they rejoined Moscow with the transportable and light wounded.

THE BAVARIAN CAVALRY (21st and 22nd Brigades)

This was taken from the 6th Corps to march with the 4th. These men were therefore with Ornano and his light cavalry. Like the Italian Chasseurs they were one of the weaker elements in such a battle, but they did charge well against Ouvarov's cavalry. It was the **Count of Preysing** who was in command with as second-in-command, **Count Seydenitz**.

There were 4 regiments of *Chevau-Légers*: the 3rd (it had 6 wounded at the Moskova), the 4th (1 officer killed and 4 wounded) and the 5th (likewise), the 6th (5 officers wounded). At Moscow, the strength of this cavalry was 700 horsemen.

AN ASSESSMENT OF THE 4th CORPS AT THE MOSKOVA

At the outset there were almost 50 000 men. After Smolensk, it was reduced to at most 30 000 men. Pino's Division must be discounted as it was absent at the Moskova, and it numbered 10 000 men. For the Russians estimated the 4th Corps at 21 200 present.

— **Delzo's Division:** on 1st September, it numbered 8 297 men and 316 officers. On 1st October, there were 257 officers and 6 589 men; 49 offciers and 1 708 men were missing but a lot joined up later from the hospitals.

— **Broussier's division** numbered about 7 000 men before the battle. The Italian Guard was not engaged.

— **The light cavalry** of the 4th Corps: there were 3 officers killed and 38 wounded.

Total count.

This is the corps which gave the most information and details, even if they are incomplete for the men. The strength of the corps can be estimated at 17 500 infantrymen and artillerymen with 2 500 horsemen just before the battle, without Pino's Division. The Russian estimate was therefore not far off.

The losses for the Corps at the Moskova were given in a roll at Moscow which stated that 435 men were killed together with 2 570 infantrymen and cavalrymen were wounded. For the officers, 48 killed and 121 wounded.

For the whole of the campaign, but with incomplete figures, the figures are: 149 officers killed, 253 disappeared and 48 returned from captivity.

An assessment of the men of the 4th Corps at Moscow, doubtlessly a little exaggerated, states that there were 1331 officers, 26 996 men and 2 679 horses present, taking into account the re-inforcements that had joined up with the return of Pino's division and the men in the Moscow hospitals or elsewhere. There were 10 cannon and 35 usable caissons.

Prince Eugène sent Davout's two divisions so generously put at his disposal into the attack which would explain the relative good condition of the 4th Corps at Moscow. It was no doubt that for this reason it was put in the front for the retreat and was engaged at Malojaroslavetz.

PONIATOWSKI'S 5th CORPS

Poniatowski

Details concerning this corps are difficult to find and those which are valid are given. Dombrowski's 17th Division had been left in the rear with the cavalry of the 2nd and the 3rd Lancers; they were not at the battle of the Moskova.

I. ZAYONCHEK'S DIVISION (16th)

— **Zayonchek** was admitted as a general by Bonaparte into the Army of Italy. Egyptian Campaign. Major -General in 1802, Prince in 1818, died in 1826. CtLH.

KAMINSKI'S BRIGADE

— The 13th and 15th Polish regiment. All these Polish regiments had 3 battalions.

MIELZINSKI'S BRIGADE

— 8th and 16th Polish Regiments.

II. KAMENIECKI'S DIVISION (18th)
ZOTTOWSKI'S BRIGADE

— The 6th and 14th Polish Regiments

GRABOWSKI'S BRIGADE

— the 12th Polish Regiment.

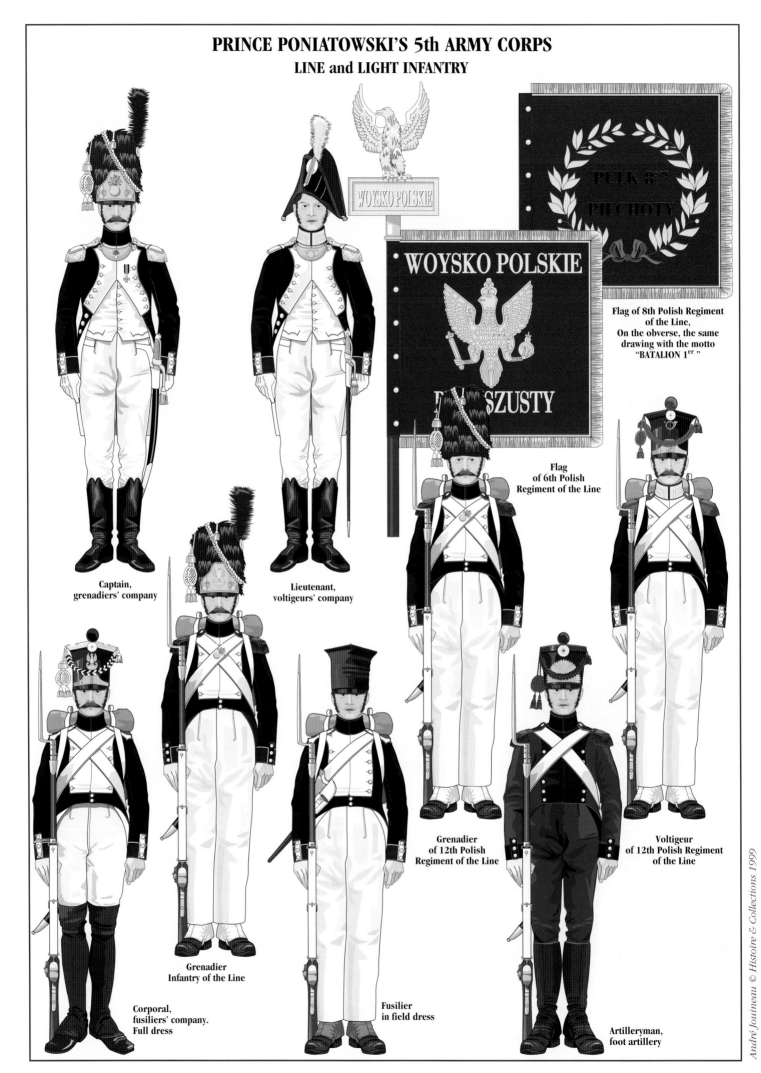

PRINCE PONIATOWSKI'S 5th ARMY CORPS
LINE and LIGHT INFANTRY

WOYSKO POLSKIE

PULK 8ᵛ PIECHOTY

Flag of 8th Polish Regiment
of the Line,
On the obverse, the same
drawing with the motto
"BATALION 1ᵉʳ"

WOYSKO POLSKIE

...SZUSTY

Flag
of 6th Polish
Regiment of the Line

Captain,
grenadiers' company

Lieutenant,
voltigeurs' company

Grenadier
Infantry of the Line

Corporal,
fusiliers' company.
Full dress

Fusilier
in field dress

Grenadier
of 12th Polish
Regiment of the Line

Voltigeur
of 12th Polish Regiment
of the Line

Artilleryman,
foot artillery

PRINCE PONIATOWSKI'S 5th ARMY CORPS
CAVALRY

Cavalryman
7th Polish Lancers

Cavalryman
7th Polish Lancers

Cavalryman
11th Polish Lancers

Cavalryman
13th Polish Hussars

Cavalryman
1st Polish
Mounted
Chasseurs

POLSKIE

LEGIAI.

I PULKLEKKI IAZDV

Officer,
Polish Horse
Artillery

Cavalryman
5th Polish
Mounted
Chasseurs

Standard
1st Polish Mounted
Chasseurs

André Jouineau © Histoire & Collections 1999

III. THE LIGHT CAVALRY DIVISION
18th, 19th and 20th Brigades

It had 3 war squadrons; they were principally: the 7th, 8th and 11th Polish Lancers and the 1st and 5th Polish Chasseurs with the 13th Regiment (Polish Hussars). On a roll of the 16th July there were the 1st, 5th and the 13th included in the 16th and 18th Divisions. In order to clarify this dispersal, we shall return to an official roll.

OFFICAL ROLL OF THE 5th CORPS AS AT 16th JULY 1812

They were near Romanov. This incomplete roll gave the following details for those going on to Moscow:

THE 16th DIVISION

The Infantry. The 3rd Infantry Regiment had 60 officers and 2 509 men. 6 officers and 607 men were to the rear or detached. The 15th had 59 officers and 2 494 men present. The 13th had 67 officers and 2 612 men and the 16th had 59 officers and 2 287 men. On the division's roll there was also the 4th Cavalry Regiment of 39 officers and 778 men. The Artillery had 10 officers and 367 men and the Engineers had 2 officers and 67 men. Many men were at the rear.

THE 18th DIVISION

The 2nd Regiment had 58 officers and 2 268 men, the 1st 59 and 2 232, the 12th 57 and 2 085 respectively. Counted with this division was the 5th Cavalry Regiment with 32 officers and 759 cavalrymen, the 13th with 27 and 632. The artillery had 11 officers and 376 artillerymen, the Engineers 2 officers and 59 men. Already there were about 20 horses missing per regiment for the riders.

THE ARTILLERY AND THE ENGINEERS

They were commanded by General Pelletier who was captured at Vias-ma and returned to French service in 1814. He served at Waterloo. Lieutenant-General in 1836, GdCxLH in 1857. The artillery was under the command of Colonel Redel who had commanded the Polish artillery in the Italian Legion, seriously wounded at Leipzig, OLH in 1813, Officier du Mérite Polonais, Knight of the Order of the Two Sicilies.

It included two heavy companies and one light. At the pool, there were in addition 5 heavy companies. All this corresponded to 6 12-pounders, 30 6-pounders and 2 howitzers. The pool had 5 companies with 11 officers and 499 artillerymen. For these artillery reserves there were 1 054 draught horses and 116 horses for the light company plus 50 horses for the heavy companies. In addition the pontoneers have to be added, 4 officers and 130 soldiers with 117 draught horses. For the Engineers, 5 officers and 116 sappers with 47 draught horses and finally for the trains, 8 officers and 640 men with 926 horses. Total: 573 officers and 21 253 men.

This roll was carried out before the Moskova but is nevertheless precious since it shows the importance of the draught horses and their large number. All along the way to the great battle, many men and many horses stayed at the rear or were combat casualties or ill. This must be accounted for in the assessment.

AN ASSESSMENT OF THE 5TH CORPS AT THE MOSKOVA

It left with about 35 000 men, this corps suffered losses at Mir, Romanov and Smolensk. In addition, the removal of the Dombrowski Division (which has been taken from the 16th July roll) which went off towards Borisov, further reduced this corps' strength. At the Moskova, Poniatowski could line up a maximum of 15 000 men and cavalry. Boutourlin in his Russian analysis counted indeed 15 000 present.

No figures for the losses at the Moskova have been found, but certain Poles criticised Poniatowski for his lack of firmness.

JUNOT'S WESTPHALIAN 8th CORPS

Junot

He was abandonned by his King, Jérôme, irritated by his bad beginnings and refusing to take orders from Davout. Junot commanded in his stead, but he was useless at Valoutina and the first signs of his mental illness were beginning to be noticeable. Napoleon had not wanted to replace him and that was a pity since he did nothing at the Moskova.

Junot's aides de camps were **Delagrave**, battalion commander (captured at the Moskova and returnd in 1814), **Captain Prévost** (wounded at the Moskova, two horses killed, major in 1814 and retired. LH in 1806).

— The Chief of Staff was **Baron Revest**, born at Sète in 1773, volunteer in 1792, Italian Campaign, followed Vandamme. Named General, commanded the Charentes in 1830, CrLH in February 1815.

I. TARREAU'S DIVISION (23rd)

The general was wounded twice at the Moskova, died from his wounds at Mojaisk on 26th September. Major-general in 1799, he was removed for having voted against the consulate for Life and against the Empire. Re-instated and made a baron in 1808, wounded at Essling, OLH in 1809.

— On his staff there was **Captain Diepenbroick w**ho died at the end of the retreat at Posen in January 1813.

DAMAS' BRIGADE.

— **Major-General Damas** must not be confused with the General Damas in command of the Berg Brigade of the Daendels Division in Victor's 9th Corps. This General Damas of the 8th Corps was killed at the Moskova.

THE 3rd BATTALION OF LIGHT INFANTRY

4 officers wounded at the Moskova; in all 8 officers disappeared and two with the Russo-German Legion in 1813.

GENERAL JUNOT'S 8th ARMY CORPS
LINE and LIGHT INFANTRY

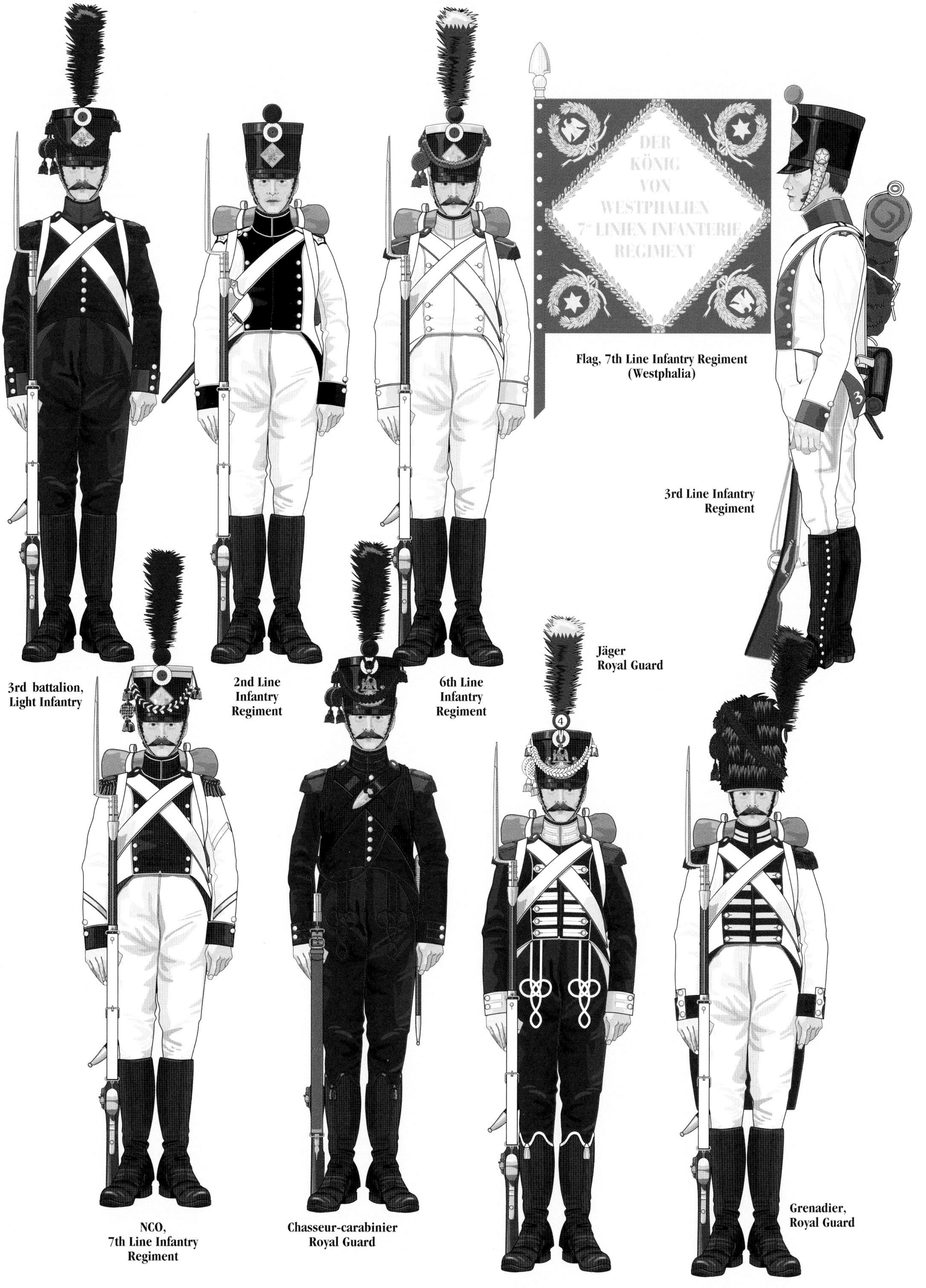

Flag, 7th Line Infantry Regiment (Westphalia)

DER KÖNIG VON WESTPHALIEN 7ᵉ LINIEN INFANTERIE REGIMENT

3rd Line Infantry Regiment

3rd battalion, Light Infantry

2nd Line Infantry Regiment

6th Line Infantry Regiment

Jäger Royal Guard

NCO, 7th Line Infantry Regiment

Chasseur-carabinier Royal Guard

Grenadier, Royal Guard

André Joutineau © Histoire & Collections 2000

THE 2nd OF THE LINE with 2 battalions.

3 officers and 24 soldiers killed at the Moskova and 4 officers wounded. In all 7 officers dead, 17 missing and 2 passed into Prussian service.

The 6th of the Line with 2 battalions.

2 officers and 56 men were killed at the Moskova, 3 officers wounded. For the whole campaign, 10 officers died, 8 disappeared and 5 captured but returned.

WICKENBERG BRIGADE

The general, Jerome's aide de camp, was a major-general in 1813, died in 1839.

THE 2nd LIGHT BATTALION.

3 officers wounded at the Moskova and in all 5 missing.

THE 3rd OF THE LINE with 2 battalions.

They lost 3 officers wounded at the Moskova, of whom one captured died in prison; and 5 men killed. In all for the Russian Campaign, 1 killed, 16 missing and 4 captured and engaged in the Russo-German Legion.

THE 7th OF THE LINE (which for some had 3 battalions).

2 officers and 78 men were killed at the Moskova and 9 officers wounded. In all 11 officers killed, 28 missing and 5 captured engaged in the Russo-German Legion.

II. VON OCHS DIVISION (24th)

The general who was Hessian, served in America. Major-General in 1811, captured in 1813, died in 1823, wrote memoirs.

— His aide de camp was **St Paul** came from Prussian service, was battalion commander in 1813. Bauermeister in 1813. The chief of staff was **Humbert**, wounded at the Moskova went to the 4th Corps then returned to the Westphalian Guard. Provisional General in 1814, he was demoted after Waterloo and put on half-pay. Three deputies were missing.

LEGRAS' BRIGADE (GUARD)

Appointed in May 1812 to replace general Wellingerode. **Legras** was an *émigré* who returned to French service in 1808; he came from the Guard, died at the end of the retreat.

THE CHASSEURS-CARABINIERS OF THE GUARD (one battalion)

8 officers killed in Russia of whom one at the Moskova. Another was wounded in the battle, was captured and died in prison. 10 officers were missing.

The Chasseurs of the Guard. 1 battalion.

54 officers were killed, 2 wounded at th Moskova and 7 disappeared. Second-**Lieutenant Puisbusque** was wounded at Krasnoi and captured with his father, in charge of the service at Smolensk, both returned.

THE GRENADIERS OF THE GUARD (one battalion)

2 officers killed one at the Moskova, one wounded during the battle. During the retreat, 7 disappeared and 4 were captured but returned among whom Second-**Lieutenants Rommel** and **von Arnim**.

DANLOUP-VERDUN'S BRIGADE

The general was a French general in 1814. Volunteer in Paris in 1791, was in the Jura in 1815 and was retired. His aide de camp, **Palmé** was captured at the Beresina and returned.

THE LIGHT BATTALION.

1 officer killed at the Moskova and 6 wounded. In all in Russia, one officer dead, 6 missing and 2 captured and returned.

THE 5th OF THE LINE, 2 battalions.

7 officers dead, 12 disappeared and 2 captured but returned.

THE 1st AND THE 8th OF THE LINE were put in the rear with the 10th Corps in Grandjean's division.

III. THE 8th CORPS CAVALRY

THE *CHEVAU-LÈGERS* OF THE GUARD.

1 officer and 9 men killed, 2 officers wounded at the Moskova among whom the son of General Ochs. The regiment lost 145 horses during the battle. In all 7 officers killed and 4 captured but returned.

HAMMERSTEIN'S BRIGADE

Major-General in 1813. His aide de camp **St-Cernain** was killed at the Moskova. The chief of staff was **de Reiche**, general in 1813 and baron. Died in 1829.

THE 1st WESTPHALIAN HUSSARS.

1 officer killed and 11 wounded at the Moskova. In all 2 officers dead and 7 missing. The regiment had 35 officers and 520 men to start with. A roll was taken at Mojaisk on 15th September where the 8th had remained to protect the hospitals. There were 15 officers and 79 cavalrymen present.

The others were dispersed as follows. At Orcha, 1 officer and 28 men. At Viasma: 1 officer and 106 men, at Dorogobug: 6 offciers and 120 men. Accompanying the Treasury: 2 offciers and 63 hussars: at the little depot 4 officers and 28 men. 7 officers and 105 men were at the hospitals. 9 were prisoners.

THE 2nd WESTPHALIAN HUSSARS.

At the Moskova, 2 officers were killed and 11 wounded. In all 5 officers were killed and 8 missing. The same roll on 15th September gave the following dispersal: at Mojaidk, there were 16 officers and 213 men; at Orch: 2 officers and 35 cavalrymen; at Viasma 5 officers and 11 men; at Ghjat: 1 officer and 47 hussars; at Koubinska: 1 officer and 66 men; at the little depot: 1 officer and 6 cavalrymen. In the hospitals: 10 officers and 139 men. 26 men were captured.

THE ARTILLERY

Commanded by **General Alix**. He served at Marengo, then Santo Domingo. Retired in 1804 accused of embezzlement, re-instated in 1808, decorated at Moscow, exiled in 1815, re-instated in 1831. 4 missing, 3 dead of whom 1 at the Moskova (**de la Chapelle**) among his aides de camp and deputies. **Schulz**, the director of the pool was listed as missing. There were two heavy batteries and one light with 26 6-pounders and 8 24-pound howitzers. For the Guard there was a light battery whose commander was **Maistre**, decorated at Moscow. He was captured at Vilna and returned from captivity. Squadron commander in French service in 1829. 38 artillerymen were killed at the Moskova. After the battle there were only 1 000 men left in the artillery. For the men of the transport train there were 3 officers killed , one at the Moskova and 10 missing.

THE ENGINEERS

Commanded by **Colonel Ulliac** who was captured at Vilna and taken to Siberia. Returned and retired in 1836.

THE LOSSES OF THE 8th CORPS AT THE MOSKOVA

The casualties can be estimated as follows using Revest's report of the 16th September at Mojaisk where the Corps was stationed: 22 officers killed and 117 wounded and for the men, 294 killed and 1 000 wounded.

ASSESSMENT AS AT 15th SEPTEMBER 1812

Theoretically the Corps numbered 18 000 men at the outset; it lost some in the fighting and on the way. At the Moskova only 10 000 were available, commanded by a general who was almost mad. For the Russians, the 8th Corps had 12 000 at the Moskova. This figure appeared very exaggerated for those present at the battle. At Mojaisk after the battle, the 8th Corps was left to defend the ambulances. It numbered 135 officers and 2 370 infantrymen, about 1 000 for the artillery and the train, together with 65 officers and 710 men, of which 548 were mounted.

A number of units were seconded as follows:

From the Infantry of the 23rd Division. The 2nd and 3rd Lights, plus two battalions of the 3rd regiment were escorting the Imperial Treasury, i.e. 76 officers and 1 946 men. 600 men were at Ghjat, others at Orcha and the rest with the ambulances, the Abbey, etc.

From the Infantry of the 24th Division. About 100 at Orcha, almost 400 at Kubinskoi, 800 at Dorogobug and 600 at Viasma, others towards Grodno and Warsaw.

GENERAL JUNOT'S 8th ARMY CORPS
CAVALRY

Cavalryman,
Westphalian
1st Hussars

Cavalryman,
Westphalian
2nd Hussars

Driver,
Westphalian
Artillery Train

Cavalryman and Trumpeter;
Westphalian Chevau-Légers
Jérôme Napoléon's motto on the saddle
blanket

Westphalian
foot gunner

André Jouineau © Histoire & Collections 2000

THE CAVALRY RESERVE

MURAT'S STAFF

The chief of staff was General **Belliard**. Born in 1769 at Fontenay-le-Comte, general at Arcola. In Egypt with Dessaix. Major-General in 1800, count in 1810, he was wounded at Mojaisk on 8th September 1812. Colonel-General of the Cuirassiers, Pair de France during the 100 Days, struck off and arrested, he was freed in 1816 and became Peer of France again in 1819. Died in 1832, Ambassador to Bruxelles. GdCxLH in 1814.

His aides de camp were **Walsh** (died in August 1813), **Colonel Robert-Dubreuilh**, Belliard's nephew, born at Sables d'Olonne. Served in 1815 on the Rhine. Dismissed. Died in 1817.

DEPUTY CHIEF OF STAFF

— **Viscount de Borelli**, born in Lozère, wounded at the Moskova, general at Moscow, lieutenant-general in 1815, then in 1830. Peer of France in 1839, retired in 1848. Gd OLH in 1828. His aide de camp was **Marbot**, brother of the general, the author of famous memoirs but he was captured by the Russians on 27th July. Returned to France in 1815 and was a brigadier in 1835.

— The commander of the Headquarters was **General Déry**. Born in the Martinique, served in America. Volunteer in 1791 with the 12th Chasseurs. Wounded and captured at Marengo. Murat's aide de camp, then colonel in the 5th Hussars with Lasalle. General at Naples and Baron, wounded at Ostrowno, he was killed 18th October 1812 at Winkovo. The Palace Marshall was **Colonel de Picerno**.

MURAT'S AIDES DE CAMP

— **Prince de Bauffremont**, lieutenant, had a horse killed at the Moskova. Colonel at Naples, taken back as squadron commander in 1821. Honorary lieutenant-colonel in 1829.

— **Berthémy**, colonel, wounded at the Moskova, brigadier at Naples in 1813, then in France in 1823. In the Reserve in 1853. CtLH in 1812.

— **Pérignon**, captain in December 1812. **Cattanéo**, colonel, a Napolitan

Murat at the time he was Grand-Duke of Berg [1]. (painting by Gérard, Coll. Princess Murat).

Belliard

lieutenant-general on 15th September 1812 at Naples. Broke his arm at the Moskova. Re-instated in France in 1817. Honorary lieutenant-general.

— **de Béranger**, lieutenant from the 7th Hussars, a friend of Stendhal, died at Dresden.

— **Gobert**, wounded at Moscow, baron and colonel in 1814, brigadier later. CtLh in 1813.

— **Romœuf**, adjudant commanding, appointed general in the Napolitan army 15th September 1812. Returned to France in 1814. Baron in 1818, retired in 1835. Brother of the general killed at the Moskova. CrLH in 1821.

— **Prévost d'Arlincourt**, went to the *Elite Gendarmerie* on 15th September. Napolitan general, he returned to France in January 1815. Retired in 1816, LH 9th August 1812.

— **de Rossetti,** Napolitan general, wounded at Austerlitz and Heilsberg. Reinstated in 1830 as brigadier. Died 1840, CrLH in 1831.

The other officers of the staff were:

— **Lieutenant de Coussy,** auditor for the Conseil d'Etat in 1813. died in 1853. Murat's treasurer. OLH in 1813.

— **General Lambert** was in the suite and returned. Died 1814.

— **de Soulaigre,** emigrated for 12 years, dismissed in 1815.

— **Second-Lieutenant de Girardin** was wounded three times in 1813, general in 1848, LH in 1815, CrLH.

— **Squadron Commander Laboullaye** participated in the campaign with Murat at his own expense, he was in the Guard of Honour in 1813.

— **General Lamer**, inspecteur des Revues, died at Beresina.

— **Commissaire Ordonnateur Clapier**, captured on 13th January 1813. Served in 1815, LH in Year XII.

— **Péborde**, Murat's Surgeon, returned.

— **Lechat**, Murat's secretary, author of memoirs, was at Vilna in September 1812.

NANSOUTY'S 1st CAVALRY CORPS

Nansouty

— **Nansouty,** colonel-general of the dragoons in 1813. Wounded in the knee by a bullet at the Moskova, died in February 1815. Grand Aigle of the LH in 1807.

His aides de camp were:

— **de Périgord,** future Duke of Talleyrand, concussed at the Moskova, brigadier in 1818, retired in 1879.

— **d'Hervilly**, lieutenant in the 9th Cuirassiers. Squadron Commander in 1814, was **Caulaincourt's brother-in-law** and was discharged in 1821 as a lieutenant-colonel. LH at Moscow.

The chief of staff was **Viscount de**

Saint-Henry, general in 1813, viscount in 1818, died of over-indulgence in 1829. His deputies were **Dentzel** (son of the general, wounded at the Moskova by a bullet, squadron commander with the 6 Hussars in 1813, arrested in 1816 for having taken the regimental eagles away, released by Despinoy), **de Prunelle**, appointed captain, was with Latour-Maubourg in 1813. The commisaire was **de Hémant de la Douie**, Egyptian Campaign, captured at Aboukir, served in 1814.

THE ARTILLERY

— **Major Chopin**, appointed colonel, was captured and returned from captivity in 1814, retired in 1815.

---

1. Murat wore a uniform decribed in three different ways at the Moskova. For Faber du Faur, he had a big hat with a soft plume and several white panaches. This is how he showed him in the picture in black. He wore a blue greatcoat covered in gold embroidery, white trousers and soft beige boots.
For Lejeune, his hairstyle was different, the coat and the trousers were light blue and he wore a cape. It was Faber's solution which was taken up by Job.

With Bruyères Division:

3 officers and 74 artillerymen of the 7th Company of the 6th Light, serving 4 6-pounders and 2 howitzers. Captain Lanson, decorated at Moscow, colonel in 1821, brigadier in 1835 at Alger. **Lieutenant Darcel** resigned after Waterloo, captain of the Guard. **Dabadie**, retired as squadron commander in 1830.

With the Saint-Germain division:

— **Squadron Commander Pons**. American Campaign, wounded at the Moskova, retired in 1813. LH in Year XII, his deputy was **Cartier**, squadron commander in 1830, decorated in Moscow.

the 1st and 3rd companies of the 5th Lights, serving 8 6-pounders and 4 24-pound howitzers.

Three officers died , one at the Moskova and 2 at the end of the retreat. Two were captured and returned from captivity, and retired afterwards.

With the Valence Division:

— **Battalion Commander Marthez**, lost his right arm at the Moskova, retired, OLH at Moscow.

The 4th and 6th Companies of the 5th Lights, serving 8 6-pounders and 4 24-pound howitzers (134 artillerymen). Two officers were killed, one at the Moskova and one captured, returned in 1814.

For the 6th, two officers listed as dead by Martinien in fact returned from captivity. **Lieutenant Judey**, born at Abbeville, was colonel in 1839.

Three officers of the 11bis transport returned. They had 255 men

I. BRUYERE'S DIVISION

— **Bruyères**, mentioned at Marengo, baron, then major-general in 1809, wounded at the Moskova and replaced by **Jaquinot**, died on 5th June 1813, both legs taken off by a cannonball. Decorated in Year XII, CtLH.

Bruyères

His aides de camp were **squadron Commander Gauthier**, born like the General at Sommières in the Gard, wounded at the Moskova, then killed at Borisov. **Vesseron** was captured at Beresina, returned from captivity, served in 1815 and dismissed, became captain of the firemen at Sedan.

The staff was composed of **Adjudant-Commander Tavernier**, wounded on 25th July, he was not definitely at the Moskova. He was wounded seven times and was Honorary brigadier in 1822. LH in Year XII. One of the deputies was missing at the end of December and the other returned

JAQUINOT'S BRIGADE

— **General Jaquinot**, volunteer in 1791, major-general in 1813, served in 1815, Peer of France in 1837, died at Metz. At the Moskova, he was mentioned as fighting to the end with his soldiers, at the head of 280 remaining mounted cavalrymen. On th 18th October, he only had 50 cavalrymen left, decorated Year XII, GdOLH in 1844.

His aides de camp were:

— **Dupuy**, author of memoirs, named squadron commander at Moscow in the 7th Hussars. Was *Sous-Préfet* at Cognac in 1830. In his memoirs he stated that the division, arriving at Moscow, only had a thousand horses left and had been heavily engaged at Ostrovno and then at Valoutina.

— **Delacroix**, a cousin of the general, squadron commander in 1813, retired in 1837.

THE 7th HUSSARS.

This regiment has been closely studied, verifying not only the officers but also the registers of the horsemen with the following results.

On 15th July there were 37 officers and 880 cavalrymen present. 3 officers and 181 men were at the little depots at Elbing and Insterburg. On 31st July there were 21 officers and 661 men present, 10 officers and 385 men were seconded to the

depots in the rear. 44 cavalrymen were missing and 46 were in hospitals in Germany. On 25th July, at Ostrovno, 3 officers were killed and 6 wounded. In the other fights before the Moskova, one officer was killed. So 4 officers killed, 11 wounded who were missing on 7th September.

At the Moskova, 1 officer killed and 4 wounded. 7 Hussars, of whom 2 officers received the LH at Moscow. During the whole campaign, 8 officers were killed in Russia, 4 missing and 3 captured but returned. The regiment thus lost 12 officers out of 37. It must be added that 12 second-lieutenants were appointed in Russia to replace the casualties. At the end of the retreat, at Gumbingen, Dupuy says that there were only 120 men left in the regiment of whom 20 were mounted and remained together during the retreat. For the men it is more difficult as the registers only give brief details. 61 died in Russia, 20 before the Moskova. 552 men were counted as missing, captured or deserted. 60 escaped or returned from captivity or joined their regiment late. Among these prisoners who returned, a certain **Robin** who served in the Zouaves in 1835. Thus, 492 men disappeared in Russia out of the 940 who were supposed to be present on the 15th June 1812 at the crossing of the Niemen. This is of course an approximation based on the registers and a lot of the soldiers returning from captivity in Russia were not accounted for. There is one important fact concerning this regiment, like many others: the origins of these cavalrymen, considered as French when many came from conquered territories of the Empire, but who had only recently become French.

The origins of these cavalrymen of the 7th Hussars has been gone into and out of the 2 850 on the registers of the period, the origins were as follows:

Escaut (Gand): 194 men; Jemmapes (Charleroi): 190; Ourthe (Liège): 67; Sambre et Meuse (Namur): 7; des Forêts (Luxembourg): 3; Dyle (Bruxelles): 10; Lys (Bruges): 31; Lower Meuse (Maastricht): 93; Roer (Cologne): 195; Mont-Tonnerre (Mainz): 174; Saar:71; Deux Nèthes (Antwerp): 66; Rhine and Mosel (Coblenz): 5 and finally 34 men of various origins.

In all this represented 1 140 men on the rolls of principally Belgian and German origins. Some, among those who had been to Russia, must have returned to their town or village, not in a hurry to rejoin the French army. Moreover, a lot of recruits came from the departments of the Upper and Lower Rhine, the Moselle and the Meurthe. This was thus a regiment where a lot of German was spoken.

Special cases:

— **Colonel Eulner**, born near Trèves, honorary brigadier in 1822, wounded and one horse killed at the Moskova.

— **Lieutenant Calvé de Soursac**, lost his right leg at the Moskova, captured at Vilna, wounded twice with a sabre, thrown from his waggon and stripped. Returned in September 1814. Served in 1821 as a captain in the 21st Chasseurs in spite of his handicap.

— **Second-Lieutenant Korte**, born in the Grand-Duchy of Berg, was colonel of the 1st African Chasseurs in 1840, brigadier in 1843, major-general in 1848. Served in Africa from 1832 to 1843, died in 1858. GdCxLH in 1857.

THE 9th *CHEVAU-LÉGERS* (EX-30th CHASSEURS).

As at the 15th June it included: 43 officers and 664 cavalrymen in four squadrons; on 31st July there were only 33 officers and 472 men with only 409 horses. Six officers and 46 men were seconded for Naploeon's correspondance. 5 officers and 100 men were in the hospitals, 79 lost and 6 captured. at the Moskova, 6 officers were wounded plus two doubtful cases. In all in Russia, they lost 4 officers killed, 17 missing and 8 captured returning from captivity.

Special cases:

— **Colonel Gobrecht**, general in 1813, served at Waterloo, taken back in 1830. Many of the officers came from the conquered territories or from abroad and among the French, 4 former émigrés had served with Austria or in Russia.

PIRE'S BRIGADE

— **General Piré**, emigrated, wounded at Quiberon. Returned to the service of France, mentioned at Austerlitz, colonel fo the 7th Chasseurs. Baron in 1808, major-general in 1813, served in 1815, was at Roquencourt. Outlawed, returned in 1830, died in 1850. Born in Rennes, LH in 1807, CtLH in 1813, GdOLH in 1834.

His aides de camp were **de Motboucher** (squadron commander in 1813, amputated at Leipzig), **de Castelbajac** wounded on 25 July 1812, wounded at the Moskova, squadron commander of the 16th Chasseurs, destituted, colonel in 1815. Brigadier in 1826. Lieutenant-general in 1840 in Algeria, ambassador to Russia in 1849. LH in 1812, Gd OLH in 1847.

THE 8th HUSSARS

— **Du Coetlosquet**, colonel of the regiment on 11th August 1812, replacing Domon, appointed general with Murat. Wounded at the Moskova, general in 1813, lieutenant-general in 1821, Minister of War, Conseiller d'Etat, discharged in 1830.

On the 31st July 1812 the regiment included 33 officers and 745 cavalrymen, short of 20 horses. 2 officers and 182 men were seconded to the depots, 3 officers and 119 were in the hospitals, 11 riders were captured. At the Moskova, 4 officers were wounded. In all for the Russian Campaign, 5 officers were killed, 2 missing and 3 captured but returned from captivity.

Special Cases:

— **Count of Argout**, squadron commander, brigadier in 1823.

— **de Ségur**, son of the Grand-Master of Ceremonies, wounded five times at Vilna on 28th June 1812 and was captured. Died in 1818, squadron commander of the Guard.

— **Potier**, colonel in 1828, brigadier in 1840, died in 1859.

THE 16th CHASSEURS.

On 31st July 1812, it had 29 officers and 557 men, missing 67 horses from the squadrons; 11 officers and 215 cavalrymen were detached to the depots, 3 officers and 72 men were at the hospitals, 2 officers and 17 men were captured. At the Moskova, one officer was killed and 7 wounded (two doubtful cases). In all for the campaign, 7 officers killed, 2 missing and 4 captured but returned.

Special cases:

— **Captain Romanet**, wounded at the Moskova, colonel in 1825.

— **Lieutenant Robert de Ste Croix**, count in 1810, inheriting the title of his brother killed in Spain. Lost a leg at the Moskova, retired in 1813, he was an auditor at the Conseil d'Etat, then Mayor of Argentan in 1849 and deputy of the Orne in 1850. Died in 1860.

ROUSSEL D'HURBAL'S BRIGADE

— **Roussel d'Hurbal** was in the service of Austria in 1782. Austrian general returned to French service in 1811. Wounded at the Moskova and appointed major-general, wounded at Waterloo, viscount in 1822. Died in 18494, GdOLH in 1846.

His aide de camp **Huot**, was battalion commander in 1813 in the Gendarmerie. He was dismissed by the King for theft.

THE 6th POLISH LANCERS

It numbered 22 officers and 246 men on 31st July 1812 instead of the 34 officers and 643 men announced on 15th June. At the Moskova, this regiment was even more reduced. One officer killed, **Major Suchorewski** and 7 officers wounded. At Moscow, 19 lancers were decorated, of whom 8 officers.

THE 8th POLISH LANCERS.

Numbered 21 officers and 462 men on 31st July 1812, commanded by **Colonel Radziwill**. At the Moskova, there were 1 officer killed and 5 wounded. At Moscow, 17 men were decorated, including one officer.

THE 2nd PRUSSIAN HUSSARS.

On 31st July, **Major von Zieten** had 22 officers and 412 men at his disposal. At the Moskova one officer was killed and 6 wounded. 11 officers were decorated on 9th August after the battle at Ostrowno. Lieutenant **von Kalkreuth** wrote his memoirs. Five officers were decorated at Moscow.

AN ASSESSMENT OF THE DIVISION

Dupuy says that there were only 1 000 cavalrymen at the Moskova, then 400 at Moscow. Murat mentioned them in connection with the fight for the Russian outposts. In all for the campaign, for the French, 24 officers killed, 25 missing and 18 prisoners returned. On 20th November 1812, the 1st and the 3rd Cavalry Corps together only had 176 officers and 157 mounted cavalrymen, together with 203 officers and 1 870

men armed with rifles or carbines, on foot. It is certain that between 31st July (192 officers ans 3 770 men) and 7th September, the loss of men increased through fighting and the men left behind. The march from Smolensk to the Moskova, done en masse by Murat, caused a number of horses to be lost before the battle.

II. SAINT-GERMAIN'S DIVISION

— **General St-Germain**, wounded at the Moskova, count in 1813, inactive in 1815, taken back in 1830, died in 1835, GdOLH in 1814.

His aides de camp were **Squadron Commander Baguet** (OLH in 1813), **Lieutenant Berger** (squadron commander in 1821, LH in 1813, OLH).

The staff was composed of **De Laville** (*émigré* returned about 1800, baron then count, general in 1813. and his deputy **Ravault** de Kerboux (2 horses killed at the Moskova, squadron commander in 1814, major in 1835, retired in 1843).

THE ARTILLERY.

7 officers and 312 men at the Moskova (1st and 3rd Companies of the 5th Light). They had 8 6-pounders and 4 24-pound howitzers.

— **Squadron Commander Pons** served in America from 1779-1782, wounded at the Moskova, retired in 1813.

— **Captain Pache**, battalion commander in 1813, lieutenant-colonel, then colonel in 1822, made baron by Charles X, retired in 1832.

— **Lieutenant Froussard** had two horses killed. One officer was killed at the Moskova, two captured and returned (listed as dead by Martinien).

BRUNO'S BRIGADE.

— **General Bruno**, born in Pondichéry, a nephew of Law of Lauriston. Grand Equerry of Holland. Served at Waterloo, died in 1861. His aide de camp was **d'Arcy**, a former page of the King of Holland, died of phtisis in 1814.

THE 2nd CUIRASSIERS.

— **Colonel Baron Rolland**, mentioned at the Moskova, amputated at Wachau and appointed general commanding the Invalides, died in 1848.

On 5th August 1812, the regiment had 31 officers and 459 cavalrymen, 6 officers and 480 men were seconded to the rear at Kovno, at Hannover, 26 were in the hospitals. At the Moskova one officer was killed and 7 wounded. In all for the campaign, 4 were killed and one disappeared, 2 prisoners returned.

Special cases:

— Ten officers were part of *the sacred squadron* and **Squadron Commander Dubois** commanded as from Moscow 4 000 cavalrymen on foot, 3 000 others being put under the command of Dessaignes of the 1st Cuirassiers.

— **Thirion**, non-commisioned officer, called *'de Metz'*, left souvenirs, was a captain in 1822. He recorded especially that the regiment was placed to the right of the Semenovskoi ravine in front of Junot's Westphalians.

BESSIERE'S BRIGADE.

— **General Bessières**, brother of the Marshall, wounded at the Moskova, inactive in 1815, taken back 1818. CtLH in 1813. His aide de camp **d'Haucourt** was wounded at the Moskova, a captain in Saumur in 1820 and dismissed in 1822.

THE 3rd CUIRASSIERS.

On the 5th August 1812, the regiment had 31 officers and 587 men Five officers and 440 men were in the rear, in the depots and 27 in the hospitals. At the Moskova, one officer was killed and 14 wounded. For the whole of the campaign, 3 officers were killed, 6 disappeared and 2 returned from captivity. Three officers were appointed in Russia.

Special case:

— **Second-Lieutenant de Rilliet** (had a brother in the 1st Cuirassiers, author of memoirs), was a general in 1848, then major-general in 1851 and died at Strasburg in 1853.

QUEUNOT'S BRIGADE.

The general was wounded at the Moskova by a cannonball on his right thigh. Retired in 1813.

FIRST CAVALRY RESERVE CORPS
1st LIGHT CAVALRY DIVISION

Cavalryman from
the 7th Hussars

Cavalryman from
the 30th Mounted
Chasseurs

Cavalryman from
the 8th Hussars
regiment

Cavalryman from
the 16th Mounted
Chasseurs

Cavalryman from
the 2nd Prussian
Hussars

Cavalryman from
the 8th Polish
Lancers

Cavalryman from
the 6th Polish Lancers

André Jouineau © Histoire & Collections 2000

THE 9th CUIRASSIERS.

— **Colonel Murat-Sestrières**, wounded at the Moskova, appointed general in 1813, lost a leg at Dresden and retired afterwards.

At the beginning the regiment crossed the Niemen with 34 officers, 900 cavalrymen and 970 horses, a theoretically official number. On the 5th August, the regiment had 34 officers and 534 cavalrymen. 4 officers and 437 men were in the rear, of which one marching squadron which did not go beyond Vilna or Borisov. There were only 100 horses left per squadron. At the Moskova, 4 officers and 10 cavalrymen were killed, one was captured and missing believed dead and 9 wounded. For the whole of the campaign, 8 officers were killed, 8 were listed as missing and 4 returned from captivity two of which were considered as dead by Martinien.

Special Cases

— Two officers received a Sabre of Honour, another was one of the first to to be decorated at the Boulogne camp. All three returned directly and were retired later.

— **Second-Lieutenant de Chalendard** ended up as brigadier in 1846. In a letter dated January 1813, one captain stated that the regiment did not charge at the Moskova.

THE 1st LANCERS.

At the Moskova, it only had two weakened squadrons commanded by **Squadron Commander Dumanoir**, who was killed at Waterloo.

On the 5th august, 14 officers and 209 cavalrymen were present. At the Moskova, 2 officers were wounded. For the whole of the campaign, there were 2 dead, 4 missing and 4 returned in 1814.

Special cases:

— **Colonel Dermoncourt**, joined up at Moscow with re-inforcements on 11th October 1812. He was promoted general in 1813. Egyptian Campaign, baron. Served in 1815 and was implicated in Belfort. In 1832 he was in Brittany, CtLH.

— **Captain Vaudeville**, born at St-Nicolas du Port (Meurthe) was recruited whilst still a seminarist in 1793. He was *"bravery itself"*. Squadron commander in 1813, dismissed in 1815, wounded 8 times. Became a canon at Nancy and died in 1840. LH in Year XII, OLH in 1813.

GENERAL ASSESSMENT OF THE DIVISION

At the Moskova, the division aligned 1 800 cavalrymen and artillerymen with their 36 pieces. 7 officers were killed and 37 wounded, of whom 1 artilleryman killed and one wounded. In Russia, in all, 17 dead plus one artilleryman, 19 missing and 14 returned from captivity. 61 officers were part of the 1st Company of *the sacred squadron*.

III. VALENCE 'S DIVISION

This general was with Dumouriez in 1793, senator. Recalled in 1808, left Moscow ill on 25th September. Egyptian Campaign, retired in 1824.

REYNAUD'S BRIGADE

The general was retired in 1824. Egyptian Campaign.

THE 6th CUIRASSIERS.

— **Colonel Baron Martin** lost his right arm at Waterloo.

At the Moskova, one officer was killed, 2 officers wounded. There were 22 cavaliers killed and 26 wounded. 85 horses were killed. It seems therefore that the regiment ensured the protection of the artillery (2 companies of the 5th Light). In Russia, in all 5 officers were killed, 3 disappeared and 4 prisoners returned.

DEJEAN'S BRIGADE

The general became Napoleon's aide de camp in 1813 and major-general. Exiled, he returned in 1818. Peer in 1824, died in 1847, GdCXLH in 1843

THE 11th CUIRASSIERS

— **Colonel Duclaux**, Egyptian Campaign, general in 1813.

In the beginning: 33 officers and 650 men. At the Moskova, one officer was wounded and six had horses killed, so this officer probably did not charge, remaining in support. In all in Russia, 4 officers killed and 7 disappeared, 7 prisoners returning.

— **Squadron Commander Gusler** was a brigadier in 1832.

LAGRANGE'S BRIGADE.

— **Lelièvre, Comte de Lagrange**, commanded the Imperial quarters during the retreat. Peer in 1832, senator in 1859.

THE 12th CUIRASSIERS

One officer killed and 6 wounded at the Moskova, three of them with their horses killed by a cannon ball, all their wounds caused by cannonballs or shrapnel. The regiment probably remained in support. In Russia, 9 dead, 9 missing and 4 returned.

THE 5th *CHEVAU-LÉGERS*.

Only one squadron to start with under the command of **Squadron Commander Guérin**. Colonel Chabert who had served in America was honorary brigadier in 1816. At the Moskova, two offficers were wounded. In Russia in all, 3 officers dead, 8 missing and 5 prisoners who returned.

GENERAL ASSESSMENT OF THE DIVISION

At the Moskova, 2 officers wer killed and 11 wounded. The division was probably kept in support. In Russia for the campaign, 20 officers were killed, 27 were missingand 20 prisoners returned.

OVERALL ASSESSMENT FOR THE CORPS

This is difficult to establish for the light division, since the rolls for the foreign regiments are missing. Jaquinot had only 280 mounted cavalrymen with him at the end of the battle. At the Moskova there were 15 officers killed and 93 wounded. The light cavalry had 5 officers killed, 44 wounded.

The cuirassiers had 9 officers killed and 48 wounded, plus two artilerymen casualties, one wounded the other killed. It can be deduced that a few more than 150 cavalrymen were killed for this corps which was not engaged very much, but which lost a lot of horses to the Russian artillery.

In Russia for the whole campaign, 65 offciers dead, 67 missing and 52 prisoners who returned in 1814 or 1815.

MONTBRUN'S 2nd CAVALRY CORPS

During the Battle, the general, a worthy successor to Lasalle, tried to find a more sheltered place for his men. At that precise moment he received a cannon ball in the chest, killing him. Auguste de Caulaincourt was appointed to succeed him.

His aides de camp were **Huber** (lieutenant-general in 1823), **Martin** and **de Lindsay** returned directly. **Calon** was captured in December but returned.

The Chief of staff was **Wathiez**, general in 1813 and baron. He was suspended for disobedience in 1814, wounded at Waterloo. Taken back in 1822, viscount in 1822, lieutenant-general in 1837, GdOLH in 1843.

THE ARTILLERY

Companies from the 2nd Light Artillery Regiment and from the 1st. Among the officers **Baron Séruzier**, captured in December and returned;

— **Captain Legriel**, brigadier in 1840, died in 1868.

— **Lieutenant Schmitt,** lost his right arm at the Moskova;

— **Lieutenant Mayol de Lupé**, captured on 18th October 1812, returned from Russia;

— **Lieutenant André**, general in 1852.

FIRST CAVALRY RESERVE CORPS
1st AND 5th CUIRASSIERS'S DIVISIONS

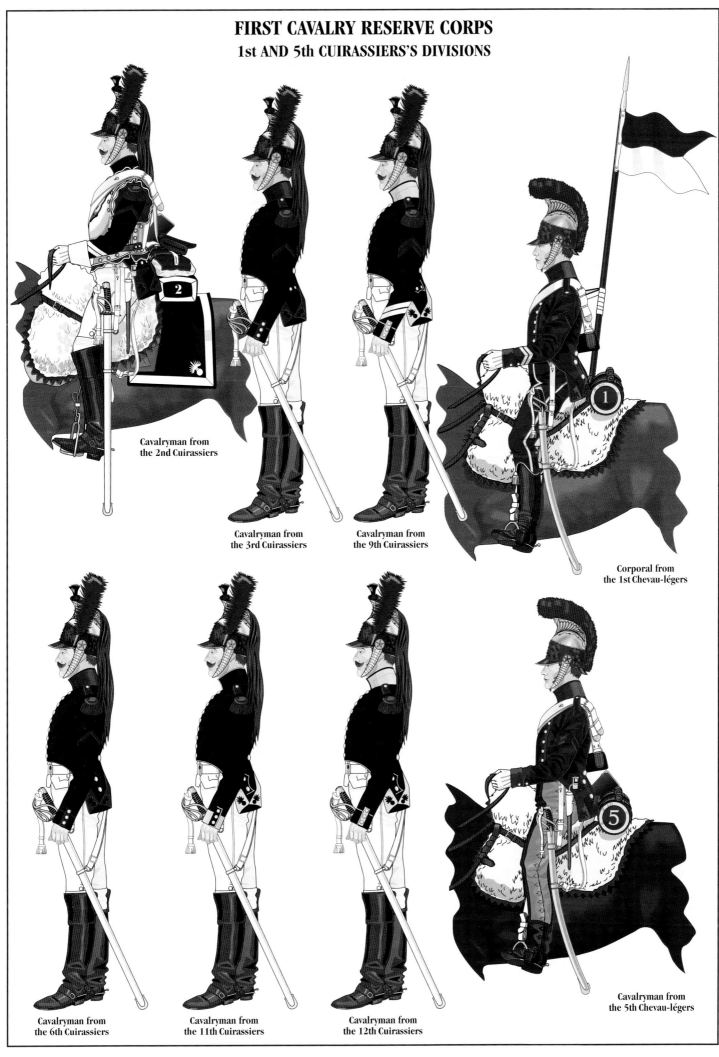

Cavalryman from
the 2nd Cuirassiers

Cavalryman from
the 3rd Cuirassiers

Cavalryman from
the 9th Cuirassiers

Corporal from
the 1st Chevau-légers

Cavalryman from
the 6th Cuirassiers

Cavalryman from
the 11th Cuirassiers

Cavalryman from
the 12th Cuirassiers

Cavalryman from
the 5th Chevau-légers

André Jouineau © Histoire & Collections 2000

Montbrun   Pajol

I. PAJOL'S LIGHT CAVALRY DIVISION

— **Pajol** was at the head of the division, he replaced Sébastiani.

BURTHE'S BRIGADE

The general was wounded at the Moskova, captured on 14th November, returned in 1814.

THE 5th HUSSARS

— **Colonel Meuziau**, wounded at the Moskova, general in 1813, then lieutenant-general in 1825.

At the Moskova, three officers were killed and 16 wounded. For some offficers, details are available of their wounds. For example some received lance wounds, others bullet wounds. **Second-Lieutenant Hartmann** was wounded while capturing an artillery piece in the great redoubt. The regiment was therefore heavily engaged to the right of the redoubt and fought also against the Russian cavalry. The regiment which on the 1st July had 34 officers and 691 men only had 28 officers and 375 men left at the review at Moscow on 20th September. Only 249 of the cavalrymen were mounted. In all in Russia, 7 officers dead, 3 missing and 6 captured who returned from captivity.

Special Cases:

— **Second-Lieutenant d'Hane de Steinhuyse**, a Belgian, was a general in 1831, and Grand Equerry to King Leopold in 1836.

— **Duval**, born in Mons, general in 1830.

THE 9th HUSSARS

— **Colonel Maignet** had two horses killed. He commanded the Department of the Charente in 1814.

At the Moskova, 2 officers were killed and 5 wounded. In all in Russia, 5 officers dead, 2 missing and 3 returned from prison. The regiment had 21 officers and 721 men of whom only 652 were mouted on the 1st July. At the Moscow review, the numbers had fallen to 20 officers and 142 cavalrymen with their horses.

Special case:

— **Squadron Commander Marquis de Faudoas-Barbazan**, exiled colonel in 1815, was a brigadier in 1829. Served in Africa, the lieutenant-general in 1838, died in Bordeaux in 1844.

SAINT-GENIES' BRIGADE.

The general, of the Egyptian Campaign where he commanded the "Dromadaries". Wounded and captured on 15th July, returned in 1814. Served in 1815, inactive until 1818, viscount in 1822. Lieutenant-General in 1835. GdOLH in 1832. His position was held at the Moskova by Colonel Désirat of the 11th Chasseurs.

THE 11th CHASSEURS.

Colonel **Désirat** was killed during the battle.

On 1st July, 27 officers and 582 men, already 19 horses were missing. At the Moskova, one officer killed and 5 wounded. One of them received 25 lance wounds and was left for dead. Captured on 18th October and then listed as missing. Among the men, 35 were killed and 52 wounded. For the whole campaign, 6 officers dead, 4 missing and 4 prisoners who returned in 1814. At Moscow, there were only 234 cavalrymen left of whom only 174 were mounted.

Special cases:

— **Nicolas**, replaced the colonel; heros of Arcola. Brigadier in 1823, died in 1854.

LH in Year XII.

— **Baron Morlant**, son of the colonel of the Chasseurs à cheval of the Guard killed at Austerlitz, wounded at the Moskova, decorated at Moscow, wounded twice in 1813, died in February 1815.

— **de Lesparda** commanded the first platoon to enter Moscow. He was a colonel with the 4th Hussars in 1838, retired in 1840.

— **Guichard**, colonel of the 3rd Cuirassiers in 1841.

THE 12th CHASSEURS.

— **Colonel Ghigny** wounded on 8th August, LH in Year XII. Replaced by **de la Bourdonnaye**, who although wounded remained at his post as long as possible. Brigadier in 1821, died in 1844.

At the Moskova, 2 officers killed and 11 wounded. The losses for the men 19 cavalrymen killed, 68 wounded or dismounted out of 280 drawn up. The Moscow review gave 29 officers and 421 men partially mounted. The numbers must have been exaggerated. LHs were awarded. In Russia, 10 officers killed, 1 missing and 5 captured but returned in 1814.

Special cases:

— **de Chabannes de la Palice**, captured in December, returned. General in 1830.

— **de Basseville**, colonel in 1840 with the 9th Dragoons. Brigadier in 1846.

— Two officers left memoirs: **Aubry** and **Ducque**.

SUBERVIE'S BRIGADE

— **Subervie** was born in Lectoure like Lannes, wounded at the Moskova. In theory he commanded, three foreign regiments which at Moscow only had 500 cavalrymen left. These regiments were according to the numbers drawn up at Moscow: the 1st Prussian Lancers (1 officier killed and three wounded), the 3rd Wurtemberg Mounted Chasseurs (1 killed and 6 wounded) and the 10th Polish Hussars (1 officer killed and 7 wounded).

II. WATIER DE ST ALPHONSE'S DIVISION

The general, a count, was at Waterloo and placed in the reserve in 1839. An aide de camp, **Dupont d'Herval**, was killed at the Moskova.

THE ARTILLERY

It included the 1st and 4th Companies of the 2 Light. They had 8 6-pounders and 4 24-pound howitzers. **Squadron Commander Romangin** was killed at the Moskova. **Captain Legriel** was general in 1840.

BEAUMONT'S BRIGADE

The general was on the Egyptian Campaign, promoted major-general in Russia. He died at Metz on 16th December 1813. His aide decamp, **Devin de Fontenat**, wounded when entering among the first the Great Redoubt. Lieutenant-colonel in 1814, died February 1815.

THE 5th CUIRASSIERS

— **Colonel Christophe**, escaped from the English prison Hulks in 1810, retired as honorary brigadier in 1830. LH in Year XII, OLH at Moscow.

On the 31st July, the regiment had 33 officers and 539 men; at the Moskova, one officer was killed and 7 wounded. 11 cavalrymen are known to have been killed and 7 captured. The wounded were wounded by bayonets. At Moscow the figures fell to 28 officers and 406 cavalrymen with only 286 horses. Re-inforcements of 4 officers and 106 men reached Moscow where 5 crosses of the LH were awarded, of which one to the **veterinary-surgeon Bourjat**. In all for the campaign, 4 officers killed, 4 missing and 2 prisoners returned in 1814.

Special cases:

— **Captain de Vergez** was squadron commander of the Gendarmerie in Algiers in 1832.

— **Captain Rémy** received a Sabre of Honour, baron in 1813 and retired after Waterloo.

— **Captain de Jouvancourt**, captured General Likhatchev in the redoubt. Dismissed in 1815, he returned to the Ile Bourbon where he was born and where he commanded the militia until his death in 1826.

SECOND CAVALRY RESERVE CORPS
2nd LIGHT CAVALRY DIVISION

Cavalryman from
the Elite Company of
the 5th Hussars

Cavalryman from
the 9th Hussars

Cavalryman from
the 11th Mounted
Chasseurs

Cavalryman from
the 10th Polish Hussars

Cavalryman from
the 12th Mounted
Chasseurs

Cavalryman from
the 3rd Wurtemberger
Mounted Chasseurs

Cavalryman from
the 1st Prussian
Lancers

André Jouineau © Histoire & Collections 2000

— **Captain de Lampinet**, born in Vesoul in 1781. Emigrated, he served in Condé's army, then in Russian service until 1801. wounded at Austerlitz and at Wagram. Wounded by bayonet at the Moskova, captured on 18th October 1812, after receiving 6 new wounds. Returned June 1814. Retired as squadron commander in 1828.

—**Second-Lieutenant du Pré** finished up as a Belgian general. Wounded and had two horses killed at the Moskova.

33% of the Cuirassiers came from conquered territories. On the registers, 117 men are stated as being back from the Russian Campaign, 431 are listed as missing and 18 returned from the prisons.

Defrance

DORNE'S BRIGADE.

The general died at Vilna on 29th November: His aide de camp, **Vast-Vimeux** was a general after 1830.

THE 8th CUIRASSIERS.

— **Colonel Baron Grandjean** was wounded in the great redoubt. Wounded at Waterloo, retired in 1816.

At the Moskova, 2 officers were killed and 16 wounded (for 6 of them "in the great redoubt" is mentioned). At Moscow, theoretically there were 34 officers and 518 men of whom 387 mounted. In all in Russia, 4 officers dead, 4 missing and 1 returned from prison.

Special cases:

— **Baillencourt** was colonel in the 1st Cuirassiers of the Guard in 1824. With him was his brother, a captain who died of his wounds in 1813 at Mainz.

— **Second-Lieutenant Gobin** wounded by bayonets when he rushed upon a group of Russian infantry which was trying to return into the redoubt. He was major with the 5th Chasseurs in 1829. OLH in 1829

On the registers there were 360 men dead or missing in Russia and 32 returned from captivity.

RICHTER'S BRIGADE

— **General Baron Richter** was at the siege of Toulon, and on the Egyptian Campaign. CrLH in 1825.

THE 10th CUIRASSIERS.

— **Colonel Franck** retired. The newly-appointed colonel in command was with another marching regiment and was not at the battle.

At the Moskova, 1 officer killed and 7 wounded for what must have been a weak regiment. At Moscow there wer 35 offciers and 415 cavalrymen of which 88 without a horse.

— **Squadron Commander Béthune** was mentioned as being the first to enter the Russian squares, breached after the capture of the redoubt. Major in 1813, OLH in 1814.

— **Captain Schneikern**, a child of the regiment, was wounded at the Moskova and his horse killed.

— **Captain Duclos**, born in Bernot near St Quentin. Amputated at the Moskova, he was retired in 1813 when he got back.

During the campaign, 6 offciers dead, 6 missing and 3 prisoners returned.

THE 2nd *CHEVAU-LÉGERS*

— **Colonel Berruyer**, wounded 18th October. General in 1814. He was accused of having abandoned Soissons. Seriously wounded on 16th June 1815, he died in July 1816. LH in Year XII for Marengo, OLH at Moscow.

At the Moskova, 1 officer killed and 4 wounded. In all 4 officers died in Russia, 7 disappeared and 4 returned from Russian prisons. The regiment was very weak, with 2 squadrons. On 31st July it included 4 officers and 223 mounted cavalrymen. At Moscow, 5 officers and 113 cavalrymen.

Special cases:

— **Captain Canuet**, general in 1835.

A lot of the officers had taken part in the Egyptian Campaign because this regiment stemmed from the 3rd Dragoons. There were 8 veterans, 6 returned and survived the Empire.

III. DEFRANCE'S DIVISION (4th HEAVY CAVALRY)

— **General Count Defrance** was the son of a member of the Convention who voted against the King's death. Wounded at the Moskova. The King's Equerry. GdCxLH in 1829. His aide de camp **De Varaigne** was a brigadier in 1843. His chief of staff was **Adjudant-Commander Mergez** awarded a Sabre and two Pistols of Honour. He was captured, wounded on 18th October, served in 1815, promoted to the rank of honorary brigadier in 1823. Founded a mill at Chalons.

ARTILLERY.

— **Squadron Commander Parizet**, 3rd and 4th Companies of the 6th Heavy.

PAULTE DE LA MOTTE'S BRIGADE.

The general followed the King in 1815. Lieutenant-General in 1821, retired in 1830. His aide de camp, **Frémaux** was wounded at the Moskova. The other aide de camp **Robinet-Malleville** was wounded and captured on 18th October. When he returned he was declared unfit for military service due to his obesity.

THE 1st CARABINIERS

— **Colonel Laroche**, wounded twice at the Moskova, general in 1813. Commandant of the Charente, deputy in 1815. LH in Year XII

On 1st July the regiment had 38 officers and 676 men. On 7th September it had perhaps 500 men not all mounted. At the Moskova, 3 officers were killed, 3 captured and 11 wounded. In all for the whole of the campaign, 4 officers died, 3 disappeared and 4 prisoners returned.

Special cases:

— **Lieutenant de Lariboisière** was killed in the fighting against the Lifeguards.

— **Cruquenbourg de Fourneaux**, wounded by three bayonets, became a Belgian general, died in 1858. In June 1815 he was with Davout.

— **Second-Lieutenant Comte de la Rochejaquelin**, served for 6 years in the English Navy. Appointed to the regiment in 1809, he was wounded and captured in the middle of the Russian squares. Returned in 1814, brigadier in 1818, dismissed in 1830, taken back in 1831, he resigned refusing to swear an oath.

CHOUARD'S BRIGADE

The general was wounded twice at the Moskova and had health problems in 1813, retired in 1815 and taken back in 1830 until 1833. His aide de camp **Benoist** was a colonel in 1845.

THE 2nd CARABINIERS.

— **Colonel Blancard**, son of a Constituant member, received a Sabre of Honour; concussed at the Moskova, was a general in 1813, wounded at Waterloo; retired and taken back in 1830, lieutenant-general in 1835.

On 1st July, there were 37 officer and 650 cavalrymen. On 1st September about 500. At the Moskova, 2 officers and 22 men were killed and 12 captured, 13 officers wounded and 4 who had a horse killed. The wounds were made by sabres and twice by lances. For the whole campaign 11 officers killed and 6 prisoners all returned. On the registers there were 440 killed, captured or missing in Russia and 26 returned from prison for certain. Moreover, 235 cavalrymen are listed as having done the 1812 Campaign. Finally 23.3% of the men came from the conquered territories

Special cases:

— **Captain Benoit**, wounded twice in the left hand by a sabre at the Moskova. Holder of a Sabre of Honour in Year XII. Served in 1815 as squadron commander. Dismissed, he returned to his home at Soissons.

— **de Mailly**, son of the Marshall, was brought back wounded in one of Napoleon's carriages together with the Prince de Bauveau, wounded as well who was also second-lieutenant with the 1st Carabiniers.

BOUVIER DES ECLAZ'S BRIGADE.

The Baron general capitulated at the Hague in 1813 and was retired.

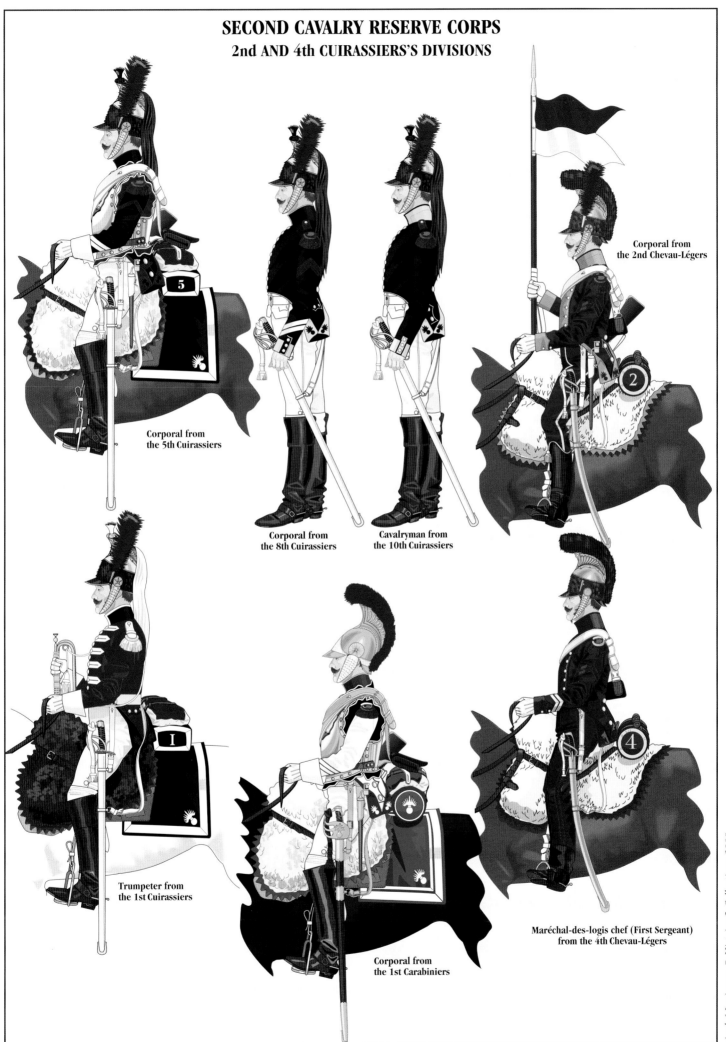

SECOND CAVALRY RESERVE CORPS
2nd AND 4th CUIRASSIERS'S DIVISIONS

Corporal from
the 5th Cuirassiers

Corporal from
the 8th Cuirassiers

Cavalryman from
the 10th Cuirassiers

Corporal from
the 2nd Chevau-Légers

Trumpeter from
the 1st Cuirassiers

Corporal from
the 1st Carabiniers

Maréchal-des-logis chef (First Sergeant)
from the 4th Chevau-Légers

André Jouineau © Histoire & Collections 2000

THE 1st CUIRASSIERS.

— **Colonel Clerc**, born in Lyon, was a brigadier in 1814, died in 1844, OLH after Austerlitz. GdOLH.

In the regiment on 1st July there were 37 officers and 475 mounted cavalry-men. In two months these figures dropped. At the Moskova, 3 officers were wounded. In all for the Russian Campaign, 3 officers died, 7 missing and 3 returned from captivity.

— **Squadron Commander Dessaignes**, received a Sabre of Honour in Year XI, commanded 3 000 dismounted cavalrymen at Moscow.

THE 4th CHEVAU-LÉGERS.

— **Colonel Deschamps** commanded a marching regiment which reached Moscow with re-inforcements for the division.

They were therefore not at the Moskova where the regiment had very little cavalry. It was Captain Faget who commanded the three companies who were present (1st July, 4 officers and 104 men). Two other regiments on the march were heading for Moscow with 121 oficers and 286 men. At the Moskova there was 1 officer killed and 1 was wounded. Captain Faget commanded 5 charges near the great redoubt.

GENERAL ASSESSMENT OF THE 2nd CORPS OF RESERVE CAVALRY

It is only possible to be precise for the officers. At the Moskova, there were 24 officers killed and 113 wounded. With regards to the number of cavalrymen killed during this battle, it must not be forgotten that this corps was fully committed so that we have the figures for casualties for the most exposed regiments. For the whole of the campaign, 61 officers died, 42 disappeared and 45 returned in 1814.

GROUCHY'S 3rd CAVALRY CORPS

— His aides de camp were **Carbonel** (wounded at the Moskova, brigadier in 1830, retired in 1841, OLH at Moscow, CrLH in 1830), **Rogé** (decorated at Moscow, heros of Vauchamp and promoted colonel on the battlefield, had seven horses killed at Waterloo where he charged at the head of the 1st Carabiniers; brigadier in 1832, died in 1854, **Gramont d'Aster** (wounded at the Moskova, decorated at Moscow, colonel in 1814, Peer of France in 1819, died in 1825), **le Doulcet de Pontécoulant**, younger brother of the Comtesse de Grouchy, straight out of St Cyr (Carbonel gave him riding lessons), wounded

Grouchy

on 24th November, presumed dead, captured, returned from prison, discharged, he left for Brazil).

— the chief of staff was the **Marquis de Jumilhac**, an *émigré*, took part at Quiberon. Taken back in 1808, wounded at the Moskova, general in 1818, then lieutenant-general he presided over the court-martial which had General Chartrand shot. Died in 1826.

ARTILLERY

— **Griois**, major in the 1st Heavy. Brigadier in 1823. OLH at Moscow. He had 16 6-pounders and 8 24-pound howitzers served by the 4th and 5th Companies of the 6th Light. One officer was reported missing and another captured but returned in 1814.

I. CHASTEL'S 3rd LIGHT CAVALRY DIVISION

—**General Chastel**, Egyptian and Italian Campaigns. Came from the Guard and served at Waterloo. Died in Geneva in 1826. CtLH in 1813.

— **De Lacroix** was his chief of staff. Made a general in 1815, cancelled then honorary. Re-instated in 1831, died in 1838.

GERARD'S BRIGADE.

No relation to the future marshall, the general was a major-general in 1813. Aide de camp to the Duke of Nemours in 1832, the year of his death. His own aide de camp, **Geoffroy**, returned and was squadron commander in 1830.

THE 6th CHASSEURS

— **Colonel Ledard** was wounded twice in the stomach in the redoubt and died the following day.

On the 1st August, the regiment had 29 officers and 460 men. It received re-inforcements later. At the Moskova, 1 officer was killed and 16 wounded, many

horses were killed. For the whole campaign, 2 officers killed and 6 missing (among whom three health officers and the holder of a sabre of Honour).

Special cases:

— **Squadron Commander Feuillebois**, took command after the colonel was wounded. A veteran from 1792, he had two horses killed but stayed at the head of the regiment. Major in 1813. LH in 1809.

— **Deconquans**, killed several Cossack but his horse was killed and he received several bayonet wounds when he entered a Russian square at the Moskova. Squadron Commander in 1813, he served at Waterloo and was a lieutenant-colonel in 1831.

— **Captain Quentin** went through the infantry twice at the head of the 1st Squadron causing terrible casualties, rallied the regiment and got his arm broken. During the retreat, he brought back 400 horsemen to the Vistula, congratulated by Murat.

— **Lieutenant Estève** had a horse killed and was wounded when entering among the first into a Russian square.

— **Lieutenant Carrion**, wounded four times and had two horses killed. One of the first to enter a square.

— **Second-Lieutenant Bezou** got himself noticed by rallying the cavalry for a charge against the Russian Lifeguards.

— **Second-Lieutenant Berger** charged 5 times and, although wounded, and remained on the battlefield until nightfall.

THE 25th CHASSEURS.

— **Colonel Christophe** received a Sabre of Honour. Wounded by a *biscayen* at the Moskova. General in 1813, retired in 1815. His brother was a colonel with the 5th Cuirassiers.

On the 1st August, the regiment had 22 officers and 436 mounted men. At the Moskova, 16 officers were wounded; in all for the Russian campaign, one officer died and 5 disappeared; one prisoner returned.

Special cases:

— **Comte de Potier**, squadron commander, replaced the colonel in spite of being concussed. Colonel in 1813, followed the King in 1815. Brigadier in 1817, died in 1840.

— **Captain Teynard** burst into a Russian square and charged against the cavalry. Decorated in Moscow, died in 1813, squadron commander.

— **Potier**, young sergeant, captured in September 1812, returned, in the Guard in November 1815. Colonel in 1848, general in 1854, went to Mexico and died in 1871.

GAUTHRIN'S BRIGADE

The general was captured "dying" on 19th November, returned in 1814, served at Ligny. His two aides de camp returned with him.

THE 6th HUSSARS.

— **Colonel Vallin**, general on 5th Decembeer 1812. Major-general during the

THIRD CAVALRY RESERVE CORPS
3rd LIGHT CAVALRY DIVISION AND DRAGOONS

Cavalryman from
the 25th Mounted
Chasseurs

Cavalryman from
the 6th Hussars

Cavalryman from
the 6th Mounted
Chasseurs

Corporal from
the 7th Dragoons

Cavalryman from
the 8th Mounted Chasseurs

Cavalryman from
the 23rd Dragoons

Cavalryman from
28th and 30th
Dragoons

Hundred Days; this was cancelled. Viscount in 1822, lieutenant-general in 1823. The son-in-law of Baron Garant, the Director of the Bank of France, LH in Year XII.

On 1st August, the regiment had 27 officers and 418 mounted men. Re-inforcements reached Moscow. At the Moskova, 3 officers were killed and 3 wounded. In all for Russia, 7 officers dead, 6 missing and 4 returned.

Special cases:

— **Nicolas**, appointed colonel of the 11th Chasseurs at Moscow. General in 1823.

—**Vilatte**, Bernadotte's former aide de camp, baron in 1818, brigadier in 1825.

— **Second-Lieutenant Raoul** was a brigadier in 1841. 2 horses killed at Ligny.

— **Urvoy de Closmadeuc**, Pirè's aide de camp in 1815. Brigadier in 1845.

— **Adjudant Moyard** captured at the Beresina, was colonel in the 1st Chasseurs in 1830 and went to Mehemet Ali in 1833. Died in 1833.

THE 8th CHASSEURS

— **Colonel Talleyrand**, nephew of Talleyrand, brigadier in 1814, lieutenant-general in 1823, OLH at Moscow.

On the 1st August, the regiment had 32 officers and 562 men. At the Moskova, 10 officers were wounded. In all for Russia, 2 officers killed and 6 missing; 4 captured returned.

Special Case

— **Squadron Commander Planzeaux**, born in Marseille in 1772, engaged at the age of 11, heros of 1813, Heros of St Dizier in 1814. Colonel in the 2nd Dragoons in 1815. Brigadier in 1831. retired in 1834. LH in Year XII, OLH.

II. DE LA HOUSSAYE'S DIVISION

The general was wounded at the Moskova, he was captured at Vilna and upon his return in 1814, was stood down. His aides de camp were captured with him One disappeared and two returned in 1814. Both were wounded at the Moskova.

— The chief of staff was **Caumont**, duc de la Force. An *émigré* who returned in 1807. Brigadier in 1814.

— Deputy chief of staff was **Dugommier**, called **Chevigny**, the third son of the general. He was qualified as a *"drunkard without talent"*. Captured he died in St Petersburg. Adjudant **Mathieu**, became a colonel in 1818; **Lauzer** died in Vilna.

ARTILLERY

Commanded by **Squadron Commander Reisser**, lieutenant-colonel in 1814. With the 4th and 5th Companies of the 6th Light.

THIRY'S BRIGADE

The general was the holder of a Sabre of Honour, was wounded three times at the Moskova. Retired in August 1815. CtLH. His two aides de camp returned.

THE 7th DRAGONS

—**Colonel de Sopransi** was the son of Madame Visconti. Captured General de Wimpfen at Austerlitz and received the LH for this act. Became Ber-

thier's aide de camp in 1807, wounded at the Moskova, general in 1813. Died in Paris in May 1814.

On the 1st August the regiment had 26 officers and 411 mounted cavalry. At the Moskova, one officer was killed and 10 wounded, many by sabre wounds or by bullets. For the whole campaign, 5 officers died, 12 were missing and 4 captured but returned. Three officers received Sabres of Honour.

THE 23rd DRAGOONS.

— **Colonel Briant**, was killed at Kovno. OLH in Year XII.

On 1st August the regiment had 25 officers and 399 mounted dragoons. At the Moskova, 2 officers and 60 dragoons were killed. 7 officers were wounded. Auvray, in his souvenirs said that half of his company only had half its numbers, the rest were dead, wounded or missing.

For the whole campaign, 5 officers dead, 8 missing and 8 returned from prison.

SERON'S BRIGADE

The general received a Sabre of Honour; was listed as missing during the retreat as well as his aide de camp **Legoupil**. The other aide, **Laveran**, from the 7th was wounded at the Moskova; served in the Scouts of the Guards and was dismissed in 1815.

THE 28th DRAGOONS

— **Colonel Pelletier de Montmarie**, commanded the Mameluks in Egypt. Wounded at the Moskova, general in 1813, killed at Wachau. LH in Year XII.

On the 1st August, 34 officers and 451 mounted dragoons. At the Moskova, 2 officers were killed and 8 wounded. In all in Russia, 9 officers dead, 8 missing and 5 captured returned from the prisons. Out of 6 Egyptian Campaign veterans, 5 returned.

THE 30th DRAGOONS.

— **Colonel Pinteville**, Heros of Spain, wounded at the Moskova, colonel-major of the Dragoons of the Guard in 1813. Honorary brigadier in 1815. Served during the 100 days. LH in Year XII, OLH on 1st July 1812.

On the 1st August, there were 28 officers and 419 mounted dragoons. At the Moskova, 7 officers were wounded, two by bullets. For the whole campaign, 6 officers killed plus one (verified) in captivity, 7 missing and 3 prisoners who returned. Two officers were awarded a Sabre of Honour in Italy. They were dismissed in 1815.

OVERALL ASSESSMENT OF THE 3rd CORPS

Theoretically present on 1st August, 223 officers and 3 556 cavalrymen. By counting the artillery and the staff, a figure closer to 4 000 is reached for the 3rd Corps at that date. A month later at the Moskova, the numbers were reduced both for the men and the horses down to about 3 000men in the line.

At the Moskova, 9 officers were killed in the battle and 84 wounded, of whom 7 in the headquarters staff. In all for the Russian Campaign: 40 officers killed, 60 missing and 37 returned from captivity in 1814, including headquarters staff.

LATOUR-MAUBOURG'S 4th CAVALRY CORPS

The general was an officer in 1782. In Egypt in February 1800, where he commanded the 22nd Chasseurs, wounded. General in 1805, wounded twice in 1807 and major-general. Made a reputation for himself in Spain. Wounded at the Moskova. Lost a thigh at Wachau. Count of the Empire in March 1814. Peer of France. Dismissed during the Hundred Days. Voted for the death of Ney and became Marquis in 1817. Wentinto exile in 1830,died in 1850. Grand Cordon of the LH and GdCxSL.

—His aides de camp were the future **general de Nadaillac** who joined up after the battle in Moscow and **de Matharel** who was brigadier in 1821.

The 4th Corps was made up of foreigners and included:

I. ROZNIECKI'S LIGHT CAVALRY DIVISION

DZIEWANOWSKI'S BRIGADE

This brigade did not take part in the battle of the Moskova. It included the 2nd and the 7th Polish Lancers.

Brigade was left with Dombrowski near Borisov.

TURNO'S BRIGADE

The 3rd, 15th and 16th Polish Lancers numbered 2 200 horsemen, of whom 147 officers at the beginning. At the Moskova this figure was greatly reduced.

The general's aide de camp was his cousin, captain and future general who, in his memoirs, recounts their rout at Mir at the beginning of the campaign thanks to Rozniecki. He confirms that after the capture of Smolensk, General Dombrowski, having been left behind to watch over Bobruisk, was given the Dziewanowski Brigade; it remained with him. This sort of division had about 5-600 horsemen maximum at the Moskova.

Latour-Maubourg

II. LORGE'S DIVISION

THIELMANN'S BRIGADE

These were the Saxon, the Westphalian and Polish Cuirassiers.

Lieutenant-General von Thielmann was concussed during the battle. His aides de camp were **von Saydewitz** of the Life Guards who was killed and **von Minckwitz** from the Zastrovs.

THE LIFE GUARDS

At the outset there were 29 officers and 613 men. In fact they left almost 200 cavalrymen behind, many of which at the depot of Mohiev. At the Moskova, there were 450 cavalrymen according to the figures given by the Saxons. It is about them that there is a mistake in the great panorama of the battle at Moscow. The two Saxon regiments wore breastplates in the normal way, but when leaving for Russia, the Guards did not have theirs, but the Zastrovs did. In the picture the Zastrovs are pictured without their black breatsplates.

Moreover, Latour-Maubourg before setting off the charge told the Guards : *Your breast plates have not come but the regiment doesn't need them to support its reputation for honour.*

And the Guards led the charge. In this fight they suffered heavy losses charging the first with 3 squadrons; the 4th squadron of the Guards came up in support with Major Hoyer and the Zastrovs. They took the still-burning village of Semenovskoi. Soon the cavalry was all mixed up and during the sort-out, Colonel von Leyser followed by Major Hoyer mistook a group of Russian Cuirasiers for Zastrovs because of the similarity of the uniforms and the black breatplates. The colonel was captured and Major Hoyer fled wounded.

At Moscow, 8 officers were awarded with the LH. The losses given were 19 officers including one aide de camp an 214 cavalrymen killed or wounded as well as 227 horses lost.

ZASTROV'S CUIRASSIERS

To begin with they were 31 officers and 596 men. At the Moskova, the colonel could assemble 400 men. This time, they wore their black breast plates and lost 18 officers and 219 men killed or wounded as well as 240 horses. 8 officers were decorated at Moscow. In his report to the King of Saxony, Thielmann claimed that his cavalry captured the great redoubt which is paradoxal considering their position on the terrain.

THE POLISH CUIRASSIERS OF THE 14th REGIMENT

This was the 14th Regiment of the Grand Duchy of Warsaw made up of cuirassiers. It must not be confused with the 14th Cuirassier Regiment of the French army which was with Doumerc's division towards Polotsk. This French 14th was however formed up with ex-Dutch cuirassiers.

The Polish Cuirassiers only had two squadrons with at the beginning 21 officers and 352 men. At the Moskova, there were only 180 left in the line. They charged with the Saxons but on their right flank. They lost 7 officers and 107 cavalrymen wounded or killed. 5 officers were decorated at Moscow.

HILLER'S SAXON BATTERY

This joined the Westphalian battery of von Lepel's Brigade. Each battery had 12 cannon. If the cannon of the light brigade were added to a company with 6 pieces of artillery, that made 30 pieces which acted on the side of the cavalry and on its right, thus helping the progression of Friant's division towards the village of Semenovskoi. Each of the 4 cavalry corps seemed to have had 36 pieces of light artillery (6-pounders and 24- pound howitzers).

VON LEPEL'S BRIGADE

The general was killed in the charge.
He had with him:

THE 1st WESTPHALIAN CUIRASSIERS.

The only roll available is that of the 1st July 1812, which gives 33 officers and 507 men for 4 squadrons. It is probable that these figures were reduced, like all the others after a month of campaigning. There were 400 maximum at the Moskova. 4 officers were killed and 16 wounded.

6 were decorated at Moscow.

THE 2nd WESTPHALIAN CUIRASSIERS.

On the 5th July, there were 32 officers and 499 men. The regiment lost one officer killed and 6 wounded. 8 were decorated at Moscow

THE WESTPHALIAN LIGHT BATTERY.

4 officers and 136 men at the start.

ASSESSMENT OF THE 4th CORPS

The numbers for the corps are difficult to establish, except for the Saxons (Thielmann) for which precise figures are available (1 130 cavalrymen and 120 artillerymen).

For the Westphalians, there were not more than 800 heavy cavalry. The light cavalry, used on the day, did not have more than 600 men. So there was a corps of about 2 500 present. 150-200 were lost at the Moskova.

OVERALL ASSESSMENT OF THE 4 CAVALRY CORPS.

The casualties for the dead are calculated approximately and must amount to 800 dead for this battle, taking into account those who died as a result of their wounds. The proportion for the men is variable in the cases where it is known. The coefficient of 10 men for one officer is without doubt a bit low, and should be rather towards 13 or 14 men for one officer. There are some surprises when one sees the figures for the 5th and 8th Cuirassiers who were the first to enter the great redoubt. As the officers were up front, they were hit hardest and were often killed, those following more likely to get wounded.

For the officers, for whom a figure is available in the case of French regiments and some foreign ones for the the whole of the campaign and especially the retreat, the following figures are to be found, taken from the 3 first corps; they are the only ones which are verifiable.

193 officers were killed in Russia, 48 at the Moskova. 172 were missing, 133 prisoners returned from captivity in 1814 or 1815.

For the 4th Corps, the only figure available was that of 71 Saxon officers killed or wounded at the battle of the Moskova.

Only the Wetsphalians state that they lost 5 dead and 22 wounded in the battle.

4th CAVALRY RESERVE CORPS
7th CUIRASSIERS' DIVISION

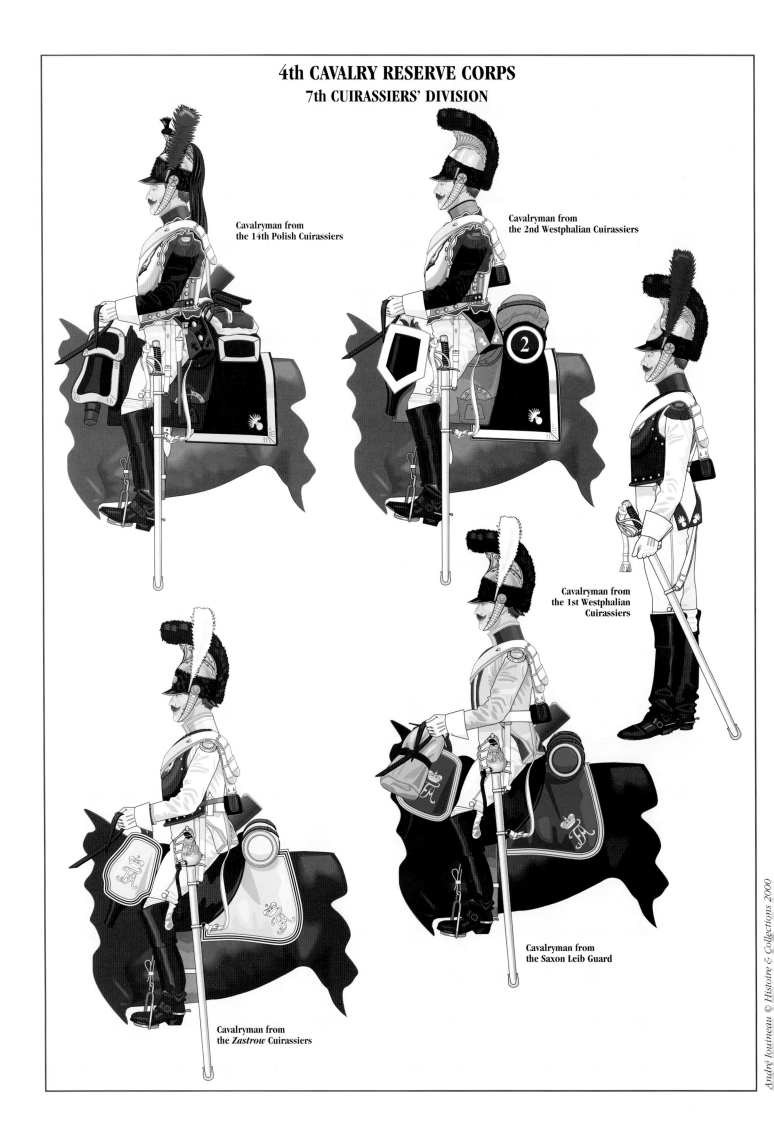

Cavalryman from
the 14th Polish Cuirassiers

Cavalryman from
the 2nd Westphalian Cuirassiers

Cavalryman from
the 1st Westphalian
Cuirassiers

Cavalryman from
the Zastrow Cuirassiers

Cavalryman from
the Saxon Leib Guard

André Jouineau © Histoire & Collections 2000

AN ASSESSMENT OF THE LOSSES

ON THE FRENCH SIDE

This has caused a multitude of interpretations because of the deliberately inflated figures given by the unit commanders. It was an opportunity to account for the men left in the rear and the missing, and thus "sort out" the numbers. Although the number of soldiers (as compared with the officers) lost is only rarely available, the numbers of officers lost can be counted for each French regiment based on their personal files. An approximation can thus be made.

1. THE INFANTRY

The best examples come from the regiments which were very heavily engaged — where there is no doubt of this — together with the units which were not engaged in the battle at all. The other units can be placed between these two extremes

The units which were most committed were those of the 1st Corps. Its five divisions were spread out over the most dangerous points of the assault: two against the great redoubt, two against the outposts and the last (Friant's) in the assault on Semenovskoia. This was the corps which did not spare its troops and which gave its utmost. It is also one of the rare corps for which the figures for the soldiers' casualties are available, along with those of the officers.

The First Corps

The dead: the number is not really debatable regarding the officers, as the place and the cause appear in their files. For these divisions, the figures are the following:

The 57th lost 20 officers and 141 men killed in the fighting on 5th and 7th September.

The 61st only has the figures of the 5th september: 1 officer and 29 men killed. The 7th, 6 officers were killed. The 111th lost 10 officers and 120 men over the two days.

These are the only really precise figures. So for the 57th and the 111th there were 30 officers and 261 men killed. The ratio is about 1:10. This is a basis for an approximation, but no more, as the fact that officers in those days were in the front leading their men and setting the example must be taken into account.

The wounded: this is a much more debatable area. The 57th had casualties of 35 officers and 975 men. The 11th 26 officers and 930 men. The rate is thus 61 officers for 1 905 men, more than 30 men for 1 officer.

The only thing that is certain is that an officer who is declared, in this book, as having been wounded always survived the battle and either continued the campaign with its attendant and implied dangers, or was evacuated directly and survived. For the soldiers it is impossible to estimate with any degree of accuracy what happened to the wounded and a great number of them must have died of their wounds.

The seriousness of the wounds

The meaning of the term "wounded" has to be explained. Firepower at that time was relatively weak, many writers who fought talk about the spent bullets found in their clothing. The power of the bullets was limited and efficient only over a relatively short distance.

Bayonet wounds however were much more serious, except for infantrymen fighting against the less accessible cavalrymen who dominated them and were thus protected. Among infantrymen during an assault it was the most fatal weapon.

Sabre or lance wounds were less often fatal. Artillery wounds were the result of biscayen-style grapeshot from the howitzer shells which were less formidable than the full cannonballs which, within a short range, caused havoc, particularly among massed troops in a square for example; but a small caliber cannonball spent itself relatively quickly. Although Napoleon's staff was only some 1 200 metres from the Russian cannon, they only experienced cannonballs rolling at their feet. Cannon loaded with grapeshot were very effective at very close range for obvious reasons. The type of wound therefore received explains how certain officers received so many wounds. Rapp for example at the Battle of the Moskova received his twenty-second wound.

What is certain is that for the officers whose files are easy to check: either they died of their wounds or they continued the campaign, rejoining their unit after differing recovery pereiods; or they were evacuated to Germany. Officers wounded at the Moskova were first cared for and were therefore missing from the first rolls, then they are to be found again at Moscow on the 1st or the 10th October with their units. The power of survival of these soldiers was very surprising; they were brought up young the hard way.

If we take as an example the 30th of the Line which seized the great redoubt alone on the first assault and was then repulsed. There were, therefore, a maximum of casualties. There were 21 officers killed and probably more than 200 men killed also.

There were 31 officers wounded at the Moskova officially. On the roll call carried out at Moscow on 15th Sepember, they were missing. Only 37 officers were left, but on the roll call of 1st October, fifteen days later,

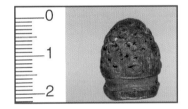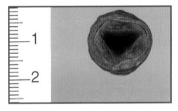

This russian bullet was received by my ancestor, a *fusilier-chasseur* of the Guard, during the night attack on Krasnoi during the retreat.
It was extracted from his left side when he came back from the Uro salt mines in 1815 (7 1/2 months' walk to get back to France).

the number of officers went back up to 68. They returned and continued the campaign. Perhaps they received reinforcements. Later one was listed as missing and three were captured but returned. The 27 other wounded officers at the Moskova returned directly.

Likewise for a lot of regiments. The 26 wounded officers of the 111th continued the campaign, one was missing on 14th November and 4 were captured during the retreat but returned from the prisons. It is certain that the recovery rate for the privates was not as high. Larrey counted one dead for six wounded. But a lot of men did like the officers and continued the campaign after having been treated.

Many who had been transfered to the hospitals in Moscow left and there were only 1 200 ill or wounded left behind in the capital.

Finally the wounded who had been amputated or were too severely wounded were made up into convoys and escorted towards France before the army left Moscow; thus they were able to reach more peaceful zones slowly in stages; many were hospitalised in Germany.

One officer took one of these convoys escorted by 1 000 soldiers, so the wounded must have been fairly numerous.

Other examples from Line units

During the final assault of the great redoubt, three regiments were at the head of the columns.

The 17th from Morand's Division, but with General Lanabère in command replacing Morand, wounded in the first attack. The 17th lost 25 officers killed and 46 wounded.

The 21st from Gérard's Division very much tried at Valoutina, on 7th September, had 5 officers killed and 18 wounded but who continued the campaign afterwards.

The 9th of the Line from Broussier's Division had 8 officers and 73 men killed, 31 officers and 713 men wounded of which 49 returned to their ranks rapidly. For the estimates regarding the dead, we have here the ratio of 10 men killed for one officer, but for other regiments it is different and it is necessary to count 15 men killed for each officer as a general average. This proportion is doubled where the wounded are concerned, 20 to 30 men for each officer.

2. THE CAVALRY.

It had to put up with the artillery firing at it whilst its units came up in support of the batteries, and filled the gaps left by the infantry who were not numerous enough to hold such a spread out line. It was the horses especially that were killed in great numbers. In a regiment from the Valence Division, for example, whose cuirassiers did not charge, there were 2 officers killed and 85 horses lost.

This battle was a carnage for all types of horses, turning thousands of cavalrymen into infantrymen. At Moscow, seven thousand formed up into two regiments armed with rifles and carbines with the necessary cartridges. Mounted men became rarer and rarer and they ended up by forming the famous *Sacred squadron* composed of heavy cavalrymen and their officers. It was only at Beresina that normally constituted cavalry units, Oudinot's or Victor's for example were to be seen again.

In the cavalry free-for-alls, losses sustained were particularly due to wounds. The heavy losses in men and horses were due to the artillery and to the attacks against the infantry, especially when the infantry was formed up into its classic squares. During the Napoleonic period, these squares very rarely gave way to the cavalry who met with very dense salvoes at very close range which were fatal. Horses were killed in very great numbers, and their riders once dismounted killed or captured. It was for this reason that the end of the Battle of the Moskova could have had no other solution than the artillery firing mercilessly on the Russian squares which stood their ground in the most unbelievable manner.

Some examples taken from the assaults on Bagration's outposts.

— the 4th Chasseurs had 1 officer killed and 10 wounded who continued the campaign. Captain Robert was mentioned.

The regiment having been disunited by three successive charges against the redoubt, he rallied thirty-odd cavalrymen and charged two platoons of Russian cuirassiers who had captured a light artillery battery, re-captured the cannon and the artillerymen, took and killed all the Russians. He had a horse killed under him during this action. He commanded a squadron in 1813.

— the 6th Lancers, from the other of Ney's Brigade, had 3 officers killed and 4 wounded. During the retreat from Krasnoi, there were 1 officer killed and 4 wounded with 34 cavalrymen killed and 49 wounded. This detail has been added to give the ratio for men lost which is so rarely available. Arriving in Moscow with 19 officers and 154 men, it received 7 officers leading 264 men in reinforcement. This showed that battalions or squadrons were on the march to Moscow, inflating the numbers slightly.

3. OFFICERS' LOSSES

These are verifiable because of each man's file; this gives the following

numbers which must be added to those of the cavalry reserve which have already been given. For the 5th Corps the figures are unknown.

— Officers killed or who died from their wounds at the Moskova

Emperor's Household:	3
1st Corps:	148
Ney's 3rd Corps:	80
Prince Eugène's 4th Corps:	48
Junot's 8th Corps:	15
Cavalry Reserve:	48 plus those of the 4th Corps

of which only 5 Westphalians were mentioned. The Saxons had 70 officers killed or wounded.

Total:	**about 360**

— Officers killed during the campaign apart from the Moskova

Emperor's Household:	13
1st Corps:	400
Ney's 3rd Corps:	207
Prince Eugène's 4th Corps:	149
Junot's 8th Corps:	44
Cavalry Reserve:	139
Total:	**952 dead**

— Officers missing

Emperor's Household:	15
1st Corps:	449
Ney's 3rd Corps:	204
Prince Eugène's 4th Corps:	253
Junot's 8th Corps:	119
Cavalry Reserve:	172
Total	**1 233 missing**

— Officers captured but returned from captivity

Emperor's Household:	12
1st Corps:	221
Ney's 3rd Corps:	149
Prince Eugène's 4th Corps:	48
Junot's 8th Corps:	31
Cavalry Reserve:	133
Total:	**594 returned from captivity.**

4. GENERALS KILLED AT THE MOSKOVA

This figure is not difficult to count; however, even here exaggerated and incomprehensible figures were to be found. Apparently 42 were killed. Here is the real list:

Generals:

— Montbrun, heros of the cavalry.

— Auguste de Cauaincourt who replaced him and was killed when entering the great redoubt.

— Romœuf, Davout's Chief of Staff.

— Lanabère from the Guard replacing Morand wounded, killed attacking the great redoubt.

— Compère, 3rd Corps.

— Marion, 3rd Corps.

— de Breuning, 3rd Corps (Wurtemberg)

— Plauzonne, 4th Corps.

— Huard, 4th Corps.

— Tharreau, 8th Corps.

— Damas, 8th Corps.

— Comte de Lepel, 4th Cavalry Corps (Westphalia).

This makes 12 generals killed at the Moskova. It is certain that Napoleon took more generals to Russia than normal and that some of them commanded false brigades with only one strong regiment. This large number of generals was no doubt justified by the need to

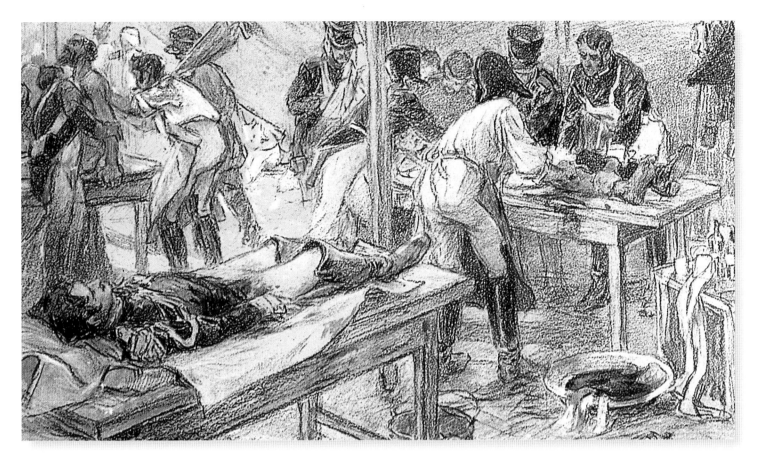

command important conquered towns and perhaps to provide the structure for troops formed up in Poland and elsewhere.

5. TOTAL LOSSES

It can be estimated that there were between 4 000 and 6 000 French or allied dead and nearly 20 000 wounded. In the number for the dead, have to be included naturally those who died from their wounds either in the field hospitals or in the Moscow hospitals. In the regimental files for the officers, the difference is made clear and the officers who were marked wounded all survived the battle.

Some wounded generals and officers returned home with their own transport. Large convoys of wounded left Mojaisk. One officer said that his convoy was escorted by 1 000 soldiers, which does suggest that it was a large one.

The men who were recoverable or transportable were moved to Moscow where the hospitals were very clean; many rejoined their units afterwards. When Napoleon left the capital, according to eye-witnesses, there were 1 000 wounded or ill in the hospitals of the town who could not be evacuated.

In the *"Bulletin français"* it was stated that all the wounded in the Moscow hospitals had been evacuated. It is known that on the 15th, 16th and 17th, convoys left Moscow with wounded soldiers. But the details refuting this are numerous, including in the officers' files where one can see "left behind" or "captured in the Moscow hospitals".

In spite of these losses, the Grande Armée still existed and was far greater than Kutuzov's. In spite of the burning town, the French found considerable ressources and took advantage of them. There was one dramatic fault in the Emperor's arrangements and this was the loss of the horses which later created problems for the artillery and also for the cavalry, where 7 000 cavalrymen had to be transformed into infantrymen.

Kutuzov, even if he was very much weakened, knew that he was going to receive reinforcements from Tchitchagov's army, which had been freed by the peace treaty with the Turks. There were good troops on the French flanks and thousands of Cossacks to harass them like flies.

Kutuzov needed time and then he would be able to count on the winter weather for support. The fate of the campaign was played out at Moscow in a matter of days. Each day lost by Napoleon in this "victory trap", increased the chances for the Russians. Could this genial conqueror resist this crisis in his dreams? When he finally left Moscow, it is estimated that he left with 100 000 men but with greatly reduced artillery and cavalry due to the horse shortage.

THE RUSSIAN LOSSES

The Russians admitted that 50 000 men were lost from their army. The infantry losses were very heavy, entire divisions were annihilated, the Neverowski, Voronzov, Paskevitch, Likhatchev and Doktorov. The Guard, shelled without firing a single shot, suffererd very heavy losses and a Russian officer said that there were 500 dead in the Preobrajenski and Semenowski regiments alone. The cavalry did not have any more horses either and its losses were very heavy too.

The artillery whose performance suffered as a result of the loss of its commander Koutaissov, was not able to fulfill its role properly when confronted with the well directed and well served French cannon. As the Russian soldiers did not surrender and got themselves killed on the spot, the number of prisoners was not excessive and did not extend beyond 2 000 men. The number of dead was considerable for one reason only: they defended themselves against the French attacks to the last man. For them it was a real masacre. Tarlé speaks of 58 000 casualties with of course a very large number of wounded, but the proportion of dead was far greater than with the French. General Ledru, going over the battlefield on the morning of the 8th, asserts that there were at least 15 000 corpses. For other witnesses there were between 3 and 8 Russians for each Frenchman lying on the ground.

When retreating, the Russians left behind them thousands of wounded in a pitiful state, that the French found on the road to Moscow. These were the real prisoners. At any rate the best troops had been reduced and the regiments of the Guard crushed by the French cannon, without firing a single shot.

The spectre of the retreat has caused the Battle of the Moskova to be badly evaluated.

CONCLUSION

The objective of this book was to find a semblance of truth in the facts with the help of the archives, which have been all too often ignored. In the case of a great battle, the difficulty increases with the multitude of testimonies, some of which are doubtful. They were often written after the events and the witnesses only saw a small part of the battlefield, mixing up time, facts and units.

Officers' reports were often more credible as they were written in the heat of the moment, but they were often partisan and falsified, to minimise the number of losses, the number of those left behind or to please those in power at the time. Finally there are the historians' frequently partisan interpretations, especially in the 19th century where the Napoleonic legend could still be said to influence politics. As far as the Battle of the Moskova was concerned, the Russians and their allies often tried to pass this huge battle off as a Russian semi-victory, as a prelude to the disasters of the retreat.

The marvellous announcement made by the English and in particular the telegram of Lord Cathcart, the Ambassador to Russia, were incredible. A huge victory for the Russians was announced; they were chasing the French. Another letter said that Davout had been killed and Ney and Eugène were prisoners. Kutuzov proclaimed his victory aloud.

The first question to answer is therefore:

WAS THE BATTLE OF THE MOSKOVA A VICTORY FOR THE FRENCH?

This question must be asked since the Russians, above all Kutuzov, claimed to have won, which is absurd; but the trace of his lies has remained. In order to leave a doubt, or by simple passiveness, Kutuzov left his troops on the battlefield until nightfall to create an illusion. Russian historians have even developped the discussions of the General-Staff which had envisaged renewing the offensive again against Napoleon on the following day. They remarked that the generals arrived to report the losses of their army; this would have made any such initiative suicidal. Leaving the

Guard thus on the battlefield formed up in serried squares, under the murderous fire of the French artillery, was to let the best troops in the Russian army be massacred. But Kutuzov did not budge from his bench, well-sheltered far from the battle of which he saw nothing. Subsequently, he was not even able to prevent or even delay Napoleon's entry into Moscow. He was beaten and he knew it perfectly well. All that he could say was that it could have been worse. So the answer is obvious: the Moskova was well and truly a French victory.

Rise and fall. After victory, retreat in the cold.

Why did he not commit it?

The answers are simple. First of all the Guard that sweeps all before it got massacred at Waterloo. Next, on this 7th September 1812, the Guard was only about 15 000 infantrymen strong. The Flankers regiment was missing and it is not known for certain if the Young Guard of General Lanusse, returning from Smolensk, had arrived at the Moskova for the 7th September.

The cavalry numbered 5 000 elite cavalrymen, but not more.

A BIG OR A LITTLE VICTORY?

This has been the subject of many arguments. Unconditional admirers of Napoleon and adamant anti-bonapartists are firmly opposed on this subject. Behind all this, the spectre of the disasters associated with the long retreat hangs over all these considered opinons. Let us try to be objective.

Napoleon was in great need of a big victory, and he had come to the depths of Russia to find it, bringing with him 115 000 men to confront the 130 000 Russians.

The forces were relatively equal. But the Russians had the advantage of the terrain, which they had chosen and reinforced with redoubts to protect their artillery batteries, placed above little ravines to make access to them even more difficult.

If one tried to turn them would they slip away again?

Napoleon weighed his decisions well but forgot that his army no longer had the same strength as at Austerlitz or Jena. But was he not infallible? "He" would compensate for all these failings.

In practice, he overcame the strong line of the enemy, causing enormous losses, opposed by men who let themselves be killed where they stood like "machines" according to Napoleon. Their massacre made his victory, a difficult one, true, but with all the glory for the attackers who, on the 8th September 1812, were certain of having won a big victory, the biggest they had ever known, a sort of Eylau, but much bigger. It opened up the gates to Moscow which they were able to admired in all its splendour and *grandeur* before it started to burn.

The answer to this second question is that the battle of the Moskova was a hard victory, with all the glory for the attackers and the inhuman sacrifices of the attacked. The idea of grandeur in this case is for the glory of the combattants. In this sense it was a great battle, a great victory.

DID NAPOLEON COMMIT MISTAKES?

Still haunted by the spectre of the retreat, Napoleon's admirers have suggested that Napoleon was ill that day. For some it was his stomach, for others his gallblader, for others a sort of 'flu; at any rate he was not himself, otherwise the victory would have been more complete. His detractors have piled it on by saying that he was getting old and that his faculties were weakening.

In his place, all of them would have engaged the Guard; one even finds the magic term of the Guard *"that sweeps all before it"*.

SHOULD THIS UNIT HAVE BEEN ENGAGED? AGAINST WHOM AND HOW?

The moment for intervening was at around 4 o'clock.The Guard would have had to advance in order to attack the Russian Guard squares. Sending the cavalry To attack these squares was to commit the same mistake that the Prussians made at Auerstadt where the cavalry, the pride of their army, got itself massacred. Sending the infantry to turn them was better, but the most efficient solution was what was adopted: massacre them with the cannon. The Russians also showed that day that their own Guard *"dies but does not surrender"*.

This does not mean that Napoleon did not make any mistakes, but he made them before and he made them after the battle. Before, it was starting this campaign without having settled the Spanish question, by leaving that country which was of no interest. One does not wage a war on two fronts, especially so far apart. Once this war had started, he was incapable of stopping it.

One mistake can sum up all the others: waiting in Moscow for his dream and his hopes to come true. He wanted Alexander as an ally and to move into India to chase out the English.

Was this the way to become master of the world? A conqueror has no limits to his ambition. At St John of Acre he had been beaten and he had returned to Egypt, which was too small for him. At the Moskova he was an Emperor, he had won and occupied Moscow, this was something different: a new power. He waited for and sent off emissaries to the Tsar; some of them behaved strangely, a little too passively. Their successful career under the Restoration revealed a suspiscious side to their activities. If only instead of dreaming, this genial conqueror had come back down to earth, in the midst of the ashes of that capital. He should have organised the intendance of his troops, evacuated the wounded and, gathering his trophies about him, returned to France. He should have installed his winter quarters better, thus creating a formidable threat for St Petersburg.

Waiting five weeks in Moscow for peace which never came, in that country, in that particular season, was a fatal mistake; only the illness of power in its conquering form could explain it, without justifying it.

He thought he had won, that is why he held out. But the conqueror had lost and it was time to fall back and abandon things.

There were signs of the old genius on the long road which brought him back to Paris, beaten. The Hundred Days and Waterloo were the final scenes of this legendary fresque.

A WORD ON FRENCH MILITARY TERMINOLOGY

In the many biographical notices to be found in this book (especially pp. 55 to 82 and pp. 101 to 111), the following rules have been adopted.

TRANSLATION OF RANKS

In order to avoid confusion, the French officers rank of '*Chef de bataillon*' (foot troops) or '*Chef d'escadron*' (cavalry) has been translated as 'Battalion commander' or 'Squadron commander' respectively. For the Napoleonic period, this rank could not be translated as 'Major' (in English), as there existed also a rank of '*Major*' (in French) immediately above it. When the rank 'Major' is used in this book, it always refers to the original French rank above Battalion commander and below Colonel – cf. plate p. 23).
- '*Général de brigade*' has been translated merely as 'General', or in some cases as 'Brigadier General' (only in the biographical notices).
- '*Général de division*' has been always translated as 'Major General' in the biographical notices.

- '*Lieutenant général*' (in the Royal French Army) has been translated as 'Lieutenant General'. This rank did not exist in the Army of Napoleon.
- '*Maréchal*' has been retained in French or translated in English as 'Marshall'.
- '*Maréchal de camp*' (in the Royal French army) has been retained in French. This rank did not exist in the Army of Napoleon.

ABBREVIATIONS USED FOR ORDERS AND DECORATIONS

LH : Légion d'honneur (*chevalier de la*).
OLH : officier de la Légion d'honneur.
CtLH : commandant de la Légion d'honneur.
CrLH : commandeur de la Légion d'honneur (*it replaced the 'commandant' mentioned above, on the 17th February 1815*).
GdCxLH : grand-croix de la Légion d'honneur (*it replaced the 'grand-cordon' on the 21th June 1814*).
GdOLH : grand-officier de la Légion d'honneur.
CrSL : croix de Saint-Louis (*chevalier de la*).
GdCxSL : grand-croix de Saint-Louis.

ACKNOWLEDGEMENTS

The author should like to thank mister Pierre Brétegnier and mister Gérard Gorokhoff for their help during the realisation of this book and misters Morgan Gillard and Patrick Lesieur for the care they have taken with the production of this work.

PHOTOGRAPHS

RMN: cover, p. 56 centre, p. 73 haut, p. 87, Roger Viollet: p. 59, p. 69, p. 80, p. 100 above left, 9e RCP: p. 90 below, Bibl. R. & J. Brunon: p. 101, Charlet: p. 118, from Faber du Faure: p. 119,
Author's collection: p. 2, p. 4, p. 34 below, p. 50, p. 51, p. 52, p. 53 below, p. 115, p. 116,
Rights Reserved: all pictures p. 33, 34 above, p. 35 above, p. 36 below right, p. 41 above, p. 42, p. 54, p. 55 below, p. 56 below left and right, p. 58, p. 59, above and below right, p. 60, p.73 center, p. 74, p. 75, all pictures p. 76, p. 77, p. 78, p. 82, p. 83, p. 84, p. 90, p. 92 above and below, p. 100 above right and below, p. 106, p. 108, p. 110, and p. 1, p. 3 above and center, all photographs p. 6, p. 7, p. 8, p. 24, p. 30, p. 32, p. 36 below left, p. 39, p. 44, p. 45, p. 46, p. 47 above and below, p. 49 above and below, p. 53above, p. 55 above, p. 66, p. 88 above and below, p. 93, p. 96, p. 101, p. 113,

SOURCES FOR THE UNIFORM PLATES

L'ARMÉE FRANÇAISE, SERIE OF PLATES IN FRENCH BY LUCIEN ROUSSELOT
Officiers généraux, plate 71
État-major, aides de camp, plate 81
Infanterie de ligne, plates 3, 17, 62 and 89
Infanterie légère, plates 5 and 33
Chasseurs à pied de la garde, plate 58
Cuirassiers, plates 37, 46, 91 and 102
Dragons, plates 7, 20, 25 and 96
Hussards, plates 9, 22 and 54
4e hussards, plate 82
Chasseurs à cheval, plates 11, 49 and 97
Artillerie à cheval 1804-1815, plate 36
Artillerie à pied, plates 28 and 66
Train des équipages, plate 90
Train d'artillerie, plate 55

LE PLUMET, SERIES OF PLATES IN FRENCH BY RIGO
Infanterie légère, 9e régiment 1804-1808, plate U7
Infanterie de ligne, sapeurs, plates 155 et 239
Infanterie de ligne, tambours et tambours-major du 88e de ligne, plates 148 and 170
Le 4e hussards, plate U2

Le 8e hussards, plate U24
Le 3e hussards, plate U10
Le 1er hussards, plate U1
Le 9e hussards, plate U25
Artillerie à cheval, 4e régiment, plate U22

ARTICLES IN THE FRENCH SPECIALIZED PRESS
Le chasseur d'infanterie légère, Michel Pétard in *Uniformes* n° 49
Le grenadier à pied de la vieille garde, Michel Pétard in *Uniformes* n° 38
Les chasseurs à cheval, Rigo in *Uniformes* n° 36
Les hussards 1805-1815, Rigo, in *Uniformes* n° 34
Le canonnier à cheval, Michel Pétard in *Uniformes* n° 43
Les généraux du Premier Empire, Alain Pigeard in *Tradition* n° 121
Les officiers d'ordonnance de l'Empereur, Alain Pigeard in *Tradition* n° 99
L'infanterie légère sous le Premier Empire, Rigo in *Tradition* n° 90/91
Les musiques d'infanterie, Alain Pigeard in *Tradition* n° 123
Le chasseur à pied de la garde, M.Pétard in *Tradition* n° 90/91

Les cuirassiers, Rigo in *Tradition* n° 54/55
Les hussards, Rigo in *Tradition* n° 74 et 77
Les artilleurs à pied, Rigo in *Tradition* n° 78/79
La musique du 3e de ligne, Rigo in *Tradition* n° 1

SPECIALIZED BOOKS IN FRENCH AND IN ENGLISH
L'uniforme et les armes des soldats du Premier Empire, L. & F. Funcken, Casterman 1968
L'équipement militaire de 1600 à 1870, Michel Pétard, volumes IV et V
Les uniformes du Premier Empire, Tome sur l'Infanterie, Cdt Bucquoy, Grancher 1979
Guide à l'usage des artistes et costumiers, H. Malibran, reprint by Olmes 1972
Les coiffures de l'armée française, J. Margerand, Leroy 1911
La cavalerie légère du Premier Empire, Rigo et Michel Pétard, Histoire & Collections
Napoleon's soldiers in Otto manuscript, G.C. Dempsey, Arms & Armour Press
Napoleonic Uniforms, J.R. Elting, Macmillan Publishing
La cavalerie au temps des chevaux, colonel Dugué Mac Carthy, EPA.

Histoire & Collections
SA au capital de 1 200 000 F

5, avenue de la République
F-75541 Paris Cédex 11

Téléphone : 01 40 21 18 20
Fax : 01 47 00 51 11

This book has been designed, typed, laid-out and processed by Histoire & Collections, entirely on integrated computer equipment.

Lay-out :Patrick Lesieur and Jean-Marie Mongin.

Printed by KSG-Elkar/KSG-Danona, Spain, European Union.
December 2000